ALL THAT GLITTERS

ALL THAT GLITTERS

THE CRIME AND THE COVER-UP

RAYMOND
CHANDLER

WINDSONG PRESS LTD.
LAS VEGAS, NEVADA

ALL THAT GLITTERS
The Crime and the Cover-Up
by Raymond Chandler

Published by:

WINDSONG PRESS LTD.
1350 E. Flamingo Road
Las Vegas, NV 89119
www.allthatglittersbook.com

ISBN: 0-9759147-2-3

LCCN: 2004110095

EDITED BY
Gail M.Kearns, GMK Editorial & Writing Services,
Santa Barbara, California, www.topressandbeyond.com

COVER, JACKET AND INTERIOR DESIGN BY
Peri Poloni, Knockout Design,
Placerville, California, www.knockoutbooks.com

BOOK PRODUCTION COORDINATED BY
To Press and Beyond,
Santa Barbara, California

COVER PHOTOGRAPHY BY
Neal Preston, © Corbis. All Rights Reserved.

Edition:

10   9   8   7   6   5   4   3   2   1

First Edition: August 2004

Printed in the United States of America

For Bea and Cynthia

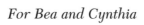

Many of the key documents discussed in this book are presented in their entirety on the internet at www.AllThatGlittersbook.com or www.ATGbook.com. Except for a few name changes inserted to protect the privacy of minors, the documents are unedited. The reader will be informed by the symbol "†" if a document is available online. It is not necessary to review any of the documents online to understand their use in this book, but the reader will gain a greater knowledge of their significance by doing so.

In chapters 32, 33 and 34, there are several discussions of important TV shows, magazine articles and books that involved the 1993 scandal. In-depth reviews of these media events are too lengthy to be included in this book, but can be found on the Web site. Again, it is not necessary to review these online in order to understand the book, but it will allow the reader to become considerably more informed.

This book contains a few four-letter words. Not many, but a few. It also contains the names of several sex acts, all of which have previously been published. It does not contain a description of these acts. Parents should use their own good judgment regarding the appropriate age for children to read this book.

RAY CHANDLER
Santa Barbara
August, 2004

TABLE OF CONTENTS

CAST OF CHARACTERS, 1993

MICHAEL JACKSON

JORDIE CHANDLER — the boy.

EVAN CHANDLER — the boy's father.

JUNE CHANDLER-SCHWARTZ — the boy's mother; divorced from Evan in 1985; married to Dave Schwartz at the time these events took place.

DAVE SCHWARTZ — the boy's stepfather.

BERT FIELDS — Jackson's attorney before and after the scandal became public; was replaced in December 1993 by Johnnie Cochran.

JOHNNIE COCHRAN — Jackson's lawyer beginning December 1993.

ANTHONY PELLICANO — Jackson's private investigator.

BARRY ROTHMAN — Evan's attorney prior to the scandal going public in late August 1993.

MICHAEL FREEMAN — June's attorney prior to the scandal going public.

GLORIA ALLRED — the Chandlers' attorney for a short period of time after the scandal became public; replaced by Larry Feldman in early September 1993.

LARRY FELDMAN — the Chandlers' attorney who filed the civil molestation suit against Jackson.

ROBERT SHAPIRO — advisor to the Chandlers; criminal attorney for Barry Rothman.

RICHARD HIRSCH — advisor to the Chandlers; criminal attorney for Evan.

MONIQUE* — Evan's wife (now divorced).

CODY* — son of Evan and Monique.

KELLY* — daughter of Dave and June.

Fictitious names used to protect privacy.

PROLOGUE

ON A WARM SPRING DAY IN 1992, pop icon Michael Jackson set out incognito on a leisurely drive down LA's boutique-studded Wilshire Boulevard. An innocent outing at first, but one that would by day's end bring him face to face with the loveliest pubescent boy he had ever seen — "I have such golden dreams for you. You are my new inspiration"[1] — and provide the spark for the most incendiary yet misunderstood scandal ever to hit the worldwide "stage."

Stranded with car trouble, the disguised star was offered the use of a phone by a kindly office worker. Moments later, after discovering Jackson's true identity, the woman was thrilled to offer additional assistance. She called her husband, an employee at a local car rental agency, who passed the request on to his boss, Dave Schwartz.

Schwartz dispatched a tow truck and limousine, then called his wife with the exciting news. Half an hour later, June Chandler-Schwartz and her twelve-year-old son were exchanging greetings and phone numbers with the King of Pop.

That, in a nutshell, is how it began. A broken widget. A helpful citizen. A one in a zillion connection. All the ingredients of a simple twist of fate. Yet mix and stir briskly — vehemently! — and from the moment Michael Jackson, "an adult male," met Jordie Chandler, "a minor child," nothing in

---

[1] From a note written to the boy by Michael. The complete text will be presented in Part Two.

this bizarre tale would be the product of chance. Every word spoken, every deed done, would emanate from the hearts and minds of responsible — *accountable* — adults.

✳   ✳   ✳

The encounter at the car rental agency was not the first time Michael and the boy had met. Jordie was little more than a toddler when he and his parents ran into Michael in a restaurant. The star picked him up, said something like, "Oh, he's so cute," and put him back down. For Michael, this brief acknowledgment was one among thousands in the day-to-day life of an icon. And little Jordie was too young to know what a superstar was. Neither would remember the event. But for Jordie's mother and stepfather, the thrill may never have worn off.

As if to be sure it wouldn't, fate stepped in and brought them together again. In 1984, when Michael was in a nearby hospital recovering from burns sustained while filming a Pepsi commercial, June penned a get-well letter on behalf of her son and hand delivered it to a bodyguard outside Michael's room. Included in the letter were Jordie's picture and phone number.

Needless to say, June and Jordie — who was now five years old — were thrilled when Michael called later that day to thank them. Surprise turned to elation when an invitation arrived several days later for Jordie to appear in an ad Michael was filming. Though Jordie was not selected to appear in the ad, and did not get to meet Michael on the set as expected, the letdown was softened by a personal invitation from the star to attend the Los Angeles performance of *BAD*.

Significant as these encounters might be, they were by no means required for Jordie, or any child, to become enamored with The King of Pop. Whether it's swooning to the music of Ole Blue Eyes or throwing panties at the Beatles, there have always been and there will always be teen idols. But with the age of satellite communications in full swing, never before had an entertainer captured the hearts and minds of a generation, in every nook and cranny of the world, as had Michael Jackson. His image was as omnipresent on planet Earth as a can of . . . Coke.

Superstar? Megastar? These words no longer adequately described the phenomenon that was Michael. John Lennon's off-the-cuff remark that the Beatles were more popular than Jesus had caused a firestorm of outrage and protest. But like it or not, in the three warp-speed decades since Lennon made his controversial statement, rock 'n' roll had solidified its position as the true religion of the younger generation. And who could deny that Michael Jackson was its reigning deity.

By age six Jordie had memorized the words to half a dozen Jackson songs and taught himself many of the star's dance moves. One evening, while walking in Westwood with his father, mother and stepfather, Jordie generated an instant crowd when he launched into his MJ routine to the sound of *Beat It* blasting from a radio Dave had brought. "Wow, look at him go," one onlooker shouted as she threw a dollar into the hat that Dave had jokingly placed on the ground.

Two weeks before his eighth birthday Jordie strutted his stuff for his entire family at a shindig back east. No sooner had he hit the dance floor when a circle gathered around the boy, three generations whooping and cheering as he twirled and moon-walked to *The Way You Make Me Feel.* Jordie's grandmother was so impressed she went home that evening and knitted him a sequined glove to add to his routine.

Jordie was twelve when he met Michael at Dave's car rental agency. The singer did not remember the boy, but Jordie sure as hell knew Michael. For more than half the child's life he had had a strong, albeit one-sided friendship with the star. Adulation would be more to the point.

So when the phone rang that fateful day in May of 1993, it was not just your basic, run-of-the-mill superstar my nephew was going to meet. It was his hero, *the most famous human being and children's advocate on the planet.* To say that Michael already had some influence over the boy is like calling Niagara Falls a leak. Jordie worshipped him, as did millions of children around the globe.

✳ ✳ ✳

PART ONE

THE TANGLED WEB

– 1 –

HE *DANGEROUS* TOUR BEGAN shortly after Michael and Jordie met, so it would be several months before the two would see each other again. But the star kept in touch by calling the child frequently from around the world. On the longer calls, often two to three hours, Jordie would take the portable phone into his bedroom and close the door, something he had never done before.

By the time Michael returned in January 1993 he and Jordie were fast buddies, and it wasn't long before the star invited Jordie, his mother and little sister to a fun-filled weekend at Neverland. Michael enjoyed their company so much that he invited them back the following weekend, which included a day trip to Disneyland. By March, one weekend had become every weekend.

At the end of March, June and her two children accompanied Michael on what was to be the first of many out-of-town trips, a four-day jaunt to Las Vegas. A week later, on April 9, June called Jordie's father from Neverland. The conversation was short and to the point. Michael has too much control over Jordie, she told her ex-husband. If you don't do something soon, you're going to lose him.

Evan Chandler had never met Michael, but all previous reports about him from June and Jordie had been positive, so this sudden warning was puzzling.

"Do you think there's anything going on?" he asked.

"Oh no!" June replied. "Absolutely not!"

Satisfied the situation warranted no immediate action, Evan promised to look into it when they returned to Los Angeles.

But the following day, after accompanying Michael to Burbank airport to see him off on a trip to the East Coast, June became saddened by the separation and realized how close she and her children had grown to the star.[2] Back home in Santa Monica she called Evan again. "Just forget about it," she said, referring to the conversation of the previous day. "Jordie is having a great time and Michael's a doll. He would never do anything to hurt Jordie."

The germ of June's now forgotten concern had originated on her second visit to Neverland, back in February, when a young boy about Jordie's age sat on Michael's lap in the front seat of the limo for the two-hour ride to Santa Barbara.[3] In full view of June, Jordie and Kelly, his four-year-old sister, Michael hugged and caressed the boy, kissing him often on the ear and cheek. Soft, lingering kisses. This affection continued the following day on the three-hour drive to Disneyland.

One month later, in the plush Michael Jackson Suite high atop the Mirage Hotel, where Jackson had been "vacationing" with little boys for many years, June awoke one morning to find her son's bed had not been slept in. The discovery upset her.[4]

Jordie told his mother that after she and Kelly had fallen asleep, Michael asked him if he had seen *The Exorcist*. When he said no, Michael played it for him. The movie frightened him and he did not want to go back to his

---

[2] Supposedly, Michael was taking Michael Milken, who was ill at the time, to see Deepak Chopra in Boston.

[3] Jordie and the boy were close in age and had spoken briefly during one of the long-distance phone calls Michael made to Jordie while on tour. The boy admits sleeping in Michael's bed, but denies any sexual contact.

[4] There is no evidence that anyone connected with the Mirage had knowledge of any improprieties.

room alone, so Michael suggested he stay with him.[5]

June might have accepted Jordie's story without hesitation had she not seen Michael's behavior in the limo. But the image of that ominous ride was in her head, so she admonished her son for spending the night with Michael and ordered him never to do it again. When Jordie told Michael what June had said, the star cautioned the boy that his mother was causing "a gap" in their friendship. "If you don't fill the gap," Michael warned, "somebody else will."

Later that evening, Jordie and Michael tag-teamed June. Not wanting to lose his first-place standing with Michael, Jordie pleaded with his mother not to be angry with them. And Michael, who claimed to be deeply hurt by June's distrust, balled like a baby as he begged her not to create "barriers" in their relationship. "I love you, you're my family," the star sobbed. "It's all about trust, love and trust."

Michael's tears had their intended effect. June apologized for having doubted him, and according to Jordie, from that point on his "sleepovers" with Michael continued on a routine basis without a word of protest from June.[6]

It was this incident in Las Vegas that prompted June to call Evan and warn him about losing control over his son. But it was not Evan's relationship with the boy June was worried about. Not really. By mid-April Michael's influence over Jordie was already rivaling, if not surpassing, her own.

On April 8, the day before June called Evan to warn him, she was anything but upset with Michael. He had invited her to Neverland to meet German Prince Albert, who, along with his governess and two sisters, was also a guest at the ranch. June was thrilled at the prospect of meeting royalty.

As it turned out, Michael snubbed the little prince, preferring instead to spend the day with Jordie. And while the prince and his entourage were assigned accommodations in the guest house, June and Kelly were given rooms in the main house for the first time, as opposed to the far removed guest quarters. Jordie, of course, slept with Michael.

Though June was pleased to be preferred over royalty, she was not happy that she, like the prince, had been excluded from most of Michael and

---

[5] They slept in the same bed, fully clothed. Michael never touched him.

[6] Jordie Chandler, interview with a psychiatrist, 1993. Coming up in Part Four.

Jordie's day. Even more upsetting was that Jordie didn't seem to miss her. In fact, he seemed to be purposely avoiding her.

Jordie Chandler had always been an obedient son. Some might say he was too obedient — a mama's boy. But under Michael's tutelage he was rapidly learning that with no parental figure around to rein in the fun and games, Neverland was truly a child's paradise. A fairytale come true.

June was losing influence over Jordie at an alarming rate. But her fears may have gone deeper than that. She had had a taste of the good life. The great life! And like her son (though for different reasons), she did not want to give it up. From that first ominous day when she saw that young boy on Michael's lap, she must have had suspicions about the wisdom of permitting her son to be alone with Michael.

"She warned *me* to do something," Evan opined months later, "because she knew it was already too late for her."

Whether June was fully aware of the choice she had made, only she can say. But according to Evan she told him very little about the Las Vegas incident and nothing about the boy in the limo. Consequently, the true meaning and urgency of her call were lost on Evan.

"When June called back to tell me everything was fine," Evan remembered, "Jordie got on the phone and told me he was having a great time. I missed him, but I figured, why spoil it." As far as Evan was concerned, June's love and devotion to her children, as well as her judgment regarding their welfare, had always been beyond reproach.

Not that Evan wasn't jealous of his son spending nearly every weekend with Michael. June had promised several times to bring Jordie over, only to cancel because Michael had invited them back to Neverland. Evan and June had had "words" about it several times over the past two months.

But Evan did his best to control his displeasure. "What kind of a selfish father would deny his son the thrill of hanging around with Michael Jackson for a few months," he told himself. "Be patient, it'll all be over soon." Michael was due to leave on the second half of the *Dangerous* tour in August.

Just twelve days earlier Evan had listened as Michael revealed his innermost secrets in a TV interview with Oprah Winfrey. Like the tens of millions around the world who watched the interview Evan had no reason to doubt the sincerity of this odd but likeable man. So he hangs out with kids all the time. So big deal, he's a kid himself.

APRIL 1993

Evan Chandler had been a dentist for over twenty years. Starting in New York City, then moving to Palm Beach and finally to Los Angeles, he had worked the gamut from high-volume, chain-store dentistry to upscale private practice. There was money to be made in both, but the latter was easier on the conscience; you could take the time you needed to do quality work. Over the past eight years, through hard work and long hours, Evan had established a solid Beverly Hills clientele.

One of his favorite patients was actress Carrie Fisher. "Carrie is intelligent and compassionate, and she always made me laugh," Evan said. "You can't part company with Carrie without a smile on your face."

Evan and his friend, Mark Torbiner, a dental anesthesiologist, were working on Carrie when Mark suggested Evan ask her opinion of Jackson. Mark believed it was unhealthy for any child to be spending that much time with Michael, and he was hoping Carrie would concur. "You respect her, right?" Torbiner urged. "Why not see what she thinks?"

Evan was hesitant. It was inappropriate to involve his patients in his personal life. But Mark, who over the next several weeks would become Evan's Jiminy Cricket, would not let up. "She has a kid too. She won't be offended."

It was apparent to Evan, even through casual conversation, that the actress had a fondness for children. And if anyone knew the skinny about the goings-on in the entertainment world it was Carrie Fisher. Who better to ask?

Evan waited until the work was finished, then, as he unclipped the bib from around Carrie's neck, asked if she had ever met Michael.

"Once," Carrie said. "But I don't think he likes me. I think he was intimidated."

Evan told Carrie that his son might be sleeping in the same bed as Jackson, and asked if she thought it was anything to worry about. Carrie was uncertain, but she offered to make some inquiries. While Evan drove her home (as he sometimes did for patients still "hung over" from anesthesia), Carrie called a close friend, Arnie Klein. Klein was not only Jackson's dermatologist, but also somewhat of a surrogate father to the star.

It was 2 AM in Philadelphia when the call jarred Klein awake, but he was genuinely happy to hear from his good friend. Carrie got right to the point. "Arnie, I'm with my dentist. His son has been spending a lot of time with Michael Jackson and he's concerned. What do you think, is it a problem?"

"Not at all," Klein replied. "Tell him he's got nothing to worry about."

Evan knew that Tinseltown's circle of power-players was tight-knit and protective, so he didn't expect Arnie would rat on Michael even if there was something to worry about. Evan also didn't put much stock in what Klein said because in a town like Los Angeles, having celebrities in your practice can pretty much guarantee success. Klein would not want to lose Jackson as a patient. On the other hand, Klein could be telling the truth.

When Carrie returned to the office two weeks later she brought new information. She had called another friend, a man high up on Michael's security team, who was as convinced that the relationship was dangerous as Klein was that it was safe.

Close as these sources were to Michael, Evan was not inclined to believe them over June's assurances. "If I asked ten people I'd probably get ten different answers. When you're famous, everyone who's ever met you pretends to know everything about you. But June was right there on the scene. And if there was one thing I was certain of, it was that she would never let any harm come to our son."

On April 22, Michael, Jordie, June and Kelly flew to Orlando on the Sony corporate jet for a three-day romp at Disney World. At night in their hotel room Michael grabbed Jordie's butt and stuck his tongue in the boy's ear. When Jordie protested, Michael began to cry and said that other boys, like Tommy Jones, must love him more because they let him do those things.[7] Michael then lamented about having to close the door when he showered, and tried to convince Jordie that it was okay to be nude in front of each other.

But Michael did not want to drive the boy away, so he refrained from doing the specific things Jordie didn't like. Instead, he continued to do whatever else he could to engage the boy in a sexual relationship. And by

---

[7] The names of all boys who Jordie claimed Michael said he had intimate relations with have been changed to protect their privacy.

the end of April his slow but steady seduction had progressed to the point where a peck on the check had become a lingering kiss on the lips, and a quick, goodnight hug in bed was now a loin-tight embrace.[8]

By the time they returned from Orlando, Michael and Jordie were inseparable. June not only condoned the relationship, she felt so strongly that the superstar had become an integral part of her little family, that she allowed him to move into her house on a permanent basis.

On the morning of May 7, Evan drove to June's to see her and the kids off on a trip to Europe. They'd be joining Michael in Monaco for the World Music Awards. "At that point," Evan later told the police, "I didn't believe anything inappropriate was going on. Jordie looked great and acted the same as always. I was happy for him."

June was ecstatic about the trip. Over and over she told Evan about the "seven-thousand-dollar first-class tickets" Michael had given her, waving them in the air as Evan helped load their bags into the limo.

"I was happy for June, too," Evan said. "Dave never treated her that well, but Michael was nice to her. I half-joked, 'Hey, maybe you'll marry Michael.' It would have been great for both of them. He'd get a new image and she'd finally have a peaceful relationship."[9]

It was no secret that June and Dave, now estranged, were not a match made in heaven. Over the years she had threatened several times to divorce him. Dave was a hard-core workaholic who was rarely at home, even on Sundays, and he often lived away from his family for months at a time.[10]

In Dave's defense, June knew what she was getting from the start. Marrying Dave provided the comfort and security that made it possible for her to stay at home, free from the need to work, and be a full-time mother.

June hoped that the birth of their daughter might alter her husband's priorities, but it was no surprise that it didn't. That's not to say that Dave

---

[8] All references to sexual contact between Jordie and Michael have been taken from Jordie's interviews with authorities and psychiatric professionals, and from my direct conversations with my nephew, all occuring in 1993.

[9] At the time, Evan believed Michael was either asexual or "waiting for the right woman," as the singer had claimed on Oprah Winfrey.

[10] Dave would stay at one the rental properties he owned in Beverly Hills, or the permanent suite he leased at the Sheraton Hotel next to LAX.

didn't love his child. He always treated her with kindness. But he was too caught up in the affairs of business to spend much time with her. And little girls don't come much sweeter than Kelly Chandler.[11]

When Evan and June divorced in 1985 Dave was already a close family friend, and it was clear that he and June had feelings for each other. But all was on the up and up. Everyone treated one another with respect and remained friends. So much so that a year later, when Evan returned from vacationing in France with his fiancée Monique, Dave and June took the couple into their home while they looked for a place of their own.

Within a few weeks Evan and Monique had rented an apartment nearby, and for the next eight years life rolled on without a hitch. The children did well in school and had lots of friends. They seemed happy and well adjusted. The adults, too, went about their lives reasonably content . . . LA style.

During the Monaco trip, Michael and Jordie took ill and spent several days locked inside Michael's hotel suite, recuperating and masturbating. To make the boy feel more comfortable with the act, Michael told him about the other children he had masturbated, and the singer masturbated himself several times in front of Jordie. They also took a bath together, which was the first time they saw each other completely naked.

While the boys were "convalescing," June rented a car and went shopping with Kelly across the border in San Remo, Italy — Michael's gold card in hand.

After Monaco they flew to Paris, where they spent much of their time having fun in the sun at Euro Disney. At night, alone in their hotel room, the fondling and masturbating between Michael and Jordie continued.

Simultaneous with their return from Europe, the *National Enquirer* released a story that disturbed Evan greatly. While he was aware that anyone hanging around with Michael would eventually appear in the tabloids, this particular story was about Michael's new family and described Jordie as if he was the singer's adopted son.

The article was pure hype, but Evan feared that Jordie might now be a target for kidnappers or jealous fans. Michael had voiced his love for many

---

[11] June kept the name Chandler for herself because it sounded better than Schwartz. She gave Kelly the name Chandler so the child would carry the same family name as her mother and (half) brother, Jordie. If this bothered Dave, he never let on. When it came to the kids, whatever June decided was fine with him.

children, all children, but never before had any one child been described as being that close to the superstar.

Knowing that Dave would share his concerns, Evan suggested he tell June to "stop yapping to her friends." It was a sister of June's closest friend who had sold the story to the *Enquirer.*

Two days later June called Evan to scold him for telling Dave she had a big mouth. No sooner had June finished with Evan when Dave called. If Evan was upset about the *Enquirer* article, Dave was livid. "That asshole [Michael] is destroying my business and my family!" he screamed into the phone. Dave told Evan he was getting calls from friends and business acquaintances expressing their sympathy for the loss of his family. He felt humiliated.

Dave also felt double-crossed. Before June left for Europe he gave her five thousand dollars and told her not to accept any gifts from Michael. Dave didn't seem to care at this point that Michael was constantly showering presents on his kids, but his wife was another story. June took the five thousand, but she was not about to pass up a Jackson-financed shopping spree just to pacify the ego of her estranged husband.

Dave was jealous, but of greater concern was the effect on his business. He was heavily leveraged in a down-turned real estate market, and things were not going well. With his family's exploits plastered all over the tabloids, his creditors became even more nervous now that his personal life was unstable.

"Calm down," Evan told Dave. "I'll call June and see if I can work things out."

But June had her own lament. "He wants me to get rid of Michael," she told Evan. "Why should I? Michael's been good to the kids and me. Dave ignores them. He hardly even bothers to call Kelly anymore. Uh-uh, no way." It appears as if June was more willing to get rid of Dave than she was Michael. Dave and June's marriage had been strained for many years and they had unofficially separated several months before Michael came into their lives.

Evan had never interfered in June and Dave's relationship, and he was uneasy about doing so now. But things were getting out of hand fast and he felt compelled to help. Despite June's position, Evan assured Dave that there was no need to worry. "Michael's not interested in June. I thought he was, too, but that's all bullshit."

Evan told Dave that when June returned from France she confided in him that Michael had no interest in her, it was the kids he wanted to be with. "This is the best thing that's ever happened to Michael," Evan explained to Dave. "Everyone thinks he's asexual or gay, now they'll think he's into June. It makes him look normal." Eventually Dave cooled off, but relations between him and June remained strictly business.

– 2 –

MAY 20

Weeks earlier, when June was in France, she had called Monique to find out the best places to shop in Europe. During that conversation June mentioned that Michael had invited her and the kids to accompany him on the second leg of the *Dangerous* tour in August. She also said that Michael wanted to meet Evan when they returned to the U.S.

Evan had been thinking the same thing. His knowledge of the star was limited to what the media had reported, particularly the Oprah Winfrey interview, and to what he had been told by June and Jordie. He had no reason to doubt any of it, but it was all secondhand and no longer enough to satisfy his concerns.

Soon after Jordie returned from Europe he called Evan to invite him and Cody, Jordie's five-year-old brother, to meet Michael. Evan was enthused but concerned. "What if Cody was to say something to Michael? You know, about the way he looks."

"Don't worry," Jordie replied. "Kids don't notice that. They like him right away."

✳   ✳   ✳

"I was shocked when I entered Jordie's bedroom," Evan recalled. "It was different than I'd ever seen it, like it belonged to another kid." Plastic army men and other such toys, all gifts from Michael, were strewn across the floor, with at least a dozen more still in their boxes piled high against the wall. A life-sized cardboard Captain EO stared from the corner, while several autographed pictures of the star in various celebrity poses covered the walls.

In another corner of the room a cabinet overflowed with hundreds of CDs, movies and video games. Except for the music and games, Jordie had long outgrown the toys that littered his room.

"Jeez, Jord," Evan said, "Cody doesn't even play with this stuff anymore. What are you doing with it?" Jordie lowered his eyes, embarrassed, then glanced toward the one corner of the room Evan hadn't seen.

Evan followed his son's gaze. "That's when I saw Michael for the first time. Ruby red lipstick, thick black eyeliner, long strands of dark hair hanging down in front of his pancaked face. But what struck me the most was how lonely he looked, huddled in the corner staring at the floor. I couldn't help feeling sorry for him."

Evan's concern about Cody's reaction proved unfounded. As Jordie had predicted, the child was instantly taken with Michael, and within minutes all four "boys" were sitting on the bedroom floor, chomping gum and blowing huge bubbles as they played war games with the action figures.

After that, they went out in the backyard to play with the slingshots Michael had brought. Tomatoes, oranges, rocks — every missile available— were loaded into the weapons, and all targets were fair game, even the million-dollar homes that lined the Pacific Palisades canyon below.

"Cody and I stayed for hours," Evan remembers. "At first I was just pre-tending, trying to make Michael feel comfortable. But you can't help becoming a kid again when you're with Michael. I got caught up in it."

That evening, Monique asked her husband what he thought of the star. "I really like him," Evan said. "He's a great guy."

And apparently the feeling was mutual. Jordie called the next day to say that Michael had a wonderful time. "He really likes you, Pops. A lot better than he likes Mom. He wants you and Cody to come visit us at the Hideout."

No sooner had Evan accepted the invitation than Michael came on the phone. "There's just one thing," the star said. "Please don't tell June I invited you."

"Why?" Evan asked. "What do you mean?" He and June had no secrets when it came to the kids.

"I don't know why," Michael explained, "but she told me she didn't want you included in anything, so I'm not sure what else to do but keep it from her."

✳   ✳   ✳

My brother had never had a problem attracting women. Blessed with movie star looks, a keen sense of fashion, and far more intelligent than the average bear, they flocked to him like ewes to a rutting ram. His problem was holding on to them.

Evan is not an easy man to get close to — and getting close is the easy part. Staying close is a bitch. Once he locks his mind on something — and his mind is always locked on something — nothing can dissuade him from attaining his goal. He becomes single-minded to the point of obsession.

As captain of his high school swim team Evan trained longer and harder than everyone else. Years before it became common practice, Evan shaved his head and greased his body to gain that extra hundredth of a second. Evan strove to be the best, *had* to be the best, even if it meant not having fun doing it.

During and after his college years Evan led a four-piece rock band and was relentless about rehearsals, demanding that every song be played over and over until each note was perfect. In the early 1990s he decided to write a screenplay, so he would come home after long hours in the office and work until the wee hours of the morning at his desk, hammering out the dialogue. He thrived on hard work and intense concentration, and demanded the same of those around him.

Unfortunately for the women who loved him, these are not the best ingredients for a relaxed, romantic relationship. Unfortunately for Evan, particularly in his teenage years, most of these young women had not yet learned the art of leaving — a daunting task at best, and damn near impossible with a guy who refuses to quit. So rather than make a clean break, Evan's girlfriends would end the relationship by starting another and allowing him to discover the fact for himself.

Not understanding the extent to which his personality had played a part in driving love from his door, Evan became increasing resentful and distrusting of women as the years passed. Then he met June.

It was 1973. Evan was twenty-nine and finishing up his senior year in dental school when the slim fashion model sat down in his chair at NYU's free clinic. Her teeth needed work, but the rest of her was perfect.

June was different from the other women Evan had dated. She seemed to thrive on his intensity, even to the point of encouraging it. They wanted the same things from life — fine clothes, expensive cars, a beautiful home. For June it meant a way out of the drab, middle-class apartment life she had tolerated as a young girl in New York. For Evan, it was simply the logical progression of his personality. It didn't matter if he was a dentist or a plumber, he had to be the best, and he would never stop until he reached the top.

To Evan's delight, June hung in there with him, through good times and bad, and there were plenty of bad. Each time they seemed to be moving up, something would go wrong and they'd find themselves starting over. Yet even as the romance began to wane from their marriage, the friendship remained intact, right up to their divorce in 1985. They had their share of fights, but neither was the type to hold a grudge, and neither ever used their son to punish the other. As far as Evan was concerned, in May of 1993, June was not only the mother of his child, she was still a close friend.

"She done me wrong, she done me bad, she done me dirt," Evan had written in one of his songs at the jaded age of twenty. But June never did him wrong. By the age of forty-nine he had known her for twenty years and she was the only woman in his life he completely trusted. Add to that trust the tremendous respect he had for June as a mother, and one begins to understand why up to this point — wrong or right — Evan had yet to interfere with the strange friendship between his son and the thirty-five-year-old Jackson.

If a psychiatrist were to describe Evan's mental state at the time he might use the term approach-avoidance. As the father a thirteen-year-old boy, something didn't sit right. And his lack of intervention went against his own inner voice. But Evan felt guilty at the thought of denying his son what every child in the world could only dream of. That guilt, coupled with his deep-seated trust in June, outweighed the hearsay Evan had picked up at his office . . . until the day he met Michael.

"What I saw in Jordie's room disturbed me not only because it was so inappropriate for his age and personality, but also because I instinctively knew that June had to know it was inappropriate, and was therefore condoning it. It was the first time I had ever doubted her motives concerning our son."

The thought that June had been hiding something from him about Jordie was so alien to Evan, and he had just begun to digest it when Michael hit him with news that June did not want him included in their relationship. More a jumble of feelings than organized thoughts, it was not as if all of a sudden Evan's trust in June, or in Michael for that matter, had crumbled. But it was cracking.

MAY 21

Evan and Cody picked up Jordie at June's and drove to Century City, a glitzy area on the border of Beverly Hills filled with boutiques, swank hotels and high-rise office buildings.

Michael's "Hideout" was a one-bedroom condo just off Avenue of the Stars. "We've come to see Richard Sherman," Evan told the security guard, using the code name Michael had given him. The guard called "Mr. Sherman" for approval, then summoned a guide in an electric cart who led them down a winding road to an underground garage.

"There it is," Jordie said, pointing to a salmon-colored garage door. Evan rang the buzzer and immediately the door began to rise, just enough for them to duck under to the other side. When they stood up, the King of Pop was there to greet them.

After a brief hello and an ogle at the vintage Rolls Royce with the gold-wired sound system — "It once belonged to the Queen of England," Michael proudly announced — their host led them through a small laundry area and up a flight of stairs. "They're all originals," Michael pointed out, as if he knew Evan was about to comment on the old movie posters that lined the staircase walls.

From the top of the stairs they entered directly into the living room. "I took a double-take," Evan recalled, referring to the life-sized statue of children playing tug-o-war in the middle of the room. "They looked so alive."

Against the far wall was a lighted display cabinet filled with tiny sculptures of famous scenes from Disney movies. Evan had had some experience sculpting teeth in dental school, but the craftsmanship here was far beyond anything he'd ever seen.

While Evan's eyes were drawn to the artwork, Cody's were glued to a stack of brightly wrapped boxes piled at the feet of the tug-o-war boys.

"They're for you," Michael said, smiling at the child.

"All of them?" Evan asked.

"Mm-hmm," the star answered. "Every single one."

Evan was mildly put off by the gluttony of boxes, yet relieved at the same time. He was concerned Cody might be jealous of Jordie and Michael's relationship, but Michael had apparently thought of that, too.

While Evan sat on the floor watching Cody play with his new toys, Michael and Jordie stood off to the side, grinning from ear to ear at the child's delight. Suddenly, Evan felt a tap on his shoulder and turned to find Michael holding a small gift-wrapped box. "It's for you," the star said, as he placed the box in Evan's hand. Inside was a gold Breitling watch.

"It felt strange being given such an expensive gift by someone I hardly knew," Evan remembered, "but I didn't say anything other than to thank him. At the time I believed he was genuinely trying to be nice and I didn't want to seem ungrateful."

Although Michael is unassuming, his presence is powerful because of his immense fame, and Evan quickly fell prey to it without realizing what was happening. He never would have accepted a gift offered by an ordinary stranger. But one does not refuse the offerings of a king.

Anxious to get on with the fun, Cody asked if he could play with the video games Jordie had raved so much about. "Sure, but why don't you look over there first," Michael said, pointing toward another corner of the room.

This sent the boy scurrying toward what turned out to be a fully stocked candy bin. Cody stuffed his pockets, then bounded upstairs to join his big brother in the game room. With both boys out of earshot, Evan turned toward Michael. "Can I talk to you for a moment?"

They sat close, Evan poised on the edge of a couch, Michael deep in a velvety chair.

"I had planned to work up to it," Evan recalled, "kind of beat around the bush for a while. But face to face it seemed phony, and I found myself at a loss for words."

After an awkward silence Evan decided the best thing to do was to jump right in, like he would with Dave or Mark or any good friend. Michael would either be offended or he'd appreciate the honesty.

Locking eyes with the star, Evan blurted it out. "Are you fucking my son up the ass?"

Michael giggled like a schoolgirl, but never batted a false eyelash. "I never use that word," he responded.

Surprised at what had tumbled from his own mouth, Evan fought to keep from blushing and stay on track. "Then exactly what *is* the nature of your relationship?"

"I don't understand it myself," the star admitted. "It must be cosmic!"

Cosmic? At first Evan thought Michael evasive. Then it dawned on him that the singer was referring to the three chance encounters he and Jordie had had over the years. Does he really believe they were preordained, Evan wondered?

"Well, what if someday you decide you don't want to hang around with Jordie anymore. He'd really be hurt."

"Oh, no, I'll always want to be with Jordie. I could never hurt him."

As they talked, Evan was on the lookout for signs of insincerity. But he detected none. "My bluntness didn't faze him in the least," Evan said. "He was aware that the relationship looked strange and he understood why I had to ask." But it was Michael's innocent, giggly response that convinced Evan that the star was being straight with him. "Suddenly it seemed so obvious. Of course he wouldn't use *that* word. He's asexual. What use would he have for it?"[12]

Months later, after the scandal broke, Evan commented on that conversation. "There was no anal sex involved, so technically Michael wasn't lying. But he knew what I meant and he gave no hint that there was a physical side to the relationship. He was brilliant. He stayed right in character: a little shy, a little embarrassed, but no anger or defensiveness."

Their business completed, the two men rose from their seats. "You're Jewish, aren't you?" Michael asked, as they strode from the room. "I have a lot of respect for Jewish people. When I was a little kid and we started

---

[12] Evan wasn't alone in this conclusion. J. Randy Taraborrelli, author of the most well-researched and in-depth biography of Jackson, *Michael Jackson: The Magic and the Madness*, came to the same conclusion.

making money, my father hired the best people to take care of our business. They were all Jewish, and very smart."

Evan relaxed.

Halfway up the stairs to join the kids, Michael spun around, all excited. "Hey, Evan, wanna see the awesome computer I bought Jordie!?"

An innocuous question, especially after the frank conversation that had just occurred, but it took Evan by surprise. Several months earlier, about the time Jordie started hanging out with Michael on a regular basis, Evan and Jordie had decided to buy matching computers. They bought one at first, to see if they'd like it. Then, a few days later, when Evan was about to buy the other, Jordie called to tell him about the "awesome computer" Michael had bought him. "He got me all kinds of games and stuff, you should see it!"

Evan was somewhat jealous that Michael had beaten him to the punch, but he was intrigued by Jordie's description of the computer and wanted to go over to June's to see it. Jordie had explained that the computer was set up at Michael's house because it wouldn't fit in Jordie's bedroom at home.

"How come it's at Neverland," Evan asked? "How can you use it for school when it's all the way up there?"

"No. It's at the Hideout, Michael's place in Century City."

"Why does he call it the Hideout?"

"Because it's like the Lost Boys' place in Peter Pan."

It wasn't until several days later, when Evan met Michael that first time at June's and saw every square inch of his son's room filled with preadolescent boy toys, that he realized why the computer wouldn't fit.

But now, sitting at the computer in the Hideout, Evan felt relieved. This was the direction he wanted his son to go in, not playing with plastic army men.

"Do you know how to work it?" Michael asked.

"I don't even think I could turn it on," Evan chuckled.

"That's okay. I hired someone to teach us. And I had great programs installed to help Jordie in school."

"Are you going to learn, too?"

"Oh yeah! I love to learn new things."

Great, Evan thought, as they started up the stairs again. You can't beat a private tutor. I guess he really is concerned about Jordie.

This was not the first, nor would it be the last, of Evan's roller-coaster feelings about the relationship between his son and Michael. Had it been the man down the street, Evan's instincts would never have wavered. But those instincts were constantly challenged by the incredible benefits he envisioned for his son. At times the glare from Michael's celebrity was blinding.

The game room was on the far side of Michael's bedroom, a dimly lit cubicle with a large bed that took up most of the floor space. Other than the bed, the only piece of furniture in the room was a display cabinet similar to the one downstairs. Inside were models of famous movie action figures like the slashed and gory head from *The Terminator.* "Stan Winston gave that to me," Michael said. "He does all the big movies."

Mesmerized by the bells and whistles of the video games, Jordie and Cody had no idea the two men were watching them. Evan stood to the side and slightly behind Michael, where he could see the adoring expression on the star's face as he watched the children at play. He obviously loves kids, Evan told himself. Maybe he just wants to experience the joy of making them happy, kind of like an adoptive parent. What could be wrong with that?

Michael can provide invaluable opportunities for Jordie, Evan thought. How can I deprive him of those opportunities just because Michael is eccentric? Aren't most of the world's great talents eccentric?

Just as these thoughts were passing through Evan's mind, Michael spun around to face him. "I'm having a slight problem with June," he said. "Can I talk to you about it?"

Michael wanted to take Jordie on the second half of the *Dangerous* tour, scheduled to kick off late that summer, but June was reluctant to take the boy out of school. "It's a once-in-a-lifetime opportunity," Michael said, making his case to Evan. "He'll see the world like no child has ever seen it."

It *was* the opportunity of a lifetime, of that Evan had no doubt. His son would travel in the style of kings. Heck, he'd *meet* kings! But that wasn't what appealed to Evan, and Michael seemed to understand. He emphasized the educational aspect of the trip.

"He'll learn things he could never learn in school," the star said. "He'll learn about music, art and history. He'll meet the greatest minds in the world!" Michael went on and on, espousing like an old wise man about the places he'd been and people he'd met. He was talking about an unparalleled learning experience, including exclusive tours of the world's greatest cities and the opportunity to meet and converse with the most powerful and successful people in their fields. Millkin, Chopra, McCartney — the names fell from his lips like raindrops — a downpour from an international "Who's Who."

Evan became entranced, not only by the content of the oration, but also by the power of the orator. It was a side of this childlike man he never expected to see. "He could carry on an intelligent discussion on a wide range of subjects, from the classics to cartoons." Coupled with the respect he already had for Michael's talent and success, Evan found it hard to believe that such a man could be anything but a positive influence on his son. He envisioned an opportunity for Jordie in which no door would be closed to him. An experience unavailable anywhere else on earth.

"Did you explain it to June this way?" Evan asked.

"Yes," Michael said, "but she's not into it."

Evan wasn't surprised; he and June never did see eye to eye on the value of formal education. She believed it was essential for Jordie to graduate from college. Evan, on the other hand, who had had four years of college followed by four years of dental school, questioned the value of it.

"Things have changed since I went to school," he told Michael. "You know how many kids get out of college and can't find jobs? Unless you're going for a graduate degree or just want to drop out of life and party for four years, it's a waste of time. I'd prefer to see Jordie involved in something where he can use his natural talents. That's what leads to fulfillment and success. The rest is just hard work and luck."

"And who you know," Michael added.

"Right!" Evan echoed. "And who you know."

To Evan, his and June's disagreement on the subject of formal education hadn't mattered much in the past. He accepted that Jordie would go on to college. But no way was he going to let his son miss out on an opportunity like this. The education alone was well worth it. Just imagine the invaluable connections Jordie would make traveling with the world's most famous entertainer!

"Don't worry," Evan said, grasping Michael firmly on the shoulder. "Jordie's going on that tour. I guarantee it!"

With the burdens of the adult world laid to rest, the two men spent the remainder of the evening with Cody and Jordie, playing video games and lobbing water balloons at the Mercedes, Jaguars and Land Cruisers passing two stories below on Avenue of the Stars.

Both men had come to this "meeting" with a pressing concern. Each *had* to talk to the other. But what transpired was more than just a resolution of their individual problems and the mutual relief at having overcome them. A bond was created. They were now allies in a common cause. Jordie.

Evan kept his promise. He worked out a compromise with June in which she agreed to let Jordie accompany Michael on tour in exchange for Michael hiring "the best tutor I can find." In the end, June so was pleased with the arrangement she couldn't wait for the tour to begin. After all, *Dangerous* promised to be five months of ultra-class travel, not to mention one of the greatest extravaganzas in the history of modern entertainment. And she and Kelly would be at the head of Michael's entourage. Right behind Jordie.

Little did Evan Chandler know how *Dangerous* a fate he had sealed for his son.

✳ ✳ ✳

"They set me up," Evan concluded seven months later. "Michael's problem had nothing to do with Jordie going on tour, that was a done deal. His real problem was that June wanted to go as well — she loved the glitz and glamour — but the last thing Michael needed was some parent hanging around. You never know how cooperative they're going to be when you want to bunghole their kid."

According to Jordie, Michael and June had an argument in Paris over whether or not she'd be going on the tour. "After Mom left, Michael became so angry he trashed the hotel room and cut himself. There was a towel full of blood on the bathroom floor."

"It was a stalemate at that point," Evan believed. "Michael couldn't take Jordie without June's permission, and June could lose the relationship with Michael if she refused. I knew that June wanted to divorce Dave, but could she get enough money from him to maintain her lifestyle? I don't think so. On the other hand, it would be pocket change to Michael to provide her with that financial security."

The Monday morning conclusions of an angry man? Perhaps. But besides the argument in Paris, Jordie remembered that when June told Michael about Evan's reaction to the preadolescent bedroom, Michael quizzed both her and Jordie about why Evan was so upset. From Jordie he learned that Evan had been urging his son to learn to use a computer, and about their plan to buy the laptops. From June he learned about Evan's opinions regarding formal education.

Two days after acquiring this information, Michael bought "the awesome computer" and had Jordie invite Evan to the Hideout, where he had made a point of bringing the computer to Evan's attention and informing him about the once-in-a-lifetime educational experience he had planned for Jordie . . . if only he could get June to allow it. "Setting it up as a me-versus-June was brilliant," Evan said. "He knew exactly what buttons to push."

From the Hideout, Evan went directly to June's to tell her of his decision and Michael's promise to hire a tutor. He also gave her a brown paper bag Michael had asked him to deliver. "When I told her that I agreed with Michael, she seemed disappointed at first, like she was hoping I'd side with her and not let Jordie go. Then she opened the bag and pulled out a ruby necklace, and her expression instantly changed from glum to glad. I thought it was a trinket . . . who delivers expensive jewelry in a paper bag? But it turned out to be worth about twenty thousand dollars."

If June really was disappointed, if she didn't want Jordie to go on tour, then maybe there was no "deal" between her and Michael. On the other hand, maybe she was doing her own scheming. She knew Evan was upset about missing his weekends with Jordie, which gave her ample reason to think he would side with her and not allow Jordie to go on tour with Michael. Then she could parlay a better deal with Michael by getting Evan to change his mind in exchange for her going on the tour also.

Of course, it could simply be that June honestly had no intention of letting Jordie go until Evan and Michael talked her into it.

In any event, June wasted no time arranging for Jordie's departure. Within days after receiving the bracelet she had made arrangements with Jordie's private school to supply his tutor with the books and assignments necessary to fulfill the school's requirements.

– 3 –

MAY 22

The day following the Hideout visit was Cody's fifth birthday, and what better present than to have Michael Jackson at your party. Michael was all for it, but Jordie knew better. The other kids would pay no attention to Cody once The King of Pop showed up.

"Won't Michael be hurt?" Evan asked.

"Uh-uh," Jordie answered. "He'll understand."

This seemingly trivial exchange was anything but trivial to Evan. That Jordie felt secure enough with Michael to be so direct was a good sign. It meant they had a real friendship. But more important, Evan was pleased that Jordie had his priorities straight.

Jordie left his father sitting in the backyard and went inside to call Michael. "Hey, Dad," the boy shouted from the kitchen, "is it okay if Michael comes over after the party?"

"I don't know," Evan said. "We have a lot of studying to do." Each year at this time Father and Son spent the weekend preparing for Jordie's final exams.

"That's okay, Pops," Jordie assured his father. "Michael will quiz me."

"Okay, I guess so. But tell him you'll call him back. I have to call Monique and check with her first."

Monique was not taken with the idea. She had no use for Michael Jackson or his music. But Cody was counting on it, and it *was* his birthday.

When Michael arrived, the four boys sat around the kitchen table talking about Jordie and Michael's recent trip to Disney World. "How do you get them to open up the rides at night?" Evan asked, then immediately felt stupid for asking. He was so relaxed around Michael he sometimes forgot who he was talking to.

"Every time I go there I'm surrounded by photographers," Michael explained. "It always gets in the papers and on TV. That's millions worth of free publicity for Disney."[13]

That led to a discussion about the business side of superstardom, and from there to the recent phone call Evan had with Dave concerning the Monaco trip and resulting *Enquirer* article.

"Dave was so angry," Evan told Michael, "he threatened to sue you for taking his family away and ruining his business."

"Ha! Ha! Ha!"

"No, he means it. He's pissed off."

"Are you kidding," Michael responded, still chuckling. "Do you know who David Geffen is?"

"Sure, who doesn't," Evan answered, wondering what that had to do with the price of fish.

Michael told him about a lawsuit where an attorney named Bert Fields had brought the immensely powerful Geffen to tears on the witness stand. Geffen was so impressed that after the suit he fired his own attorney and hired Fields. "When David told me that story," Michael said, "I hired Bert, too."

Bert Fields was unquestionably the most feared attorney in the entertainment industry. He had not lost a case in thirty years. With such a man in his corner, the threat of a lawsuit from Dave Schwartz — a wealthy man in his own right — was a joke to Michael Jackson. Literally.

But it was no joke to Evan. About a year earlier, shortly after he and his writing partner, J.D. Shapiro, sold their screenplay, *Robin Hood: Men In Tights,* to Mel Brooks, a dispute arose over writing credits. Believing that Brooks was claiming more credit than he was entitled to, Evan and J.D. brought their complaint to the Writer's Guild. According to Evan, the guild sided with him and Shapiro, but the head of the guild told them privately that it would be best if they gave Brooks equal credit. When the two men refused, the guild informed them that the issue would have to be reviewed one more time.

Why is the guild so afraid of Brooks, Evan asked, knowing that Brooks was no longer the powerhouse he used to be? Because Brooks threatened to hire Bert Fields and sue us, the head of the guild replied. Fields, it turned out, had

---

13 Disney, of course, returned the favor by providing luxurious accommodations for Michael and his entourage. Jordie was molested in the finest Mickey had to offer, from Florida to France. (Unbeknownst to Disney, of course.)

defeated the guild in a previous suit and they were loathed to face him again.[14]

"Bert Fields, I think I've heard of him," Evan told Michael, without revealing the story.

"He'll take care of Dave," Michael mused.

It was during this brief exchange that Evan caught his first glimpse of yet another facet of Michael's personality — one he would soon come to know all too well. Apparently, this fragile and innocent man had a tough side.

"Then Michael did something strange," Evan remembered. "He began pronouncing judgment on members of the family. He said that June was lazy and had a big mouth and that he had no respect for her, although he accepted having to support her for the rest of her life because she was Jordie's mother.[15] He respected Monique, though, because she was educated and worked hard.[16] Then he said I was a good father because Jordie had told him that many times, and he could see it for himself. But Dave was a bad father because he was more interested in making money than he was in his children."

Despite his own penchant for doing so, Evan thought it weird that someone would just come out and say things like that. He couldn't help wondering if Michael was buttering him up, and if he said the same things to June about him. But he let it slide.

Evan, it seems, was more enraptured by the relationship than he realized. Had an ordinary man made such inappropriate comments my brother would have given him hell. But not the King of Pop. Evan could not see the virus that was slowly infecting his family.

The boys spent most of the day in the backyard, shooting BB guns and pelting trees with cherry tomatoes. Later in the afternoon they moved to the front yard to play basketball in the driveway. Every now and then

---

[14] The final decision was that writing credits were published in alphabetical order, beginning with Brooks. In exchange, Evan was given associate producer credit, a reward he neither wanted nor earned. How much of the final script Brooks actually wrote is unknown.

[15] At the time, Evan accepted this statement at face value. Later, it became the basis for his theory that Michael had agreed to support June in exchange for letting Jordie go on tour. "If you're a pedophile and making a hundred million a year, what's a million or two for carte blanche access to the kid you desire most?"

[16] Ironically, Michael's respect for Monique had been bolstered when he learned she was completely unimpressed by his stardom. "It's rare," Michael told Evan, "to be around an adult who wants nothing from me."

Michael would duck inside the garage to avoid being spotted by a passerby. It was a quiet residential street, but when it came to Michael Jackson all hell could break loose from just one glimpse.

By dusk the foursome had worked up a gnawing appetite, and though everyone wanted to go out to eat, no one, especially Michael, was in the mood to be mobbed by adoring fans.

"I'll pick something up," Evan suggested. "What do you guys want?"

"I'll have whatever Jordie's having," Michael answered.

"Are you sure?"

"I'm sure. I'll like whatever Jordie likes."

When Evan returned, they sat around the TV and pigged out on Chinese food as the Lost Boys fought off the evil Captain Hook (Michael's pick). Evan was surprised at how much food the scrawny star could pack away. He took it as a sign that Michael was content and felt at home.

When the movie was over they cleared the dishes and set about deciding what to do next. "Let's watch another movie," Michael suggested, much to the approval of the group. This time they let the birthday boy choose. "Hey, how about *The Terminator?*" Cody said.

"Oh, I love that movie!" Michael exclaimed.

"That's my favorite!" Evan blurted out at the same time.

For the remainder of the evening, well past midnight, they sat oohing and aahing like a bunch of sports freaks watching Monday Night Football, playing and replaying *The Terminator.*

During the course of the evening Evan and Michael discovered they shared a passion for film, as well as a reverence for this particular movie. Everything about *The Terminator* was genius they agreed: the story, the characters, the cinematography, and most of all the special effects. When Michael revealed that he had conceived some of the effects, like the part where the checkered tile floor morphs into the bad terminator with the knife arm, Evan was flabbergasted.

"What! That was your idea! That's brilliant! How come you didn't get credit for it?"

"I just did it for fun," Michael explained. "I don't care about credit."

Wow, Evan thought, in a town where people would kill to get credit for things they haven't even done, Michael got his reward just being involved in the creative process. Now that's a *real* star.

"I'm involved in a lot of new things," Michael said. "I'm creating video games for Sega. I'm designing theme parks. I have deals with two studios to develop movies. I'm doing another album."

Evan was overwhelmed. "The first indication I ever got that Michael had an ego was that night. But his mind was fertile with ideas and I'm sure he did all the things he said, and more. His enthusiasm was infectious. On the other hand he also had a humility about him that made him seem like any ordinary human being."

"I'm going to be very big in movies," Michael predicted. "I'm going to bring back the musical."

"If anyone can do it, Mike, it's you," Evan said.

"You and Jordie wrote a movie, too, didn't you? Jordie said you guys had a lot of fun doing it."

"Yeah. We wrote it with a friend of mine. It's pretty stupid, really. I don't even like talking about it."

"You shouldn't think that way, Evan. It's amazing you got your first screenplay produced."

"I know. Jordie and I had a great time. But it's no *Terminator.*"

"Do you have any other ideas?" Michael asked.

"Oh yeah, plenty. We just finished another screenplay. A first draft, anyway."

"What's it about?"

"Jordie and Cody, actually."

"It's about kids? That's great. What's it called?"

"'Joe-Bob, Billie and the Cap Gun Kid.' About these three kids from a dried up western town who go to New York to look for their dad. There's a character in it that's like you. He's a kind of street person and . . ."

Michael chuckled.

"Well, not that part. But he teaches one of the kids — who was sort of forced to become the man of the family when their father left — how to become a kid again."

"That sounds like a great story. You should finish it."

"Maybe. But I'm burnt out. I really appreciate what writers go through now that I've done it."

"You can't give up now, Evan. It's not only a good story, it's also commercial."

"You think so?"

"Sure. I'll help you with it if you want."

"You're kidding!"

"Uh-uh. I wouldn't waste my time if I didn't think it was good. We can all go up to Neverland and work on it."

"Wow! Wouldn't that be incredible!"

"Yeah. And I've got some ideas for a musical, too. Something like 'Mary Poppins,' but I don't have a story yet. We could work on that as well."

"I'm really good with story ideas," Evan said. "And you know Jordie, everything's a joke to him. Whatever we do will be a comedy if he's involved."

"Yeah," Michael agreed, gazing adoringly at his young pal. "He cracks me up."

By 3 AM, with Cody crashed on the couch and Jordie barely able to keep his eyes open, Evan and Michael decided to call it a night. As the two men rose from their chairs they spontaneously reached out and hugged each other. No words were spoken.

Michael slept in a trundle that rolled from beneath Jordie and Cody's bunk bed.

The following day was devoted to serious studying. "We were a team," Evan recalled, referring to Michael. "I saw him as a valuable addition to Jordie's life."

That night, before Jordie and Michael left for June's, Evan took his son aside to ask him if Michael was serious about them going up to Neverland to write.

"Oh yeah," Jordie said. "I *know* he is. I asked him to give you a job so we could all be together."

"Oh . . . I see. Well thanks, Jordie. Thanks for trying to include me in."

Jordie couldn't help but notice the dejected look on his father's face. "C'mon, Pops. It'll be fun."

"I'm not so sure,"Evan said. "It sounds like he'd be keeping me around just to do you a favor."

"No! He likes you. He told me."

"Well I like him, too, but I doubt we'd end up working together all that much."

Evan let it drop, but there was something else he needed to talk about. Earlier in the day Jordie mentioned that he and Michael no longer wanted to live at June's, they wanted to move in with him and Monique. The proposal caught Evan off guard, so he waited to discuss it until he could collect his thoughts.

"So, Jordie says that you guys want to live here?" Evan asked, as Michael reentered the room. Michael nodded yes. "Well that's fine, but the boys' room is way too small for three people. We'd have to add a room on to the house."[17]

"Do it!" Michael responded instantly. "I'll pay for it."

Out in the driveway, Jordie and Michael exchanged hugs with Evan, Monique and Cody, then climbed into the limo for the two-minute ride back to June's. As they pulled away, Evan ran the new plan by Monique.

"Absolutely not! I don't want him living here."

Evan wasn't surprised. "You should give him a chance. He's a nice guy when you get to know him."

"I don't care. I don't want him living in my house. Let him stay at June's."

"They don't want to stay at June's anymore. They want to stay here."

"Who told you that?"

"Jordie. He said Michael likes it better here."

"Jordie told you that?"

"Yeah. He also told me Michael's going to give me a job working for his production company."

"Are you going to take it?"

"I don't know. What do you think?"

"You won't be happy, I know you. You'll be living under his thumb."

"You're probably right, but I don't want to hurt his feelings."

"And Jordie, are you going to tell him he can't live here, too?"

"That's the hard part. I'd love him to live with us. He's the one who asked Michael to give me a job so we can all be together. I'm not sure what to do."

"It's moot," Monique pointed out. "June will never go along with it."

---

[17] Jordie and Cody's bedroom was 9' x 12'.

"Oh, yes, she will," Evan argued. "She knows he's at the age where boys need to be with their fathers."

"Huh! That's not what I meant. It's Michael she won't give up."

"C'mon. You're just saying that because you don't like her."

"That's not true, Evan. I never said I don't like her. I said I don't respect her. There's a difference."

"Well, apparently she's not all that fond of you, either. But let's not get into that. All I want is for the kids to be together. That's all that matters. Don't you want Cody to be close to his brother?"

"Of course I do. But under no circumstances do I want Michael Jackson living in this house. This relationship is wrong and I think you should stop it. If I had the right, that's exactly what I'd do."

"Okay, okay. I get the message. Michael doesn't live here. But I'm not sure breaking up their friendship is the best thing. Michael can do a lot for Jordie, and I'm not going to take that away from him unless I have a good reason."

"Do whatever you want, Evan. But I wouldn't promise Jordie he can live here until you talk to June. She has custody, remember?"

Custody? In the eight years since Evan and June divorced, this was the first time the word had ever been mentioned.

✳ ✳ ✳

Back at June's, Jordie and Michael resumed their routine. They awoke each morning, dressed, ate breakfast and left to begin their day — Jordie off to school, Michael off to sing. When Jordie returned, Michael returned. They played or did homework, watched movies and went to bed. Side by side in Jordie's double bed. Masturbating and more. Night after night for an entire month.

– 4 –

MEMORIAL DAY WEEKEND

Jordie returned to Evan's the following Friday to continue his studies. No sooner had he arrived when Michael called, wanting to speak to Evan.

"I don't want to hurt your feelings," the star said, "but there's something you should know."

"What?" Evan asked, wondering what Michael could possibly have to say that was so terrible.

"I probably shouldn't be telling you this," the star continued, "but June said she hates you. She thinks you're selfish and you don't really love Jordie. And she thinks Monique's a bitch. Before I came over she told me she was like Hitler and I'd really hate her when I met her."

"What!"

"I'm sorry, Evan. Maybe I . . ."

"Look, Michael, I don't know where you heard that, but June would never say such things."

Michael apologized again, but insisted it was all true.

Jordie was standing next to his father, listening to the phone call. "Is it true?" Evan asked his son. "Did Mom say nasty things about Monique and me?"

Jordie hung his head. "Yeah, Pop, she did."

"Please don't be upset!" Michael pleaded. "I love you. Jordie loves you. I'm sorry. I really love you."

"That's okay, Mike," Evan said, tears welling in his eyes. "You did the right thing."

Michael arrived after dinner as Evan was clearing the dishes to make room for the study session. Evan sat at one end of the rectangular table, reluctantly finishing Jordie's overdue history paper, while the boys sat at the other end, talking about *Huckleberry Finn*. It didn't take long before Michael and Jordie's discussion degenerated into a laugh fest, punctuated by spontaneous bouts of dancing.

"Watch this!" Michael exclaimed, as he twirled round and round in place like an ice skater.

"That ain't dancin'," Jordie said. "That's choreography. Here, watch me. I dance street, see. I don't have to count, 'cause I got natch'l rhythm."

Michael howled with laughter. "Where'd you learn to dance, Rubbahead, in a wotamelon patch?"

"Uh-uh. Y'alls confused. Dats where y'all was bowun."

And on and on they went, poking fun of each other's dancing, skinniness, blackness and anything else that came to mind, till their ribs ached from laughter.

"Michael's hungry," Jordie announced to Evan after several hours of fun and games. So off they went, Jordie and Michael giggling away in the back seat as Evan, the dutiful chauffeur, drove to the restaurant, picked up the food, served dinner and then cleaned up while the two boys ran off to play.

Evan went upstairs to bed early that night. He opened the trundle for Michael in the boy's room, and then went to talk things over with Monique. Michael and Jordie had been off in their own little world all day, as if Evan didn't exist. This was a complete turnaround from the previous weekend, and it left Evan hurt and confused.

Monique had made her position clear several times over the past weeks, but Evan felt she was overreacting, especially when her comments came intertwined with sarcastic remarks about June. Yet after this weird weekend Evan had to admit that Monique had been more clearheaded than he about what made Michael Jackson tick.

Monique reiterated her opinion that Michael was taking up too much of Jordie's life. But this time she offered an additional observation. "Jordie doesn't even know you're in the room, Evan. Can't you see what's going on? They're in love!"

The minute the L word left Monique's mouth, Evan believed she was right. "It should have been a dead giveaway," Evan recalled weeks later, "when Jordie came walking in the house that night wearing tight black pants, white socks, black loafers and a black fedora, and Michael came walking in right behind him wearing the same thing. Or when they ran off into the living room together after dinner and closed the door behind them, leaving me to work alone on the history paper. Or that Michael never once called Jordie by name, referring to him instead by affectionate nicknames like 'Applehead' and 'Doo Doo Head.'"[18]

"Do you think it's physical?" Evan asked his wife.

"I don't know?" Monique answered. "It could just be infatuation. But whatever it is, it's not good for Jordie."

---

[18] Evan and Monique's belief at the time, that Jordie and Michael were "in love," is significant to the problem of understanding sexual molestation in older children. It did not occur to them that the thirteen-year-old was not a willing participant.

"You're right," Evan admitted. "Do you see how different Michael's acting now?"

"Oh, absolutely! He took last weekend as some sort of approval. Now he's showing his true colors."

"I can't believe I didn't see it coming."

"Well, June's been encouraging him all along. Now he thinks you are too."

"What should I do?"

Monique pondered a while. "Maybe you should come right out and ask them."

"Ask them! Are you kidding? There's no way they'd admit that. Besides, it might do more harm than good right now. Michael thinks he's got me fooled so he's letting his guard down. I think we should let it play out over the weekend and see what happens."

"Okay," Monique agreed, "he's not going to try anything here. Not with Cody in the room. But make sure you tell him he can't stay with us any more."

Considering that the majority of Monique's information about Jordie and Michael came secondhand from Evan, her take on things was pretty sharp. But it takes a professional to understand the mind of a pedophile. So what if Cody was in the room. All the better. Especially if he turned out to be as cute as his brother.

The King of Pop masturbated Jordie that night.

Michael awoke around eight with a splitting headache and sent Jordie to seek Evan's help. Evan was in the bathroom when his son made the request.

"I'll be there in a minute," Evan said, and as Jordie turned to leave, added, "Hey, Jordie, are you and Michael doin' it?"

"That's disgusting!" Jordie reacted. "I'm not into that."

"Just kidding."

Evan explained it this way. "It was crude, but I was so anxious, I decided on the spur of the moment to say it because I figured it would elicit an unplanned response." Jordie's repulsion brought Evan great relief. So much so, that he felt quite chipper as he walked down the hall to check on Michael.

The singer was walking in circles, holding his head. "I didn't sleep all night," he complained. "I've got a bad headache. I get them all the time."

"Do you know what causes them?" Evan asked.

"Yeah, I've had them ever since my hair caught fire. They said it's from the surgery."

Evan offered the standard remedies, aspirin and Tylenol, but Michael insisted they had no effect on him and that his doctor usually gave him a shot of something, he didn't know what. When Evan suggested that he call his doctor, Michael refused. He didn't want to bother the man on a holiday weekend. Instead, he asked Evan if *he* could give him something stronger.

Evan rattled off a list of drugs to see if he could find out what Michael's doctor used. When he mentioned Demerol, Michael said that sounded familiar. Evan did not use Demerol in his practice, so he called Mark Torbiner for advice. The anesthesiologist suggested an injection of Toradol, a non-narcotic equivalent to Demerol, and offered to pick some up at Evan's office and bring it to his house.

Evan injected 30 mg, half the maximum dose, into Michael's gluteus. But one hour later the star claimed he was still in a lot of pain, so Evan administered the remaining half and instructed him to lie down and try to relax.

"Keep an eye on him," Evan told Jordie. "It'll take a few minutes to kick in. I'll be right back.

"When I went back to check on him, maybe ten minutes later," Evan recalled," he was acting weird, babbling incoherently and slurring his speech. Toradol is a pretty safe drug, and I thought that either he was having a rare reaction or had taken another drug and was having a combination reaction."

Other than the drunk-like symptoms, Michael's pulse and respirations were normal and he appeared to be in no real danger. So Evan took no further action.

But Jordie was scared. He had seen his friend "acting strange" before, but never like this.

"Don't worry," Evan assured his son, "Right now Michael's the happiest person in the world. All we need to do is keep him awake and talking until the drug wears off."

Four hours and a serious case of cottonmouth later, Michael began to sober up. While Jordie was downstairs fetching water, Evan decided to take advantage of Michael's still uninhibited but somewhat coherent condition. "Hey,

Mike, I was just wondering . . . I mean, I don't care either way, but I know some of your closest people are gay, and I was wondering if you're gay too.

"You'd be surprised about a lot of people in this town," Michael mumbled, as he rattled off the names of a few prominent Hollywood players who were still in the closet.

Evan tried to get back on track before Jordie returned. He stroked Michael's hair and reassured him. "I don't care if you're gay, Mike. I just want you to know you can tell me if you are."

"Uh-uh," Michael slurred. "Not me."

Given Michael's willingness to talk openly about everyone else's sexuality, his consistent denial about being gay reinforced Evan's belief that the singer was asexual.

Michael remained in bed all day, with Jordie sitting by his side on the edge of the single bed. Cody joined them about ten, and by ten-thirty the three boys were fast asleep.

Evan was tired, too, but the thought that Michael might awake during the night and take more drugs caused him to get up several times to check on the star. On his third visit, around 3 AM, Evan found the boys still fast asleep. But Jordie was now in Michael's bed, spooning, with Michael's arm wrapped tightly around the boy, his hand resting on the boy's crotch on the outside of the covers.

Ever so gently, Evan picked up Michael's arm and moved it to the side, then slowly pulled back the covers. Thank God! They were both fully clothed.

Evan dozed off at dawn, but he and Monique were awakened shortly thereafter by Cody crawling into their bed. "What's the matter, Honey?" Monique asked.

"Is it okay for two men to get married?" the boy asked. Evan and Monique were stunned. They asked why he wanted to know, but the child was in no mood to reveal his thoughts, only to cuddle up and cling to his mother.

In the weeks that followed, Evan and Monique tried again to find out what Cody had seen or heard. But the boy remained secretive and depressed. Three months later, during dinner one night, Cody turned to his parents and announced, "Michael Jackson is bad. He did bad things to Jordie." After that release the little boy began to perk up.

A picture is worth a thousand words. And the sight of his son in bed with Michael finally made it clear to Evan that he *must* end their relationship. Even if there was no sex, Jordie's personality had been seriously altered. As he morphed day by day into a pint-sized clone of Michael, he withdrew further and further from his family and friends.

Evan's initial reaction was to separate them then and there, but he and Monique talked it over and agreed that a sudden split could be traumatic and might cause Jordie to bond even deeper with . . . his lover?

On a more practical level, June had legal custody of Jordie and controlled his daily routine. They would need to coordinate with her for a separation to have any effect.

Monique insisted, however, and Evan agreed, that Michael must be told that day that he could not move in with them. Not wanting to arouse the star's suspicion, lest he assert even more control over Jordie, Evan lied.

"You know, Mike, I checked with the building department and they said we're not zoned for an addition. I guess we'll just have to forget . . ."

"Then we'll build a new house," the superstar vowed, as if it were already a done deal. "Just don't tell anyone I paid for it, okay. It'll create problems."

Concerned he'd tip his hand if he pushed further, Evan thanked Michael and let it drop. When Evan called June the following morning to discuss the situation, Michael answered and said that Jordie was ill and confined to bed. Jordie had a history of severe asthma that had sent him to the emergency room several times. So Evan grabbed his stethoscope and raced over to check on his son.

Jordie was sitting up in bed glued to the TV, unaware that his father had entered the room. As Evan made his way around the end of the bed, Michael, in pajamas and a felt fedora, sprang to his feet. *"I'm* taking care of him," Michael proclaimed, in a booming voice that nearly halted Evan in his tracks.

"What are you doing for him?" Evan asked.

"I'm giving him his medication and keeping him warm," Michael answered, retreating back to the chair in which he had been keeping his nurse's vigil.

As Evan listened to his son's lungs, his eyes perused the toy-laden room and landed with a jolt on the opposite side of the bed. The covers were pulled back as if someone had recently gotten up, and the deep mold of a head remained in the soft pillow. Evan said nothing, but when he was satisfied his son's lungs were clear he hurriedly left the room to find June.

"What the hell is going on in there?" he demanded.

"Michael wants to take care of Jordie himself," June said. "He doesn't want me to do it. But it's okay. I showed him what to do."

"Don't you think that's a little screwed up? He's our kid but we're not allowed to take care of him?"

"He loves Jordie," June defended.

"No shit! Is he sleeping in bed with him?"

"Yes."

"Why can't he sleep in Kelly's bed?"

"Because that's Kelly's room."

"Don't give me that crap! She never sleeps in her bed. She sleeps with you."

Realizing that he and June were seconds away from a major blowout, Evan reined in his anger. "You're as sick as they are," he scolded, then broke off the argument and walked back to Jordie's room. "I'm leaving now," he told Michael. "Call me if he gets any worse."

The following day Evan went back to June's to insist she kick Michael out and end the relationship. June refused, and a nasty argument ensued.

– 5 –

At work the following morning, Mark Torbiner, the anesthesiologist, informed Evan that he had inadvertently discovered that Michael's dentist had recently bought his practice from Dr. Saunders, who was thought to have contracted AIDS.[19]

Evan was terrified. Whatever damage Jordie may have suffered from his relationship with Michael, it paled in comparison to the threat of AIDS. The odds were slim, sure, and Evan still had no idea if there was anything

19 To protect his privacy, Dr. Saunders' real name has not been used.

sexual going on, but the thought brought little consolation. You don't gamble with your child's life![20]

Evan knew he wouldn't be able to function until he had the truth. So the following morning he called Michael at June's and asked the star if he had ever been a patient of Dr. Saunders. Michael claimed he had never heard of the man.

Michael sounded sincere and Evan had no reason to doubt him. So with a genuine concern for both his son's and Michael's welfare, Evan explained why he had called. "This is just between you and me, Mike, so please don't tell anyone. But Dr. Saunders has AIDS."

Evan didn't want Michael to get the impression he had anything against gays, because he didn't. He just wanted him to understand the reason for his concern. "I'm concerned about you, Michael, so I got worried when I heard you might have been his patient."

"That's nice of you, Evan, thanks. But there's no need to worry. I'm fine."

"Well, you know, a lot of your key people are gay, and . . . "

"That's true."

" . . . and now your dentist and maybe some other people I don't know about, so I'm . . ."

"Well, I'll tell you what, you're my dentist now, okay, so we don't have to worry about that."

"Uh . . . okay, Mike. Thanks."

Whatever the nature of his son's relationship with Michael, Evan believed the singer truly loved Jordie and would not put either of their lives in jeopardy just to conceal his own homosexuality. No decent human being would. So this little talk brought Evan such great relief that he couldn't help but wonder if *all* his concerns about Michael were nothing more than manifestations of his own paranoia.

The following day, after Evan reamed Mark for getting him so upset, Mark informed Evan that he had seen the chart and x-rays at Dr. Saunder's former office. "He has beautiful teeth," Mark said.

Evan's heart sank, but his mind lagged in disbelief. "Yeah, he has great teeth. But they could have been someone else's x-rays. You know how . . ."

---

[20] Evan did not think that Michael was sleeping with his dentist. He was concerned that a dentist with AIDS might not take the proper precautions when treating his patients.

"Wake up!" Mark snapped. "They were his. They had his name on them."

"Fuck, Mark! He lied to me! I can't believe he lied to me!"

As Evan's hands worked through the rest of the day, his mind sifted through the possibilities. As far as he knew, there had never been a gay member in his or June's family. So on the surface at least, that ruled out genetics. And there was nothing in Jordie's environment that would explain it. Evan and Dave, the boy's primary male influences, were heterosexual.

On the other hand, the boy, now age thirteen, had yet to show any overt signs of a sexual preference. No ogling girls or making verbal comments about them. So it could just as well be that Jordie's natural orientation was to be gay, and that his relationship with Michael was now bringing it to the surface.

Even so, what about the age difference? Would the father of a hetero-sexual thirteen-year-old girl want her involved with a thirty-five-year-old man? Certainly not, even if they were in love.

In the end, Evan realized that his immediate concern was not to analyze the relationship but to end it. The question was, how to find a way to do it that would be the least traumatic for the two . . . whatever their relationship.

✳ ✳ ✳

Jordie and Michael spent the weekend at Neverland, masturbating in front of each other, playing at the water fight park, masturbating one another, watching movies in Michael's private theater, hanging around the zoo, Michael performing oral sex on the boy.

JUNE 9

When June, Jordie and Kelly sat down beside Evan at Cody's preschool graduation, Evan was joyously surprised. Other than a brief phone call, he and June hadn't spoken since their argument when Jordie was ill. June had ended the argument by threatening to boycott the graduation, and Evan was now relieved to see that June still honored their long-standing practice not to use the children as ammunition in the battles between adults.

This was not your average preschool. One by one the graduates marched to the podium to receive their diplomas and say a few words about their plans for the future. When it became Cody's turn, the five-year-old announced that unlike the other children who talked of becoming doctors, lawyers and presidents, his goal was to be a house painter.

Cody was all smiles when the audience broke out in laughter, but his face radiated with glee when Jordie stood up in front of the entire crowd and high-fived him.

"Any parent would swell with pride watching their children interact that way," Evan explained. "But to me it drove home the reality that I was an inch away from losing it all, and suddenly the joy was gone and I felt pressured, like if I didn't do something immediately I might not get another chance."

Evan was anxious to talk to June again about Jordie and Michael, and he intended to do so right then and there. But it was not to be. June had to leave immediately after the ceremony and asked him to take Kelly back to his house to play with Cody; she'd pick her up later that afternoon. Just as well, Evan thought, they'd have more privacy at his house.

While Cody and Kelly mingled with the other kids and their parents, Evan led Jordie to a nearby bench to have a chat. "What if I asked you not to go on tour with Michael? What if I wanted you to stay home with us? What would you say?"

"I'd go anyway," the boy answered, without a moment's reflection.

"You mean, if I asked you not to go, you're telling me you'd go anyway?"

"You'd have to give me a good reason why not."

Evan was surprised at the strength of his son's defiance. Six months earlier the boy would have complied without argument. But okay, Evan thought, he's not a little kid anymore, and there's nothing wrong with him challenging me. It's got to happen sometime. Besides, I'd want a good reason, too, if someone told me I couldn't go on tour with Michael Jackson.

"What if I said you could be dead in five years if you went on tour?"

Jordie looked puzzled. "Well, of course, I don't want to die. But why would I?"

"Because you guys lied to me!" Evan erupted. "And you know how much I hate liars. You're not going on the tour. Now let's go, I'm taking you home."

Jordie was aware that his father was more liberal than most parents. But he also knew that of the few things that pissed Evan off, lying was at the top of the list. Evan had told him time and time again that whatever mistakes he might make in life, lying about them was worse and would only compound the problem.

"Thank God he didn't ask me what they had lied about," Evan later recalled. "I don't know what I would have said, other than Michael had lied about his dentist. Then I would have had to tell him about the AIDS thing. But I knew he'd go home and tell Michael that I was really angry with them, and I hoped it would make Michael think twice about taking him on tour. Not that I was relying on that. I was relying on June. I still believed that once she truly understood my concerns, she'd put a stop to everything."

"The reason I didn't ask Dad what he meant by me and Michael lying to him," Jordie explained months later, "was because I thought he already knew what Michael and I were doing and I was freaking out he'd ask me about it."

Evan wanted to tell Jordie about Dr. Saunders, and Michael's lies. He wanted Jordie to say, "Oh my God, Pops, he doesn't really love me!" But painful as it was to admit, Evan believed that his son's loyalty now belonged to Michael, and that if he revealed the truth the boy would tell Michael everything and the two of them would then create a story for June. No, Evan thought, I need to get to June before they do. She was coming to pick up Kelly at his house before going back home to Jordie and Michael. That would be his opportunity.

During the ten-minute drive back to June's, Evan placed a call from his car phone. "There's this list of names," he told his son. "I'm calling to find out if Michael's on it. You guys better pray he's not."

"Hello," Evan said into the phone as he swung the car into June's driveway. "Is he on it? Take your time. It's important you get it right." Evan was calling a friend who had been involved in the sale of Dr. Saunder's practice and had a list of the patients who transferred over to the new dentist. Jordie had no idea what the call was about.

Alone at his mother's house, Jordie called Michael at the Hideout and told him everything. Half an hour later, Michael was at June's trying to figure out with Jordie what Evan meant about "lying" and "the list."

As Evan drove home, he, too, began speculating about the day's events. Mark Torbiner was a good friend, and Evan was certain he wouldn't kid around about something so important. But Michael's name was not on the list. So perhaps Michael hadn't lied after all.

At home, Evan paced around the house muttering to himself. "Cosmic, my ass! So he's not on the list, big fucking deal! They can't fool me; I know what's going on!" But Evan knew that he was partially to blame for this dire predicament. *"You,"* he said, confronting the man in the mirror, "are a fool."

When June came by to pick up Kelly, Evan took June into the backyard where they could talk privately. "I'm worried about Jordie," he began. "I'm afraid he might be gay."

According to Evan, June shrugged her shoulders and replied, "So what. So he's gay. Who cares?"

Evan couldn't believe what he had just heard. In his mind, June was admitting their son might be gay and having sex with Michael, and that it was no big deal. He became instantly enraged and screamed at June, "Who cares! Who cares! Are you crazy!!" Barely in control of his temper, Evan ordered June to leave his house.

That June saw nothing wrong with Jordie being gay was not what angered Evan. "Though what straight parent would be pleased at the prospect," he later explained. "It was the way she flipped it off, like there was nothing to be concerned about, or even talk about. Maybe I should have tried to talk to her more. But I just lost it. Anyway, looking back, I doubt it would have made any difference. She was already locked on course."

When June arrived home, Michael and Jordie told her what had transpired at the graduation, including Evan's decree that Jordie could not go on tour. June called Evan immediately, and with Michael and Jordie listening on speakerphone she launched into a tirade.

"You're a terrible father! You're just using him for his writing talents." June accused Evan of reneging on his promise to give Jordie five thousand dollars from the sale of *Robin Hood.* She announced that she was now managing their son's career and if Evan wanted to collaborate with him again he would have to sign a contract with her.

"What are you talking about?" Evan said. "Jordie didn't write one word of that screenplay and you know it. He doesn't know the first thing about it." The only contribution Jordie had made was the original suggestion that it be a comedy, and occasionally he reviewied the script to see if it made him laugh. "I'm not going to give a thirteen-year-old five thousand dollars to spend at will," Evan continued. "The money's in the bank. He knows it and you know it. Please, June, let's not argue about this. It's stupid."

Evan later surmised that the real reason June had read him the riot act was to make it clear to Michael that she had total control of Jordie. That she and she alone could give Michael what he wanted.

June ended the call by bashing Evan over the head with the very weapon he had so conveniently provided to her just a few weeks earlier, when he had joined forces with Michael to convince her about the once-in-a-lifetime educational experience awaiting their son. "We're going on the tour," June proclaimed, and hung up.

Since the day Jordie was born, Evan and June had never questioned the other's motives when it came to their son's well-being. Nor had either of them made even the slightest attempt to wrest control of him from the other, or desired to.

Evan believed that June felt threatened by the relationship developing between himself and Michael. "To Michael she was Jordie's mother, period. He couldn't play with her like one of the boys. She was scared of being pushed out, that's why she told Michael she didn't want me included in their relationship."

Evan knew that June had been receiving expensive jewelry from Michael and using his credit card on elaborate shopping sprees, but he had previously considered those material benefits to be a windfall, nothing more. Now he realized that there was more to it, and it scared him. Because no matter what plan Evan devised to separate his son from Michael, he always came to the same conclusion — June. She had legal custody and control of the boy. She had control of them all. And Evan feared she would fight him to the bitter end.

If one had to pick a day on which the die was cast, it would have to be June 9 — the day communication broke down between Jordie's mother and father and a line was drawn in the sand.

Did Michael act subconsciously, or did he play the two parents like a dime store kazoo? Probably both. What is clear, however, based on Jordie's sworn statement and on the evidence gathered by the police and private investigators, is that Michael Jackson had only one objective in mind, to have Jordie sexually. A goal he had already achieved, many times over.

In retrospect, Evan knew that he waited too long to act. "June was in way too deep, morally if not legally. Had I not been influenced by Michael's smooth talk and success and acted on my instincts, I might have been able to prevent it, or at least the bulk of it. I was starstruck and stupid, and there's no excuse for it."

The following weekend, June allowed Jordie to go to Neverland alone, his first time at the ranch without her. As he had been doing since their trip to Las Vegas in March, Jordie slept with Michael in the star's high security bedroom.

June called the ranch over the weekend to see how things were going. Jordie said he was having a good time. Michael spoke to her, too, but he was nearly incoherent. A shot for back pain, he claimed.

– 6 –

JUNE 13

The entire left side of Barry Rothman's face had slid down his lap and was now oozing over the side of the dental chair. At least that's what it felt like after the massive dose of anesthesia Evan had given him. All the more reason why the right side seemed so sensitive. "Hey, what's that!" Rothman said, as the cold splash of Evan's tear burst on his cheek.

"I'm sorry, Barry, I'm kind of upset right now. Would you mind if we quit for the day?"

"Why? What's wrong?"

"I wish I could tell you, but it's . . . it's too personal."

"Excuse me," the attorney garbled, not happy that he had been on the chair only long enough to be anesthetized, "I think you owe me an explanation."

He was right, of course, and Evan felt obliged to tell him. So after extracting a promise not to repeat what he was about to hear, Evan relayed his story.

"That's an amazing tale," Barry remarked.

"Yeah," Evan said, and since the cat was out of the bag, he asked the attorney for his take on things, from a legal standpoint.

"You know, it just so happens that I have a son Jordie's age, so I can empathize with you. And you're right, it's definitely in Jordie's best interest to get him away from Michael as soon as possible."

To Evan's delight, Barry claimed that such a separation would be easy to accomplish. So easy, in fact, that he offered to do it free of charge as his way of repaying Evan for all of the weekends and nights he had worked to accommodate him. "Call me at the office when you're ready," he said. "It's really no big deal."

Wow! Evan thought. Just wait till Monique hears about this!

But Monique was far from thrilled. "Is Rothman a litigator?" she asked.

I don't know," Evan answered, undaunted by his wife's concern. "What's the difference, I'm not suing anyone."

Anxious to get things settled, Evan went to Barry's office the following day — a stone's throw from the Hideout. Evan filled him in on the details and gave the attorney a copy of his divorce agreement with June.

According to the document, June had full "care, custody, and control" of Jordie, and Evan had visitation rights. In the past these had been "just words" to Evan, because there were never any limitations on his relationship with Jordie. Now these words were coming back to haunt him.

In an uncontested, do-it-yourself divorce filed in 1985, "Petitioner" Evan Chandler voluntarily gave "Respondent" June Chandler full custody of their son. "It seemed appropriate at the time," Evan said. "Jordie was only five and it was best that he live with his mom during the school week. She didn't work and could spend all her time raising him, whereas I was busy trying to build a practice and could only spend quality time with him on weekends."

Barry Rothman laid out a two-part plan. First, Evan was to ask June one more time to end the relationship between Jordie and Michael, warning her that if she refused to comply he would file a restraining order against Michael. Unless June contested it, Barry counseled, the restraining order would be granted automatically because Evan was Jordie's father, whereas Michael had no legal connection to the boy. Phase two of the plan, a custody suit against June, would be initiated only if she fought the restraining order.

Barry didn't believe it would go that far, but just to be sure, he suggested they hire a private investigator to watch June's house in order to verify that Michael was entering every night and leaving in the morning.

"What good will that do?" asked Evan. "It doesn't prove they're sleeping together."

"No," Barry answered, "it doesn't. But a signed affidavit from a licensed P.I. will be enough to convince a judge to hear our complaint, and the last thing June and Michael want is to have the court prying into their lives."

As it turned out, the P.I. reported that it would not be possible to do an adequate surveillance of June's house, so the idea was scrapped.

While Evan and Barry were conceiving a plan to separate Jordie from Michael, the superstar was performing oral sex on the boy in a luxury suite at the Riga Royal Hotel in Manhattan.

On June 23, the Jackson entourage boarded the Sony corporate jet en route from New York to Disney World, where Jordie and Michael played and sexed at The Grand Floridian Hotel for four days before flying home to Neverland.[21]

Back in Los Angeles, Evan grew more and more despondent as Father's Day had passed without a call from his son. But he did speak to June several times; conversations that turned loud and hostile each time she refused his demand to put Jordie on the phone. "He doesn't want to talk to you," she said. "And I'm not getting involved."

June's statement of neutrality infuriated Evan. "How can a mother remain uninvolved when her son all of a sudden stops talking to his father?" When June called several days later to let Evan know they were back in town, Evan assumed he would finally get to speak to Jordie, but it was not to be.

"You get him on the phone right now!" Evan exploded.

"Look," June said coolly, as if she were reporting the weather, "this is between you and Jordie."

"Let me tell you something, June. He better call me, and it better be soon, or you're all going to be sorry. You know me. I've had enough!"

At this point, Evan hadn't seen or heard from Jordie since June 9, almost

---

[21] Michael, together with his little boys, was a frequent flier on the Sony jet, one of the many perks he enjoyed as the label's top recording artist and cash cow.

three weeks. "Michael had been telling me my dad was a bad person because he didn't want me to go on tour," Jordie later revealed. "He said I shouldn't talk to him." According to Jordie, June did not try to convince him to talk to his father, or even discuss it with him.

EARLY JULY

After nearly a month with no contact from his son, it was now clear to Evan that extracting Jordie from Michael's clutches would be more difficult than anticipated. Evan became despondent and desperate.

Evan and Dave were good friends, but Dave was also June's husband — estranged, yet her husband nonetheless. Evan did not want to drag Dave into this dispute any more than he wanted to be in the middle of Dave and June's problems. But things had gone too far for such niceties. Recalling how angry Dave had been with Michael and June as a result of the *National Enquirer* story that described Dave's family as Michael's new family, and believing that Dave genuinely loved Jordie, Evan was positive his son's "other dad" would join him in rescuing the boy.

Not only could Dave put pressure on June to do the right thing, but Evan was under the impression that Dave had the money to help pay for high-powered attorneys should it come to that. Evan felt confident that between his legal rights as Jordie's father, and Dave's added financial resources, they could rid themselves of Michael Jackson once and for all.

"I need you to help me get Michael out of the family," Evan began. "Jordie is really getting screwed up." The two men were sitting in Dave's private office at his car rental business.

Dave seemed anxious to help. He recalled all the reasons he hated Michael — the humiliation he suffered and how his business had been ruined by Jackson's interference with his family. Just talking about the subject made him upset.

"Come with me, Evan!" Dave exclaimed, as he jumped over his desk and ran out of the room, "I want to show you something." He led Evan to a TV room and slammed a tape into the VCR. "Just look at this! It's on the fucking Joan Rivers Show!" When the tape was over he whipped out a stack of newspaper clippings to show how he had been disgraced at the hands of

The Gloved One. Dave was furious. Michael's relationship with June and Jordie was all over the media.

"So what do you think we should do?" Evan said, ready to start mapping out a plan.

"Well," Dave answered, "as much as I'd like to help, I can't right now. Nobody around here can do anything right. I'm just too busy. I'd like to help you, but I'm under a lot of pressure."

If it were any other situation Evan would not have been all that surprised at Dave's reaction. "I'd seen it before," Evan said. "He'd get all worked up over something, then refuse to get involved because it would take him away from 'the business.' But this was about Jordie, for God's sake!"

Evan tried again to solicit Dave's help, but to no avail. "You're all talk! You don't give a shit about the kids! All you care about is money!" Inside, Evan was screaming at Dave. But he said nothing out loud. "I didn't want to alienate him," Evan explained. "I knew he wasn't suddenly going to become someone he'd never been, but I was desperate to have him as an ally."

"Okay, then do me one favor," Evan asked. "Don't give June money for a lawyer. I may have a chance if she can't afford to fight."

"Don't worry," Dave promised. "I'm not giving her a fucking dime!"

It wasn't until several days after Dave turned him down that Evan realized how much he'd been counting on his friend's help. "A custody battle seemed unavoidable at that point, and Dave was the only one who could have put enough pressure on June to prevent it. I wasn't about to give up, but I can't remember ever feeling so powerless."

JULY 7

Barry Rothman was still optimistic. He had prepared two legal documents: a restraining order aimed at Michael to keep him away from Jordie, and a modification of custody to prevent June from taking Jordie on tour. When filed with the court, Barry told Evan, these documents would guarantee an end to the relationship.

His lawyer's assurances notwithstanding, Evan was hesitant to take the legal route. He had an intense distrust of the courts, and feared, as did Monique, that they'd all end up losing if "the system" became involved. Not that he wouldn't do it in a heartbeat if that's what it took to get his son back, but he preferred to use it only as a threat to pressure June into getting rid of Michael.

The problem now was how to get June and Michael to meet with him. Evan had already asked June half a dozen times to talk to him about Jordie. He had asked nicely, and not so nicely. He had screamed and begged, but all to no avail. What was left? Evan figured that if he made it crystal clear that this would be their last chance to avoid a legal confrontation, they would *have* to talk to him. "Did they think I would just give up and never see my son again? Surely June knew me better than that!"

Rothman approved of the plan, but advised Evan not to mention anything about having a lawyer; it might be interpreted as a threat and sour the chances for a meeting. He suggested that Evan prepare a written message and read it to June over the phone. Not only would that avoid any misunderstanding on June's part about what Evan wanted, it would prevent the phone call from degenerating into an argument — the fate of all of Evan and June's communications over the past few weeks.

June was out when Evan called and he was about to hang up when it dawned on him that leaving his message on her answering machine was better than talking to her in person. There'd be no arguing, that's for sure, and Michael could hear it directly from the horse's mouth, as opposed to June's interpretation.

> It's Wednesday, July 7. June, make sure you play this message for Michael and Jordie. I'm going to repeat that. June, make sure you play this message for Michael and Jordie. All three of you are responsible for what is going on. No one is a neutral party. Since Jordie has repeatedly refused to return my phone calls, this will be my last voluntary attempt to communicate. I will be at your house at San Lorenzo this Friday, July 9, at 8:30 in the morning. Take my word for it, there is nothing else any of you has to do that is more important than being at this meeting.

June and Michael picked up the message later that evening when she called her answering machine from the limo.

Despite the numerous arguments Evan and June had had over the past month about Jordie and Michael, and that June knew Evan had not seen or spoken to Jordie for over a month, and despite the fact that Evan's message specifically mentioned Jordie's refusal to talk to him, June later testified that she had no idea why Evan wanted to meet.

When asked, under oath, if Evan had voiced his concerns about Jordie and Michael to her during the month he did not see his son, June's attorney would not permit her to answer.

June testified that she found Evan's message "threatening" and "ominous," and that her immediate response was to call Dave to see if he could figure out what Evan had wanted — though she and Dave "had not been on speaking terms" at the time.

Dave testified that when he heard Evan's message, he, like Evan, "was very frustrated about what was going on with Michael Jackson. I can't tell you the frustration and depression and gut-ripping feelings I had about Michael Jackson . . . maliciously and with intent trying to disrupt my family."

Despite these strong admissions from Dave, and his further testimony that between March and August he asked June numerous times if she thought there was any sex between Jordie and Michael, and despite Evan's coming to him just five days before to seek his help in ridding the family of Michael, and despite Evan's clear reference to Jordie on the message, Dave also swore, so help him God, that he had no idea what Evan wanted to talk about.[22]

When Michael heard the message, he immediately called his attorney, Bert Fields. What happened next is best heard from Fields himself, in a 1993 interview he gave to *Vanity Fair.*

> He [Fields] remembers hearing in early July that Jordie's father was very angry and was demanding a meeting with Michael, because Jackson called Fields about it. "I stopped Michael from going to a meeting," Fields says. The next thing Fields did was call Anthony Pellicano to say the father was accusing Michael of molesting Jordie. Then they got on a conference call with the mother and stepfather. On the very first call, Fields says, the stepfather told him that he thought the father "wants money." In an effort to help his wife, the stepfather secretly recorded three conversations with the father, and reported back to Fields and Pellicano."[23]

---

[22] Dave testified that each time he asked June about the sex she denied it, so he accepted her answer and was positive there was none. Why did he keep asking if he was so positive?

[23] Maureen Orth, "Nightmare at Neverland," *Vanity Fair,* January 1994. By far the most in-depth and evenhanded coverage in any media format during the entire scandal.

Anthony Pellicano, the well-known Hollywood gumshoe, had been working on and off for Michael Jackson since 1988. Under oath, he defined his working relationship with Fields and Jackson by stating that he had performed more than ten jobs for the singer, each time having been paid for his work through Fields' law firm.

Pellicano claimed that he had been "involved in an active investigation relative to an extortion attempt for two and a half months."[24] In other words, at either Jackson's or Fields' request he had been keeping an eye on things since mid-June, when Jordie had come home from his brother's preschool graduation and told Michael and June that Evan knew they had lied. Evan, of course, was referring to Michael lying about being a patient of the dentist with AIDS. But Michael, June and Jordie naturally assumed he knew about them sleeping in the same bed, and that he believed it was sexual.

Nevertheless, Evan had made no precipitous moves, so Pellicano had not taken any action against him. On July 7, however, everything changed. As Pellicano would later state under oath, he was "retained" by Fields' law firm "in regard to an extortion attempt by Evan Chandler." When asked *when* Fields retained him, Pellicano testified, "Will you define the word retained. You mean when I was retained to perform services? It would have been on the seventh (of July)." July 7, of course, is the day Evan left his message on June's answering machine.

✳ ✳ ✳

After the matter became public, Jackson's defense was that Evan had tried to extort him. The evidence, Jackson claimed, was a secret tape recording of Evan made by Dave Schwartz on the evening of July 8, which Dave then turned over to Pellicano and Fields the following day. Dave has always maintained that he made the tape of his own volition. But there's no doubt that there was contact between Schwartz, Pellicano and Fields the day *before* the tape was made. This was confirmed in the information Fields gave to *Vanity Fair* about how and when he came to hire Pellicano, and was further confirmed by Pellicano's subsequent testimony under oath.

PELLICANO: I think that I was involved in a conference call the day before. I

---

24 Anthony Pellicano, interview by Larry King, *Larry King Live*, CNN, August 24, 1993.

think the call originated from Mr. Fields' office. I can't say that for a fact. One of those two parties [Dave or Fields] originated the conference call. I think it was Mr. Fields.

ATTORNEY: And this was the day before he [Dave] came to your office and gave you the original of this tape?

PELLICANO: Yes, I believe that's — that's the facts. My best estimate was probably sometime in the afternoon.

JULY 8

Early on the morning of July 8, Dave called Evan at his office. Evan was busy with a patient and told him to call back. At 9 PM Dave called Evan again. Evan's initial thought was that Dave had changed his mind and was calling to lend a hand, but his hopes were quickly dashed. "I just happened to be at June's house and heard your message," Dave began. "I've got to tell you, Evan, I think you're crazy."

Wait a minute, Evan thought, wasn't Dave the one who only a week ago was fuming about Michael interfering in our lives, yet he refused to get involved? Now all of a sudden he's changed his mind and is getting involved, to tell me that *I'm* crazy? He's the one who's crazy.

Evan also knew that, at this point, Dave hadn't been living at June's house for several months, and that with the exception of haggling over money Dave and June had rarely communicated since May, when June's escapades in Cannes became fodder for the tabloids. That Dave should suddenly find himself at June's on the very day Evan left his message was strange indeed.

Evan had a bad feeling about this call from the start, but communicated none of these feelings to Dave. He desperately needed the man's help and still held out hope he could talk him into joining forces.

Throughout the conversation Dave tried to convince Evan that his real problem was that he was under too much pressure at work. Dave could relate to such pressure, he told Evan, because he, too, had similar problems. Evan responded that his concerns were strictly about Jordie and had nothing to do with work.

"No, no, you don't understand," Dave insisted. "You're under a lot of pressure but you don't know it. You've learned to deny it after all these years, like I have." Dave then offered a solution to the pressure problem. "Do you need money?" he asked. "Is this about money?"

Evan reminded Dave that he had just netted over one hundred thousand from the sale of his screenplay. But Dave paid no heed and insisted that money *had* to be at the root of the problem. He was so relentless in trying to shove money down Evan's throat that Evan finally blew up. "I don't give a shit about money, you idiot! I want my kid back!"

The two men bantered back and forth for nearly an hour, at which point Evan said he was exhausted and had to go home. Dave insisted that Evan call him back from the car on his way home, and Evan reluctantly agreed. Mark Torbiner had been standing at Evan's side during the entire conversation. They had just finished a case when Dave called. "What the fuck is his problem," Evan said, frustrated and bewildered as he hung up. "He knows damn well what I want, I told him last week."

"Take it easy," Mark said. "You'll burst a blood vessel."

"I don't get it, Mark. A week ago he told me he doesn't want to get involved. Now he calls to tell me I'm crazy."

Evan called Dave back from the car as promised. They talked until Evan arrived home, then a third time after Evan was inside the house. It wasn't until six weeks later, as he watched Anthony Pellicano and Howard Weitzman (Michael's criminal attorney) hold an internationally televised press conference, that Evan first discovered Dave had taped their conversations.[25]†

After making these recordings, between 8 and 11 PM on July 8, Dave left his office and drove directly to his house in Bel Aire, where June, Michael and Jordie were spending the night. Both Dave and June testified that Dave did not bring the tape home from work that night. But according to Jordie, Dave not only brought it home, he played it for June and Michael.

Though it was now 2 AM (July 9), Michael called Bert Fields to tell him they had the tape, whereupon Fields instructed Dave and June to meet him at Pellicano's office the following afternoon and to bring the tape.

---

[25] Dave, not Evan, initiated each of the calls. Dave testified that he did not tape the first call to Evan in his office, only the second and third calls. But the evidence soon to be presented suggests otherwise.

"Don't worry," Dave assured Michael that night, "I'll handle Evan." Dave was confident he could convince Evan to back off, and in so doing become a hero in both June's and Michael's eyes. It might not get him back in June's bed, but it would surely put him in good stead with Michael.

"Worried?" Michael replied. "Who's worried? I've been in this situation before. Bert and Anthony will take care of it."[26]

JULY 9

Evan and Monique arrived at June's sharply at 8:30 AM ready for the meeting Evan had demanded in his message. "Are they here?" Evan asked, as Dave opened the door. "There's nobody here but me," Dave answered with a grin, thinking Evan had no choice now but to deal directly with him. Instead, Evan and Monique turned their backs and walked toward their car.

"Wait!" Dave shouted. "We have to talk!" But the couple paid him no mind and drove directly home.

A few minutes later a loud knock sounded on Evan's door. Peering through the window, he saw Dave standing on the landing with June out in the driveway, leaning against Dave's car.[27]

Evan played possum at first, hoping Dave and June would leave. He had made it clear in his message and in his conversations with Dave the night before (it's on the tape) that Michael and Jordie *had* to be at the meeting — that he had no intention of meeting alone with Dave and June. But Dave kept pounding and screaming, "Open up! We have to talk! "

"I have nothing to say!" Evan shouted back. "Get off my property!"

"No! You have to open the door!"

"I said get off my property. You're trespassing!"

"I'm not leaving until you talk to me!"

"If you don't leave right now I'm going to call the cops!"

---

[26] Dave and Michael's conversation, as quoted by Jordie.

[27] June testified that she was home when Evan and Monique arrived at her house, but failed to make her presence known. Why she did this seems strange, considering she also testified that "We were very upset that it ended that way. We thought we were going to come to some kind of solution (as to) why Evan was so upset. We needed to get to the bottom of this, and we thought, as adults, we could get to it . . . "

"Just open the door and tell me face to face. Then I'll go!"

Evan relented and began to pull the door back slowly, intending to stick his face in the narrow opening and order Dave to leave. But as he flicked the lock, Dave pushed hard against the door and sent it smashing into Evan's head.

Furious, Evan ran outside and shoved Dave off the landing, then quickly retreated back inside the house when Dave raised his fists and came at him. Dave was a boxing fanatic and had taken lessons. "You destroyed the family!" Evan shouted as he slammed the door safely behind him. "It's all your fault! It's all your fault!"

Far from having "handled" the problem, Dave and June were now forced to report to Bert Fields that the situation had deteriorated. Fields understood that with tempers flaring, the possibility of the authorities becoming involved had increased exponentially. It was time to unleash Pellicano.

Dave had told the P.I. that Monique was a reasonable person. After all, she was an attorney — working out disputes was what she had been trained to do. Figuring he could get to Evan best through Monique, Anthony Pellicano called her at her office. But she was at lunch, so he left a message to call him back.

When Monique returned his call, Pellicano introduced himself by saying, "I work with Bert Fields," leading Monique to believe he was an attorney in Fields' firm. Although Dave and June testified they had no idea what was bothering Evan, Pellicano seemed to know exactly what it was, though he had talked only to Dave and June at this point and not to Evan.

According to Monique's detailed notes of the conversation, Pellicano told her that he, like Evan, was a father, and that he understood how Evan must feel thinking his son may have been "the victim of *a molestation.*" "Whatever it takes" to resolve the problem can be "accomplished between fathers," Pellicano assured, and Evan would have his "undivided attention" toward that goal.

Monique refused to discuss the subject and reminded Pellicano that it was improper of him, as an attorney, to contact the opposing client directly without going through his attorney. "I had no reason to think he knew that Barry Rothman was representing Evan," Monique explained months later. "I just assumed he did. But he never protested. He never said, 'Oh, sorry, I didn't know,' or anything like that." Monique called Rothman to tell him about her conversation with Pellicano.

That afternoon, at about 2 PM, Dave and June met with Fields and Pellicano as previously arranged, in a back room at the Pellicano Investigative Agency on Sunset Boulevard. They began by playing the tape. "I listened to it for ten minutes and knew right away it was extortion," Pellicano would later claim.[28] Then they got down to business.

"How many people know Michael slept in the same bed with Jordie?" Fields asked during the course of the meeting. Frequently, he and Pellicano would excuse themselves to confer in private, and then return with more questions, which Dave and June did their best to answer. They cooperated with Michael's underlings in every way.[29]

Dave and June would eventually testify that the first time they spoke to Fields or Pellicano was *after* the tape was made. Fields and Pellicano have stated that they were in contact with Dave and June before it was made. But all four insist that Dave acted on his own. If this is true, it was miraculously fortuitous for Jackson that just twenty-four hours after Pellicano was "retained to perform services," Dave just happened to catch the so-called extortion evidence on tape.

This might not seem so far-fetched if Dave had made the tape because he, too, expected an extortion attempt. But he didn't. According to June and Dave's later testimony, it all began with Evan's "ominous" and "threatening" message on her answering machine. "He sounded like a crazy man," Dave agreed, also under oath. But since neither knew what was bugging Evan, or so they testified, Dave decided to call and find out.

Dave swore that the only reason he recorded the last two calls (Evan in his car and at home), was because Evan was so "very irate and very threatening" in the first call (in Evan's office). "I thought that Evan was going to come and kill everyone," Dave said, claiming that he wanted to capture Evan's threats on tape, as evidence, should Evan carry them out.[30]

---

[28] Mary A. Fischer, "Did Michael Do It?" *GQ Magazine*, October 1994, 220.

[29] The description of this meeting, including the quote of Fields, is from Dave and June's depositions. According to Dave, at one point during the meeting, Pellicano looked at Fields, rolled his eyes and sighed, "Here we go again."

[30] Contrary to Dave's testimony, Fields told journalist Maureen Orth that the stepfather recorded three calls with Evan. Only the last two calls were on the tape. Maureen Orth, "Nightmare at Neverland," *Vanity Fair,* January 1994, 131.

When Dave was asked if Evan had threatened to kill any particular individual, he testified, "It was all implied. . . . The implication was that he was going to kill everyone, including Jordie."

Dave was asked what, specifically, Evan had said that led him to that conclusion.

"I just can't remember the exact wordage, but that was my feeling."

Did Evan ever use the word "kill" in the conversation?

"I don't think he did."

Did Evan use any words synonymous with kill?

"I don't know if he did, but that was the implication."

Did Evan threaten to kill Jordie, June or Michael?

"I don't remember."

By the end of that first telephone call, did you feel Evan was going to kill anyone?

"Maybe."

Did you notify the police after the call?

"No."[31]

Oddly enough, in the first minute of the tape we find Dave asking Evan to come to his office so they could talk face to face. This was very brave of Dave, not to mention inconsistent with his testimony that Evan had just threatened "to kill everyone."

Dave then made several offers to set up a meeting for the following morning between Evan, Jordie and Michael, two of the people Evan had allegedly just threatened to kill. Dave later admitted that he went home after making the recordings and tried his best to talk Michael into meeting with Evan the next day.

Does a man send his stepson, or anyone, into a situation where he truly believes they might be physically harmed, or even murdered?

Also curious is that the morning after Evan allegedly threatened to kill everyone, including June, Dave and June chased after Evan, pounded on his door and demanded that he come out and confront them.

---

[31] California law allows a person to record another without their consent if there is reason to believe that the other is going to commit a violent crime. But the purpose is to bring the tape to the police so the crime can be prevented.

To support his allegations of Evan's violence, Dave testified that when Evan finally came out of his house on the morning of July 9, he did more than just push him off the stoop. Dave claimed that Evan pushed him to the ground and repeatedly struck him.[32]

Yet despite this severe beating, Dave testified that his clothes didn't even get soiled and that he did not seek medical attention for several weeks. In fact, the only damage Dave claimed to have suffered was that the alleged beating negatively affected his ability to negotiate business deals, thus causing him financial loss.

And, as with Evan's alleged threats to kill everyone, Dave did not report the battery to the police. Instead, he turned to Bert Fields and Anthony Pellicano for help, two people he swore under oath he had never met. Total strangers.

Dave also testified that two months after the first beating, Evan knocked him unconscious again while they sat in a meeting with Jordie's legal team. According to Evan, two attorneys who were present at the time denied in sworn statements that such an event occurred.

To further support his claims of Evan's violence, Dave testified that although he had never known Evan to be violent before these incidents, he had heard from June that Evan had beat up several people, including Monique, June's mother and Evan's own mother. June testified that she had heard of one incident, in January of 1992, when an argument between Evan and Monique turned physical. Other than that 18-month-old event, she knew of no other reason why her son would not be safe with Evan.[33]

Last, but certainly not least, Dave claimed that after making the secret recordings of Evan, he and June went to the meeting with Fields and Pellicano for the purpose of eliciting their help in "fending off" Evan's violence. Yet at that meeting they agreed to let Jordie spend a week with Evan, who, according to Dave, had just threatened to kill the boy!

These abundant lapses of logic in Dave and June's testimony should be proof enough that Dave did not make the recordings for the reasons he and

---

[32] Dave made these claims in an assault and battery suit against Evan in 1994.

[33] Evan's mother and June's mother, an angel of a woman, are deceased. May they rest in peace.

June claimed — out of fear that Evan was about to become murderously violent. Yet there exists more empirical evidence that the decision to record Evan was premeditated.

Dave testified that his decision to record Evan was made on the spur of the moment: after hearing Evan's violent threats in the first call, Dave ran down to Radio Shack, bought an automatic voice-activated recording attachment for a tape recorder he had lying around the office, then came back and recorded the second and third calls.

On the first day of his deposition Dave agreed to produce the recording attachment the following day. But the next day he claimed he could find neither the device nor a receipt for its purchase. Radio Shack submitted that it had no record of such a sale on July 8, 1993, at any of the three Radio Shack locations where Dave testified he would have made the purchase.[34]

As for the hundreds of glitches on the tape, Dave testified they were not intentional edits.

> [At] Radio Shack they have these attachments that will — oh, they're voice activated, and it's a long cord with a little switch in it, which I actually incorrectly hooked up 'cause, like, if you notice in the tapes . . . it would go off about every eight seconds. I'd have to go "uh huh" or talk to get it going again. It just didn't go. I didn't know how to work it.

The first question that comes to mind is this: assuming Dave did use such a device, could it have created the glitches found on the tape?

According to its 1993 catalogue, Radio Shack sold four devices that attach to any standard tape recorder for the purpose of turning it into a voice activated unit. (Remember, we're talking about an adapter, not a single-unit tape recorder with built-in voice activation.)

Contrary to Dave's testimony, there is no way to hook up these devices incorrectly and still have them activate the recorder. If you fail to plug in any of the lines correctly, the devices will not activate. You get nothing.

In addition, these devices are not "voice activated" in the true sense, meaning they are not "voice sensitive." They go on and off with the electrical impulse generated when you pick up the phone and are completely

---

[34] Anyone who shops at Radio Shack knows how diligent they are about entering sales in their computer.

independent of the voice. If a voice gets too low, or even if no one speaks at all, the tape recorder continues to roll. It is either on or off, period. The bottom line is that none of these devices are capable of producing the editing glitches found on the tape.

But the most compelling evidence regarding the making of the secret tape is this. The conversation between Evan and Dave takes up about 75 percent of the tape. The rest of the tape contains twenty-nine separate conversations between employees and customers of Dave's car rental business. Apparently, Dave Schwartz was routinely taping phone calls at his business.

Dave certainly didn't keep the device in plain sight; it must have been hidden from both customers and employees. And he wasn't personally monitoring the calls because when two customers asked to speak to him they were told that he was involved with other customers. In other words, he wasn't controlling these recordings. Yet despite many long periods of silence in these employee-customer conversations, the tape never stops rolling. *There is not one glitch in any of them.*

So, if Dave's device was not even capable of producing the glitches, and, in fact, was hooked up and operating without producing glitches, how did they get on the tape recordings of Evan?

Dave Schwartz, car salesman, had neither the expertise nor equipment to add them. But *the very next day* he gave the tape to a world-renowned audio surveillance expert with the most sophisticated equipment available, Anthony Joseph Pellicano Jr., who according to his own testimony was hired by Bert Fields "to perform services" the day before the tape was made. Anthony Pellicano, "The best suppressor of confirmable gossip."[35]

Dave and June's story about why and how Dave made the tape, and why they met with Fields and Pellicano and turned the tape over to them, is, at best, not credible. At worst it's a pack of lies.

The true facts paint an ugly picture.

When Evan left his message on June's answering machine on July 7, it was the first indication he had given that he intended to take some action.

---

[35] Peter Wilkinson, "The Big Sleezy," *GQ Magazine*, January, 1992, 114. There is no evidence that Dave participated in the editing or wanted it done.

In response, Michael called his heavies, Fields and Pellicano.

Dave testified that Michael called Pellicano his "007 man." Pellicano's job was to find a way to make Evan back off. Trapping him into saying something incriminating on tape, then using it to threaten him would do just fine. The only problem was that Pellicano had never met Evan, and June and Evan were on the outs. To bait the trap, Pellicano needed someone Evan trusted.

"[When I] came over to talk to you," Evan told Dave on the tape, referring to their conversation at Dave's office one week earlier, "you seemed pretty damned upset that everybody was telling you that Michael Jackson has taken your family away from you. You even went so far as to tell me you couldn't get bank loans because of that [tape irregularity]."[36]

"I'll tell you what I'm concerned about," Dave answered. "I'm concerned about Jordie. . . . I've been there plenty for him. I mean, in the thirteen years I've been there a lot."

"I agree," Evan replied. "So why all of a sudden do you not want to be there?"

"Because I've been in a survival mode. . . . I would die for that kid — you don't know what I've done for that kid."

"Easy to say that, Dave, but when you tell me you're in a survival mode so you can't pay attention to your children, it doesn't jive with 'I would die for that kid.'"

"I'm ashamed of that. I'm not proud of that, but . . . I would do anything for Jordie. I would lose everything. I would die for Jordie. That's the bottom line."

"Then why don't you just back me up right now and let's get rid of Michael Jackson?"

"Because I don't know the facts, Evan."

What facts *did* Dave know prior to making the tape? He testified that prior to July 1993, during the very period Jordie was being molested, he asked June if she thought Michael was sexually abusing the boy. She did not think so, Dave said, and he believed her.

---

[36] "Tape irregularity" appears in the official transcript of the tape. It's the official term for "glitch."

But several weeks later, Dave asked again. June still did not think so, so again he believed her.

Then he asked again. And again. And again.

Despite June's denials, Dave felt compelled to ask at least five times over a period of four months, according to his own testimony.

Dave also testified, "I'd kid Jordie, 'Who's on top?' . . . I'd be kidding him, but checking him out." In other words, Dave had suspicions about Jordie and Michael's relationship that preceded Evan's by several months.

In 1994, after Jordie's suit against Michael was settled out of court, Dave filed his own complaint against Michael in which his attorney claimed, "As his concern grew, Schwartz on numerous occasions inquired of Jackson whether Jackson was having improper and/or sexual contact with Jordie."

Dave testified that as far back as April 1993, when June and the kids accompanied Michael to the World Music Awards in Monaco, "I was trying to figure a way to wean the family away from Michael Jackson. . . . It was Christmas every day for the kids. . . . If this lasted too long, it was really going to be harmful to the kids. . . . It was very unhealthy for them."

Dave testified that prior to the day when Evan came to solicit his help in ridding the family of Jackson, he was already of the opinion that the singer was *"maliciously and with intent* trying to disrupt my family."

Yet with all this, and with all his professed love and willingness to die for his children, Dave still refused to help Evan oust Michael from the family. He had no choice, he claimed, he was in "survival mode."

Survival mode?

Dave Schwartz had become a wealthy man since founding the world's first discount car rental agency. Wealthy enough to be featured on *Lifestyles of the Rich and Famous.* But by July of 1993 he was heavily leveraged in a depressed Los Angeles real estate market and his fortune was precarious.

A day or so before Evan went to Dave's office to seek his help, Dave approached June with a request. One of his creditors was demanding payment of a five million dollar note but was willing to settle for a lump sum of four million. Dave asked June to present a proposition to Michael in which the star would loan him four million as part of a business deal. June agreed to pass the request on to Michael.

Survival Mode. Dave was starved for cash and waiting for Michael Jackson to feed him. According to his own testimony, Dave already suspected that the relationship between Jordie and Michael was sexual. But rather than help Evan get rid of Michael, he helped Michael get rid of Evan.

It is possible that neither Fields nor Pellicano came right out and told Dave to record Evan. Maybe they beat around the bush and said something like, "You know, Dave, famous people like Michael are constantly the target of extortion. If we could just catch the attempt on tape . . ." Maybe it *was* Dave's idea and they just went along with it *after* he brought them the tape.

One thing is clear. By the time they met at Pellicano's office the following day to listen to the tape, all four participants were of one mind — to stop Evan from upsetting the status quo.

Follow the money. June was living the life of a fairy princess and did not want the dream to end. Dave was waiting for Michael's word on the four million. And Fields and Pellicano were being paid huge sums, pail and shovel in hand, to trail behind the circus elephant that was Michael Jackson.

If Fields truly believed that Evan was out to extort Michael, wouldn't he have called the police, paid Evan off or simply told him to get lost? The tape made it clear, however, that Evan was concerned for his son and therefore the only way to diffuse the situation was to allow Evan to see his son. That's why Fields decided that he would call Evan's attorney, Barry Rothman, and arrange for a visitation between the boy and his father.

Fields would have preferred to stay in the background and let Pellicano negotiate the visitation agreement with Rothman. But he was forced to step into the spotlight when Rothman refused to deal with Pellicano. Not that it would have made a difference, morally or legally. Fields became inextricably tied to every dirty trick his dog pulled the moment he unleashed him.

By actively involving himself in a dispute between the mother and father over their child's relationship with the alleged molester, while at the same time representing the molester, Fields placed the noose around his own neck. And later that evening, as we shall now see, this ace litigator unwittingly began to strangle himself.

Though Fields knew that Evan had engaged the services of an attorney, at no time during the meeting were Dave or June advised by either Fields or Pellicano to seek legal representation elsewhere.[37] On the contrary, though they never signed a retainer with Fields, by the time they left Pellicano's office they were under the impression that Fields and Pellicano were working with them toward a common goal. "[We were] planning, we were discussing strategy together. We were discussing how to fend off Evan together," Dave testified regarding the July 9 conversation between himself and Bert Fields.

Two decisions were reached at this meeting. First, as Bert Fields later testified, " . . . the upshot of the meeting was that I was going to speak to Mr. Rothman" to work out an arrangement in which Jordie would be allowed to visit Evan for several days. This would help Evan blow off a little steam, Fields told Rothman. Second, the meeting's participants would meet again that evening at Michael's Hideout.

Later that afternoon, Barry Rothman and Anthony Pellicano spoke for the first time. Pellicano again introduced himself as being "with Bert Field's office." Barry, like Monique, assumed Pellicano was an attorney, but he refused to discuss the matter with anyone other than Fields.

No sooner had Rothman hung up with Pellicano when Fields called, anxious for a meeting. But it was not to be; they were both booked up for the remainder of the afternoon and Fields was due to leave for New York the following day, which also happened to be the day Rothman's son was being Bar Mitzvah'd.

Knowing the situation was critical and could not wait, Fields and Rothman negotiated the visitation agreement over the phone. Jordie would be delivered to Evan by 7 PM the following day, Saturday, July 10, and be returned to June at the same time one week later.

While June and Dave were meeting with Fields and Pellicano, Jordie and Kelly were being driven around town by Michael's chauffeur, Gary Hearne. Gary was ordered to keep the children busy for a few hours, and then drop them off at the Hideout at 6 PM.

---

[37] In his deposition, Fields was asked if he understood that "Barry Rothman was Evan Chandler's agent speaking on his behalf." "Absolutely," Fields answered.

Jordie stated that when he arrived, Michael took him aside and explained that a private investigator named Anthony Pellicano was coming over to ask him a few questions. When Jordie asked why, Michael replied with an accusation that would not only be repeatedly drummed into the boy's head, but over the next few years into the public's mind as well: "Your father is a bad person. He's causing trouble."

While Michael fed Jordie the correct answers to Pellicano's forthcoming questions, the Inquisitor himself was on his way over with June, whom he had picked up at her house as previously planned. Dave, too, was en route. And Bert Fields, though not present in body, was there in his capacity as an attorney via his subcontractor, Pellicano.

Consider the following exchange between Pellicano, under oath, and Larry Feldman, the attorney who was hired in September of 1993 to represent Jordie in his civil lawsuit against Jackson.

> FELDMAN: "What was the purpose of the conversation with Jordie?"
>
> PELLICANO: "The purpose was trying to ascertain what the difficulty with his father was."
>
> FELDMAN: "Why did you feel it was your business to find out the difficulty of what him and his father were having?"
>
> PELLICANO: "June Chandler told me."
>
> FELDMAN: "What did June Chandler tell you about the problems that Evan and Jordie were having?"
>
> PELLICANO: [Refused to answer. His attorney asserted the attorney-client privilege.]
>
> FELDMAN: [to Pellicano's attorney] "Is that your position? That on July 9, Mr. Pellicano was the investigator for Mr. Jackson in some dispute between Jordie Chandler and his father?
>
> PELLICANO'S ATTORNEY: "He has said that everything he's done for Mr. Jackson has been under the supervision and the direction of counsel and that would make it [privileged]."
>
> FELDMAN: "A lawyer for Mr. Jackson has something to do with the custody dispute between Jordie and his dad?"
>
> PELLICANO'S ATTORNEY: "Everything is [privileged]."

The attorney under whose supervision and direction Pellicano operated is, of course, Bert Fields.

While Jordie was downstairs being cross-examined by Pellicano, June and Dave remained upstairs in Michael's bedroom; June watching TV, Dave on the phone to work. Both were apparently unconcerned about what the tall stranger they had met for the first time that afternoon was doing with their child. At one point during the forty-five-minute session Dave started downstairs to see Jordie, but Pellicano stopped him. I just need a few more minutes with him, the P.I. declared, and ordered Dave back upstairs.[38]

According to Pellicano, Jordie not only denied having sexual relations with Michael, he stated his father was just out for money. When asked by the press why he didn't tape the session, Pellicano responded, "You have to understand, that was a whim."[39]

A whim?

Anthony Pellicano, a family man with nine children, just happened to be driving around on a Friday night, picked up June at her house, drove to Michael's apartment where Jordie had been recently dropped off at a pre-arranged time, interrogated the boy for forty-five minutes about his relationship with Michael, all just hours after a decision had been made to turn the boy over to his father, who happened to be claiming Pellicano's client had molested his son.

Wow! What a whim!

What bullshit, too. It was Pellicano's job to make sure the rehearsing Jordie had been subjected to over the past year held up.[40] If Jordie admitted the truth to Evan . . . well, no telling what might happen.

"Michael scared me," Jordie later recalled. "He told me an investigator would be there to talk to me, then went over all the questions I would be asked. He was, like, really worried and made me all worried. He said, "Just smile and say no. That's all you have to do is say no."[41]

Consider the following comments of a well-known attorney about the interrogation of minors.

---

[38] From Dave and June's depositions.

[39] Orth, "Nightmare at Neverland," 131.

[40] To be discussed in Part Four.

[41] Jordie quoting Michael.

[LAPD officers] have subjected them to high-pressure interrogation, *sometimes out of the presence of their parents.* . . . These tactics are not merely *inappropriate,* they are *disgraceful.* They should not be employed by an enlightened, modern police force. Certainly, they have no place in the LAPD. Your officers should do their job, but do it fairly and *ethically* . . . especially when those witnesses are minors. *They should not interrogate minor witnesses at all in the absence of their parents.* (Italics added.)

This is from a letter dated October 28, 1993, addressed to LA Police Chief Willie Williams. It was written two months after Pellicano questioned Jordie. In the letter, the attorney was admonishing the chief for alleged misconduct by his officers during their questioning of other young boys who might have been molested by Jackson.

The signature on the letter? Bert Fields.

On October 29, *just one day* after sending the letter to Chief Williams, Fields filed a motion in Santa Monica Superior Court in response to Jordie's molestation suit. In support of Michael's innocence, Fields attached a declaration signed by Pellicano in which the P.I. stated,

[I] personally interviewed the plaintiff [Jordie], *at length and in detail.* I did this *alone,* so that he would be under no pressure from having Michael Jackson *or his parents* in attendance. (Italics added.)

The alleged perpetrator did not pay the police. But he did pay Pellicano.

Fields knew that Pellicano would be questioning Jordie that night; the decision to do so had been made only hours before in the meeting at Pellicano's office. But it would be naive to think this top-of-the-heap litigator wasn't looking far beyond what Jordie might tell his father. Bert Fields never made a move without considering potential litigation. That's what made him so formidable.

By his own admission, both to *Vanity Fair* and under oath, Fields knew that Evan had already hired an attorney, and that that meant a potential lawsuit. So certain was he of looming litigation that he used it as the core of his defense against Barry Rothman's 1995 defamation suit.[42]

Jordie, as the victim-witness, would be the first to be questioned by the

---

[42] Discussed in Part Three.

authorities. Fields had to be sure that if Evan went to the cops, the boy's answers would stop their investigation cold.

By July 9, Fields must have realized that he had crossed over the line. Why else would he have denied that he was in league with Pellicano? Despite the P.I.'s declaration that he was hired by Fields — *a declaration submitted to the court by Fields himself* — Fields swore under oath that, "He [Pellicano] never worked for me."[43]

Harry Cain would never have approved.[44]

While Jackson and Pellicano were rehearsing his son, Evan was home with Monique discussing the events of the day, including her afternoon phone conversation with Pellicano. "When she told me Pellicano said I was concerned about 'a molestation,' the significance didn't register immediately. I had never thought of gay behavior as molestation. If not asexual, I was coming to believe Michael was gay. I had never used the word 'molestation,' much less thought it."

It's telling that Bert Fields (to Pellicano on July 7)[45] and Anthony Pellicano (to Monique on July 9) were the first to label the relationship a molestation, and that they used the word to describe Evan's thoughts before they had met or talked to him.

Fields and Pellicano had been working for Jackson for many years, and one can't help but wonder what they knew about Michael's relationships with little boys. After all, they had followed this elephant before. "Here we go again," Pellicano had said, as he rolled his eyes to Fields at the July 9 meeting. It appears that in their minds it was all very clear, and so they assumed it was clear to Evan as well.

They were wrong.

---

[43] From Fields' deposition in a 1995 civil suit between Dave and Evan. This was the first and only time (to this author's knowledge) that Fields had been placed under oath regarding his role in the Jackson affair.

[44] Under the pen name D. Kincaid, Bert Fields authored several works of fiction about Harry Cain, an attorney known far and wide for his sterling successes in high profile law suits — remarkably similar, in some respects, to Fields' real life cases. Harry Cain's cardinal rule was that he would never lie under oath. (Fields' books, *The Sunset Bomber* and *The Lawyer's Tale*, are quite entertaining, if you like that sort of thing.)

[45] Orth, "Nightmare at Neverland."

– 7 –

JULY 10-11

Evan slept soundly Friday night — he was finally going to see his son — but awoke early in a cold sweat. "Something was going to go wrong. I could feel it."

Monique tried to comfort him. "Why worry about something that hasn't happened yet?" she advised.

But by 5:00 PM Evan was a wreck. "These people are sadistic," he lamented. "They had all day to bring him. They're waiting for the last minute just to fuck with me." An hour later Evan flat out declared, "They're not coming. I know it."

Saturday passed with no communication from the other side.

On Sunday Evan was awake and pacing by daybreak, anxious to call Barry Rothman with the bad news.

"H'lo?" Rothman grunted.

"He didn't come, Barry."

"Wha? Who is this?"

"It's me, Barry. It's Evan. Jordie didn't show up."

"What!" Barry jarred awake. "What do you mean he didn't show up?"

"They didn't bring him. He's not here."

"That can't be! Bert gave me his word he'd be delivered yesterday by seven."

"So much for Bert's word. I'm going to get them, Barry. They're not going to do this to me and get away with it!"

"Take it easy, Evan. There must be some mistake. Don't do anything. I'll make some phone calls."

Barry eventually reached Bert Fields at the Plaza Hotel in New York. Bert insisted Barry had the wrong day; Jordie was to be delivered on Sunday, not Saturday. Barry was positive it was the opposite. So round and round they went until one finally tired of the game. "I'm sorry," Fields' said. "I must have made a mistake."

Meanwhile, June, Jordie, Kelly and Michael sat comfortably in the back of the limo as Gary Hearne drove north, up the Pacific Coast Highway toward Santa Barbara. It was Kelly's birthday and June wanted to celebrate it at Neverland. On the way they stopped at Mike Milken's beach house in Malibu, where June and Michael went into a back room to call Pellicano.

Michael was angry as hell. Though stoned on pain killers from a recent minor surgery, the star was acutely aware that the mix-up might push Evan over the edge and the police would be called, so he screamed his displeasure at Pellicano for allowing things to get out of hand. Michael's speech was broken and slurred, but the P.I. got the message.

"I'm working for you, Michael," he pleaded. "I only care about you."

Across town, Barry Rothman was having similar problems with his client. By the time he tracked down Fields in New York, it was afternoon in Los Angeles and Evan had been near desperation for almost twenty-four hours. On top of that, little Cody, who had been excited at his big brother's pending arrival after not seeing him for a month, was now crushed.

"Forget it, Barry," Evan ordered. "I don't want to see him."

"What!" Barry screeched into the phone. "What are you talking about?"

"I can't take it any more! I've had it! He doesn't care about me and I don't want him in my house. I have two other children who are suffering. I can't do this to them. If Jordie wanted to see me he would have come yesterday. It's over. Let him go. I have to maintain my sanity."

"Do you realize what you're saying?" Barry insisted. "You can't do this to him, he needs you. And you can't do this to me. I gave my word to Bert. We made a deal."

Monique also prevailed on her husband. "You can't let him go, Evan. He needs you more than ever."

They were right, and Evan knew it. He was angry, but he was also frustrated and tired and just wanted to make the whole thing go away.

It was about that time when Pellicano called (having been chewed out royally by Michael) to assure Evan that there had been a mistake. But Evan had gone for a walk to calm down, so Monique took the call. "We're tired of you people lying to us," she warned. "This will be your last chance to make it work."

When June finally called to ask if it would be okay to bring Jordie over around 7 PM, Evan went ballistic at her for lying to him. June apologized, claiming Bert had told her Sunday, not Saturday.

In retrospect, there was nothing to be gained by Fields having lied to Rothman, or having purposely relayed the wrong information to June. In fact, if it was Fields' goal to keep Evan from going to the authorities by giving him "a chance to blow off a little steam," it would make no sense for Fields to have sabotaged the deal. Most likely it was an honest misunderstanding.

But not to Evan. Not in his state of mind at the time. He took it as a personal attack. "It destroyed any trust I had left. From that point on I accepted nothing they said as the truth."

As with everything else in life, Murphy had a hand in this, too.

Jordie was dropped off at 10 PM, Sunday night. Evan would have one week with him and was determined to find out the truth before he gave the boy back. "I wanted to hug him the minute he walked through the door, but I held back. I needed him to know that I loved him, but that things were not the same as the last time he was here with Michael."

"Don't even think about lying to me," Evan cautioned his son. "This whole thing is about lying, nothing else. If someone lies to you, then you can't trust them. And if you can't trust them there's no sense having a relationship. Just so you know, I had your bedroom at Mom's house bugged and your phone tapped. I know everything you and Michael did. This isn't about that, this is about lying. Do you understand?"

Evan had done none of those things. "I was sitting there lecturing him about lying and then proceeded to lie to him. But I was desperate. What choice did I have? I knew he wasn't going to come right out and tell me. I prayed he would, but I knew he wouldn't. As far as I was concerned it was a matter of life and death for my son — emotionally speaking."

Jordie listened to his father politely, as he always had, and then nodded yes, he understood. "He gave no indication he was even remotely concerned," Evan remembered. "His performance was spectacular. For a moment, I wondered if my suspicions were wrong."

Over the next few days, Evan spontaneously "tested" Jordie. "Hey, look at that babe!" he'd comment, whenever they passed a pretty girl. But Jordie showed no reaction.

Maybe he is gay, Evan thought.

JULY 12

Barry Rothman was putting in considerable time on the case, much more than he had originally expected, and it was apparent that working for free was no longer appropriate. Evan was grateful and readily signed a formal retainer.†

With the formalities out of the way, Evan and Barry reviewed their options. Going to the police was out of the question. They had no proof that a crime had been committed, and it was unlikely they'd acquire any. What type of complaint would they file? That Jordie didn't spend enough time with his father? That he wanted to be with his mother, who had custody of him anyway, and with Michael Jackson, the Pied Piper of children? At best, the police would tell them it was a civil, not criminal matter.

"If we had called the police at that point," Evan joked months later, "they probably would have investigated just long enough to get Michael's autograph for their kids."

If they proceeded civilly, by filing the restraining order and custody documents, it was certain there would be repercussions. The most critical, as far as Evan was concerned, was Jordie's reaction. He had given no indication that he wanted his relationship with Michael to end. If forced to give it up, he might be resentful, which could drive him further from his father and deeper under Michael's influence.

Also to be considered was the likelihood of the court documents becoming public. Michael would then be forced to throw his entire, crushing weight against them. And what could Rothman do against Michael's phalanx of lawyers? Rothman was an unknown solo practitioner. Fields was a famous partner in a large, prestigious firm. That, combined with the star's immense popularity and squeaky-clean reputation, not to mention his endless connections, made him virtually omnipotent. Going head to head with Michael Jackson, especially when Jordie was still under his control and June had legal custody, would be a tough fight indeed.

But Evan didn't rule it out altogether. If that's what it took to protect his son, he would do it. And he wanted Michael to know that. "It was obvious, even in my thick head, that these people were game players. I wanted to let them know I wasn't like that. Play games and I'll ratchet things to the next level."

So Barry and Evan decided to fire a warning shot across the enemy's bow — to put Fields and Pellicano on notice that they were willing to take them on legally if necessary, regardless of the odds. Barry drew up a custody agreement that modified the terms of Evan and June's divorce. Among other things, the agreement provided that June would not be permitted to take Jordie out of Los Angeles County without Evan's written consent.†

The document did not include a change of legal custody or a demand that Jordie be prevented from seeing Michael. It stipulated only that June could not take the boy out of the county, which would preclude him from going to Neverland, and more important, prevent him from going on tour. Jordie leaving U.S. jurisdiction with Michael was Evan's biggest fear. It would be party time for five months and Evan was certain his son would be irreversibly damaged . . . if he wasn't already.

The document was sent by messenger to Anthony Pellicano on the afternoon of July 12, with a cover letter from Barry Rothman. In the letter Rothman reiterated something he had discussed with Pellicano while negotiating the agreement. "As you are aware, this firm represents Dr. Evan Chandler. . . . It is our understanding that June Chandler is not represented by counsel and that you have agreed to use your good auspices to effect the execution of this stipulation."†

June went to Pellicano's office the following day and signed the document. Evan claims that both June and Dave told him that Bert Fields advised June to sign. The agreement was promptly returned to Barry with a cover letter from the Pellicano Investigative Agency.[46] †

With this accomplished, Evan could breathe easier. But there was more to resolve. Jordie was no longer his son; "emotionally speaking he belonged to Michael." And June apparently had no intention of ending the relationship. Also to be considered was Dave's inexplicable switch from a detractor of Michael's, to a neutral party, to completely going over to the other side, all in just one week.

Though Evan still had no direct proof there had been sex between his

---

[46] Is it any wonder that in June and Dave's minds Fields was acting as their representative? Not only had he negotiated the visitation of Jordie with the opposing counsel, he supposedly advised June to sign a contract that his private investigator had negotiated with the same opposing counsel.

son and Michael, his level of suspicion was rising rapidly. What else could explain Michael and June's aggressive efforts to keep Jordie away from him — efforts that shifted into high gear after the June 9 confrontation about the possibility of Jordie being gay.

And then there was the seed Pellicano had sown when he used the word "molestation" in his conversation with Monique. Now, five days later, the significance of the word had taken root.[47]

JULY 14

Evan and Barry decided that the only way to truly understand what was going on between Jordie and Michael was to consult a professional. The only hitch was that California law requires a psychiatrist to report suspected child abuse to the police, and the two men were certain that involving the authorities would only make matters worse. Evan was fearful that anything with Michael's name on it would become public, and that the result of that publicity would be more devastating for Jordie and the rest of the family than whatever had occurred between Michael and Jordie.

Not only did Evan distrust "the system" in general, but on a more practical level, why would anyone believe Michael Jackson was sexually involved with a child when the father had no concrete proof and both the child and his mother denied any wrongdoing?

The only way to get a professional assessment and avoid the reporting requirement was to tell their story without supplying names. Barry called several psychiatrists but they were hesitant about getting involved. "If it ever gets into a courtroom," one doctor said, "you'll need someone with a lot of experience in this area." Of the five or six psychiatrists Rothman contacted, several recommended the same man, Dr. Mathis Abrams, MD, JD. "He's the best there is," one therapist told Barry. "A psychiatrist and a lawyer all wrapped up in one."

"Jordie had been with me for three days at that point," Evan remembers, "but we never talked about Michael. I came close several times but I was

---

[47] The sexual implications of the word, not the criminal. At this point they still believed that if there was a sexual component it was a gay love relationship. Neither Monique nor Evan thought of Michael as a criminal.

afraid to alienate him further, and he never gave any indication he wanted to talk about it. At the time I walked into Dr. Abrams office I had every intention of returning Jordie to his mother [in four days]. I knew it was not in his best interest, but Barry had warned me that the law was on June's side and she could exercise her rights anytime she pleased."

"I was after the truth, not an ally," Evan commented. "The most important thing I could do to help Dr. Abrams render an accurate opinion was to give him accurate information. It was critical I did nothing to influence his thinking, since my decisions were going to be based on what he said. I specifically stayed away from any inference to sex. I only told him what I knew to be provable fact."

Notepad in hand, Dr. Abrams listened carefully as Evan told his story, then offered a lengthy response that boiled down to the opinion that Jordie was in acute psychological danger. From a legal standpoint, Dr. Abrams believed that a thirty-four-year-old man consistently sleeping in the same bed with a minor when other sleeping accommodations are available is a violation of the law regarding lewd and lascivious conduct toward children. He urged Evan to bring the unnamed child in for an interview.

Evan declined, explaining that he needed more time to decide what to do because he feared that if his son and the adult were truly in love, which they appeared to be, and he separated them by involving the authorities, the separation would be traumatic and his son might hate him for it. "I might lose him forever if they're ripped apart like that," Evan told the psychiatrist.

Dr. Abrams responded with a dismal pronouncement, "You've already lost him," and repeated his advice to bring the boy in.

Dr. Abram's warning penetrated Evan to the core, leaving him even more frightened for his son than before, and more despondent about the eventual outcome. Jordie's devotion to Michael, coupled with June's legal control, was daunting enough. Then there was Michael, himself. Had he been any ordinary Joe, or even any ordinary famous Joe, the battle would not have seemed so daunting. But was there anyone more powerful?

Emotionally and physically drained, a strange peace came over Evan that evening. "Like standing at the bedside of someone you love and watching them gasp their last breath, knowing it's over and feeling relieved." It was the first and only time, in what was to become a lengthy battle, that Evan, in his own mind, totally gave up. He accepted that his son was lost to him — that the boy was going back to his mother and there was nothing he could do about it.

This acceptance brought Evan great relief, because now he, too, could go back to a normal life. Or so he had convinced himself.

"You know what, Jordie," he said, before going to bed that night, "I think you should come into the office tomorrow. You're going to be gone a long time and I haven't checked your teeth in ages." Jordie had a baby tooth that had never fallen out and Evan had been meaning to pull it for some time. With the boy out of town for much of the past months, it kept getting put off. "It was the one thing I could rely on," Evan realized months later. "The one thing that was consistent in my life. My work."

"Okay, but no shots," Jordie insisted.

"C'mon, Jordie, I filled six of Kelly's teeth at one time and she didn't say a word."

"I don't care. I don't want any shots. Use anesthesia."

"I can't. It's too dangerous."

"Come on, you do it all the time."

"Not on kids. It's a whole different thing."

"Well, how about Mark? Can't he do it?"

"Yeah, but I hate to ask him. Though I guess he won't mind, he likes you."

JULY 16

Jordie and Evan met Mark at Evan's office at 8:30 AM. As it turned out, the x-rays showed that Jordie had no cavities, just the overretained baby tooth that was causing the permanent one underneath to come in crooked. Evan cleaned his son's teeth while Mark set up his equipment, and when the boy was sedated Evan performed the thirty-second procedure. When Jordie was safely out of sedation, Mark packed up and left.

"That was great," Jordie said, fully awake. "I didn't feel a thing! Can we go eat now?"

"In a minute," Evan answered.

Jordie sat quietly in the chair while his father cleaned up around the operatory.

"Hey, Jordie," Evan said, trying to sound nonchalant. "Since this is our last day together, is there anything you want to tell me before we go?"

"Yeah," Jordie replied. (Evan prayed for a miracle.) "I'm thirsty."

"Uh, okay. You can get up and walk now. Go to the kitchen, there's some bottled water in the fridge."

Evan had waited all week for the right moment to talk to his son, but he was concerned that forcing him to speak before he was ready would drive him further away. The end result was that the right moment never came. Or that Evan had passed it up.

"I was standing there thinking, Oh, well, I guess that's it, he's not going to talk. But while he was out in the kitchen it hit me that I'd been taking the wrong approach. Here I was tiptoeing around him because Dr. Abrams had scared the hell out of me. But Jordie was about to go away with Michael for five months, so how much worse could it get! If he wasn't totally screwed up yet, going on tour was sure to finish the job. That realization changed my whole way of thinking. I could be as tough on him as I wanted. I had nothing to lose."

When Jordie came strolling back from the kitchen, Evan went on the attack. "Have a seat, and listen very carefully to what I'm about to say. Do you remember when you came over to the house I told you that if you lied to me I was going to destroy Michael?" Jordie nodded that he did. "Good. Keep that in mind, because I'm going to ask you a question. Do you care about Michael?"

"Yes," the boy answered.

"You could say you love him, right?"

"Yes."

"And you wouldn't want to hurt him?"

"No."

"Okay then, let me remind you of something. Remember I told you I bugged your bedroom?" Jordie nodded. "Well, I know everything you guys did, so you might as well admit it."

The boy remained silent, seemingly unimpressed by his father's strong-arm approach. Sensing this, Evan quickly changed tack.

"Look, Jordie, lots of famous people are bisexual and nobody gives a shit. They're not embarrassed. It's sorta cool, in a way."

After ten minutes of meandering monologue Evan had elicited nothing from his son but a blank stare. Frustrated, he switched back to his original approach. "I'm going to give you one last chance to save Michael. If you lie to me, then I'm going to take him down in front of the whole world, and it'll be all your fault because you're the one person who could have saved him."

Nothing.

In his heart, Evan already knew the truth; he didn't need Jordie to confirm it. But he believed if his son could just hear himself say it, if he could just spurt it out quickly and painlessly like the tooth, it would release him from the prison in his mind. Without a plan, Evan began babbling away again, saying whatever came to mind in the hope of eventually hitting on something that would push a button in his son and free him.

"I know about the kissing and the jerking off, so you're not telling me anything I don't already know," Evan lied. "This isn't about me finding anything out. It's about lying. And you know what's going to happen if you lie. So I'm going to make it very easy for you. I'm going to ask you one question. All you have to do is say yes, or no. That's it. Lie and Michael goes down. Tell me the truth and you save him."

Jordie remained silent for what seemed to Evan a hopeless amount of time. Then, "Promise?"

"Have I ever lied to you?"

"No."

"And I never will."

"You won't hurt Michael, right?"

"Right."

"And I don't want anyone to know. Promise me you won't ever tell anyone."

"I swear, no one."

"Okay. What's the question?"

"Did Michael touch your penis?"

Jordie hesitated. Then, almost inaudibly, he whispered "Yes."

Evan would press no further. He had heard all he needed to hear. He reached out and hugged his son, and Jordie hugged back, tight.

"We never talked about it again," Evan later told the L.A. district attorney. To Evan, the details didn't matter. "The prison walls had cracked and I was confident the rest would take care of itself."

– 8 –

After lunch, Evan went to Barry Rothman's office to tell him he was not going to return Jordie the next day as planned.

"Why not?" Barry asked.

"Because I love him. That's why."

"See," the attorney bragged, "aren't you happy I talked you into taking him back?"

"You're a wise man, Barry."

"Yeah, but not wise enough. I can't tell Bert you're not returning him because you love him."

"Then don't tell him anything. I'm sure they'll find out tomorrow when he doesn't show up."

"I can't do that, Evan. I have to give them a reason."

"I just gave you one."

"C'mon, that's not good enough and you know it. By the way, how is Jordie?"

"Better than ever, Barry. Better than ever."

"Why is he better than ever?"

"You talk like a lawyer."

"I am a lawyer, Dumb-Dumb. Now why is he better than ever?"

"Where have I heard that question before?"

"Don't bullshit me, Evan! I'm your lawyer. You have to tell me *everything.*"

"Because he eats like a pig and he looks at girls. Or is it the other way around? I'm very confused."

"It's nice to see you so happy. Now would you mind telling me why?"

"Because he's going to be okay and they're not going to fuck with him anymore."

"Did he tell you something?"

"No."

"He told you something, didn't he? What did he tell you?"

"I can't tell you."

"What do you mean you can't tell me!? You *have* to tell me! How am I supposed to help you if you don't tell me everything?"

"I'm sorry, Barry. I promised him I wouldn't say anything and I'm not going to break my promise."

"This isn't working, Evan. I can't do this alone. You have to give me some help here."

"Look, Barry. Let's just say I know something happened because he's my kid, and I know my kid."

"Are you telling me . . .?"

"I'm telling you, you can go ahead on the assumption that something happened because I'm his father and I know him, and I believe very strongly that something happened."

"You're being very difficult."

"No, Barry. He trusts me and I'm not going to do anything to make him not trust me. How do you think he got so fucked up? His mother lied to him. Michael lied to him. The people he trusted most in this whole fucking world betrayed him. Forget it. It's not going to happen. Call Bert and tell him whatever you want. You're the lawyer."

July 16 was turning out to be a big day. Besides the decision not to return Jordie, Barry also received the following report from Dr. Abrams.

A 13-year-old male (the child), whose parents are divorced, lives with his remarried mother and younger half-sister. Her husband is not consistently in their home at this time. The male child has had, for several months, an intensely emotional, personal relationship with an idolized male who is more than 20 years his senior, is a celebrity of some sort, and is not a relative by blood or marriage. The child spends much of his time in the company of this adult male, and their relationship is described as 'inseparable'. The child's mother and half-sister often accompany the child and adult male on trips and/or to events, and the child's mother has received numerous and substantial gifts, both monetary and material, from the adult male. The child has, on many occasions, spent the night in the same bed with the adult male, though separate beds are available. The child and adult male have been observed in the same bed, under the covers, by both the child's mother and father, on separate occasions, and by the child's half-brother. The child's father expressed his concern to the child's mother, who was unconcerned (or impotent) about the nature of the relationship between her son and the adult male. The father is gravely concerned about the psychological (and physical) impact of the child's relationship with the adult male, the message to the child by his mother's condoning attitude, the ramifications of the father's efforts to terminate the relationship between his child and the adult male, and any need for psychotherapeutic intervention. Based upon the above, there are several persons for whom psychotherapeutic intervention is indicated: First and foremost, the child appears to be at risk whether his relationship with the adult male continues or is terminated. . . . Section 11166(a) (of the Penal Code) requires the reporting to a child protective agency by a health practitioner (inter alia) who has knowledge of . . . a child whom he or she . . . reasonably suspects has been the victim of child abuse. Child abuse is defined (11165.6) as including sexual abuse of a child. Sexual abuse is defined in 11165.1 as meaning sexual assault or exploitation as defined therein, which includes 11165(a) conduct in violation of 288, relating to lewd or lascivious acts upon a child under 14 years of age. Such conduct is described to include, but not to be limited to, those examples enumerated in 11165.6(b)4: 'The intentional touching of the genitals or the intimate parts (including the breast, genital area, groin, inner thighs, and buttocks) or the clothing covering them, of a child, or of the perpetrator by a child, for purposes of sexual arousal or gratification. . . . The events as presented above provide the basis for the conclusion that reasonable suspicion would exist that sexual abuse may have occurred. Because such a reasonable suspicion would exist, such awareness by a health practitioner (defined in 11165.8), or other required reporter, would require the reporting of the suspicion to the required agency. In addition, these circumstances raise the possibility of issues regarding, but not limited to, child neglect and/or prostitution (aiding and abetting) not addressed further herein.

Barry called Bert Fields (Bert was still out of town) and left a message that Evan would not be returning Jordie because new information had become available indicating the boy would be "at risk" if he were returned to his mother. Fields' reaction, as he later told *Vanity Fair*, was to "refuse to talk to that son of a bitch Rothman" ever again. And he didn't. He had Pellicano deliver the message.

Pellicano then called Dave and June to inform them that Fields would not talk to them anymore because Rothman's actions were reprehensible.

The couple was stunned. They had met with Fields several times and had followed his counsel each time, including signing the stipulation. In their minds he was looking out for their interests. It made no sense that he would suddenly leave them high and dry because of the opposing lawyer's attitude.

But for Fields, if a conflict of interest had not already occurred, the potential was now enormous. He had interjected himself into a dispute between two parents that revolved around allegations of improper conduct perpetrated by his own client. With Evan's refusal to return Jordie, the likelihood of a legal confrontation between the parents had reached critical mass, and there was no way Fields could continue to help June.

Dave and June tried to contact Fields directly but he would not return their calls. Only Pellicano would speak to them. The legal implications of Pellicano's ties to Bert Fields was lost on the estranged couple. All they knew was that Fields would no longer help them and Pellicano would.

Working in concert with Pellicano, Dave called Rothman to set up a meeting with Evan. Though Evan had not yet learned about the tape, or the real reason why Dave refused to help when he came to him at Dave's office, he was painfully aware that his good friend had taken up arms against him and Jordie.

"No," Barry told Dave, "Evan won't meet with you. He won't even talk to you. The talking is over. He begged all of you to talk to him for weeks. Now he doesn't trust you. And he's convinced Jordie's in danger."

"Why does he think that?" Dave asked.

"Because I have a report from a child psychiatrist that says, 'the child is at risk whether or not he is in the presence of the adult male.'"

"What's that supposed to mean?"

"What it means to Evan is that Jordie is not going to be hanging around with Michael anymore, and that Jordie is at risk being with June even if Michael isn't there. That's what it means."

"I don't believe that," Dave said.

"I have it right here in the report. And on the psychiatrist's recommendation, Evan refuses to put Jordie back into any situation that might pose a risk for him."

"What does he want?"

"He wants a new custody agreement so he can protect him from June and Michael."

"I'll call you right back."

JULY 17

When Dave called back he said that he and June would come to Barry's office to see the report, and if it actually said Jordie was "at risk," June would sign the new custody agreement.

"Sounds reasonable," Barry replied. "Do you have a lawyer?"

"We don't want a lawyer," Dave said, "they only screw things up. We know how to read. If that's what it says, then that's what it says."

"Okay. As long as you've been advised."

"But we want Jordie there," Dave added. "So we can talk to him and see that he's okay. And we want Evan there too."

"Evan? Why Evan?"

"We want to talk to him."

"I sincerely doubt that will happen," Barry said. "But I'll try to talk him into it."

Try as he might, Barry could not talk him into it. "It will turn into a shouting match," Evan said. "And nothing will be accomplished." Evan also refused to let Jordie go, fearing Dave and June would snatch him.

Barry felt the meeting was important. With the lines of communication wearing thin, it might resolve the entire mess before it blew up in everyone's face. He called Evan and advised him that while his presence could be excused, the meeting would never take place without Jordie. He gave Evan his personal assurance that as long as Jordie did not want to leave with Dave and June, it would not happen.

"If they take him," Evan warned, "he's going to end up on that tour and be permanently screwed up. If that happens, I'll hold you responsible."

"Don't worry," Barry said. "I have Dave's word that as long as he sees the words 'at risk,' June will sign the agreement. And he *will* see the words, Evan, so you can relax. It's almost over."

Evan was incredulous. "You know, Barry, you're as stupid as I used to be.

They're not going to sign anything. They're coming to get Jordie . . . or something, I don't know what." Evan's voice was getting louder by the word. "Those people are fucking sick, Barry! They don't give a shit about him!"

"You're getting hysterical, Evan. Hang up and go enjoy your son. And calm down for God's sake."

"Fine. We'll try it your way. And don't tell me I'm hysterical. I'm not hysterical, I'm pissed. There's a difference."

"Okay, I understand. But don't worry, it's all going to work out."

The meeting was set for July 20.

JULY 20

Evan signed the new "Stipulation Re: Child Care, Custody and Control," kissed his son and left him with Barry.

When June and Dave arrived they exchanged handshakes with Barry, said "hi" to Jordie, and got right down to business. Barry showed them the psychiatrist's report and pointed out the section with the words "at risk." He then handed June a copy of the custody agreement to read and sign.

The document called for physical custody of Jordie to switch from June to Evan, and it restricted June's time with her son to a maximum of two days per week. June would also have to agree that Jordie would have no contact or communication "with a third party adult known as Michael Jackson." If June violated this condition she would only be allowed to see Jordie in the presence of a court appointed monitor.

Dave refused to let June sign, objecting, in particular, to the amount of time she would get to spend with Jordie. He said he wanted to take the document home for further review.

When Barry reminded them that they promised to sign if the report said Jordie was at risk, Dave became angry and accused Barry of trying to coerce them into signing their kid away.

"Do you think we're stupid enough to sign anything that important without a lawyer?" Dave shouted.

"You said you didn't want a lawyer!" Barry yelled back, and the meeting quickly degenerated into an argument.

Caught in the middle, Jordie did his best to calm the two men. "Wait!

Wait!" he said. "I'll call Dad. He'll change it. I know he'll change it." He
called Evan at his office and explained what was happening, but Dave and
Barry were arguing so fiercely neither would take the phone.

Evan bolted from his office, leaving his patient stranded in the chair, and
raced over to Barry's. By the time he arrived, Dave and June were gone.
They had left without a hug or even a goodbye to Jordie, brushing right past
him in a huff.

"I heard everything," Evan told Jordie. "It's not your fault. You did everything you could." Then turning to Barry, "I told you they were liars, didn't I?"

"I had to try, Evan. You know that."

"I know, but this kid is never going to recover from all this bullshit.
Thank God they didn't take him, that's all I can say. Why did they even
bother? What was it all about?"

"This," Barry said, holding up Dr. Abrams' report. "They came for this."

"You stupid shit! They never had any intention of signing. He intimidated
you and you fell for it. I told you not to give them that report no matter
what. It's a damned good thing you whitened out Abrams' name and
address. You did white it out, didn't you? Please tell me you did."

"Don't worry, Evan, I took care of it."

It was Evan's idea to white out the psychiatrist's name, address and
phone number. He feared Dave and June might contact Dr. Abrams and
tell him a different story, in which case Evan would be forced to take Jordie
in to verify his side. That would trigger a report to the authorities, a catas-
trophe for everyone.

Dave delivered Dr. Abrams' report to Pellicano.

JULY 21

Barry was at his desk reviewing another case when his receptionist
informed him an attorney named Michael Freeman was on the phone. "I
represent June Chandler," Freeman began.

Then, Barry told Evan, the man became exceedingly hostile. "He called
me every name you can think of. He said I was a stupid motherfucker and
he should have my license pulled for trying to coerce June into signing the
stipulation without counsel. I couldn't get a word in for two minutes."

Barry wondered if Freeman had even read the document, which contained a paragraph stating that June has been given the opportunity to seek legal advice but had declined to do so, and that she would be signing the agreement voluntarily, with no undue influence or duress.

Dave later testified that he did have a consultation with Freeman just prior to meeting with Barry. He didn't officially hire him, mind you, just had a little chat. Monique, who claims to have seen the bills Freeman sent to Dave, says he charged Dave for telephone conversations with Pellicano on the day *before* June and Dave came to Rothman's office.

After "introducing" himself, Freeman told Barry to draw up a new agreement and June would sign it. Barry was wary, but acquiesced.

"Why do you always buy into their lies?" Evan asked.

"Because this time they have a lawyer, so they can't say I coerced them. Freeman and I will work out the details before I put it in writing. Then he'll check with June to ensure everything's okay before you two sign it."

"You finished, Barry?"

"Yes."

"Didn't you forget something?"

"What?"

"The part that goes, 'and that will be the end of it.'"

Freeman and Rothman went back and forth for the next two weeks, attempting to finalize an agreement both sides could live with. Evan told Barry he was agreeable to anything, as long as Jordie and Michael could not be in the same place at the same time. In the end, June refused to sign the new agreement. "Sorry," Freeman told Barry. "She changed her mind."†

AUGUST 1

Although Evan was certain Michael's actions toward Jordie were harmful, he still did not believe them to be intentional. As twisted as Michael was, Evan believed Michael genuinely cared about Jordie, and that if he could talk to Michael alone and explain his concerns, Michael would understand and together they could work out a solution, "without the damn lawyers."

With Barry's blessing, Jordie called Michael at the Hideout to suggest a meeting. But the number had been changed, so Evan called Barry, who called Pellicano, who called Michael, who called Jordie. Jordie asked Michael if he would meet with him and his dad. When Michael refused, Evan took the phone and asked again. This time Michael agreed, but only if Bert Fields or Anthony Pellicano could attend.

"I just want to find out what's going on between you two," Evan explained. "You don't need a lawyer. We can work this out ourselves."

Michael wouldn't budge: Pellicano or Fields had to attend.

"We may talk about some embarrassing things for both of you," Evan cautioned.

"Anything you say to me, you can say to Bert," Michael insisted.

"But I don't think anyone else should hear these things. I don't want you to get in trouble. I just . . . " Click.

This phone call was a turning point for Evan. "I understood that a man in Michael's position needed lawyers for everything, but this was not business, not to me. I really thought we could work it out if we could get all the lawyers out of the picture, and I thought Michael would want that too. If I wasn't bringing a lawyer, why did he need one?"

This was a completely different Michael than Evan had seen before. His defensiveness and unwillingness to communicate about Jordie's welfare left Evan "with serious doubts" about the star's true feelings.

Minutes after the phone call with Michael, Barry called to say he had just received a call from Pellicano, who claimed Evan had threatened Michael. Pellicano warned that Michael was about to file a libel suit, though he didn't say why.

Barry knew it was a bluff; the last thing Michael Jackson wanted was a public airing. The only real oomph behind Pellicano's threat was Michael's immense power, financial and otherwise, which was not to be trifled with.

But Barry was not intimidated. He informed Pellicano that Evan had made no public statements or defamatory remarks about Michael in any way. And further, that Evan, as a dentist, was a mandatory reporter governed by the same requirements as any licensed health professional. Not only was he required to report his suspicions to the proper authorities, but he could not be sued for doing so even if they turned out to be incorrect.

Barry's argument knocked the wind from Pellicano's sails, and he quickly changed tack. He called Barry the next day and announced he had a way of working everything out. Michael would help Jordie and Evan "reestablish their relationship" by assisting them in setting up a screenwriting career. That way they could spend lots of time together doing what they loved best.

Barry relayed the offer to Evan and a meeting was set for the following Wednesday at the Westwood Marquis Hotel.

Evan was enthusiastic about the meeting. A face-to-face with Michael was what he had been wanting for two months, and was long overdue. Besides, what harm could there be in just listening to what the other side had to say?

✳ ✳ ✳

"I understood Evan's desire to settle things out of court and out of the media," Monique later explained. "But what needed to be settled was Michael's sexual abuse of Jordie. That was the only thing that should have been open for discussion, with attorneys present in a formal setting. The minute I heard that Pellicano had suggested some sort of screenplay deal I knew it was a setup."

Monique advised Evan to avoid meeting with Pellicano at all costs, and had she been his attorney and not his wife he may have listened to her. But he didn't, and the decision would come back to haunt him — to stigmatize him — in every subsequent issue, legal or otherwise, that arose from the Jackson scandal. A screenplay deal for the father as compensation for the molestation of his son, that's all anyone needed to hear. How and why it came about wouldn't matter. Even those who believed that Jordie was molested, and that Evan did attempt to stop it, would have a hard time accepting Evan's willingness to even listen to such an offer.

"I can see how people might take it that way," Evan admitted months later. "I probably would, too, if I were them."

– 9 –

AUGUST 4

Michael's chauffeur, Gary Hearne, was waiting in the lobby when Evan and Jordie emerged from the elevator. Evan and Gary had met several times and always enjoyed a pleasant conversation. Now they walked in silence, both nervous as hell, as Gary led them to a room at the end of the hall.

Anthony Pellicano played the gracious host, all smiles as he ushered them in and offered food and drinks from a buffet. Evan exchanged a quick handshake with the man, but Jordie wouldn't go near him. He remained slightly behind but very close to his father.

Evan then walked over to Michael and embraced the star with a big, happy-to-see-you hug, patting him on the back like an old friend. Jordie wouldn't go near Michael either. "I was scared of him. I knew my dad was going to say that I told him what happened, and I thought Michael would get mad."

"Are you sure you aren't Jewish," Evan joked with Pellicano, as the investigator showed everyone to their seats. "You look just like a cousin of mine."

As he sat down, Evan noticed that the chairs were arranged tightly around a small table — a perfect setup for recording. "Pellicano was so pleasant that for a moment I forgot who I was dealing with. Then I noticed the table. That's when the tension came back."

Evan asked Pellicano if he was taping the meeting. "Absolutely not," the investigator replied. But just in case, Evan read a prepared statement Rothman had supplied concerning laws prohibiting secret recordings. Everyone remained relaxed and smiling throughout the opening formalities.

"So," Evan began, directing himself to Pellicano, "Barry tells me you have a plan to help Jordie and me reestablish our relationship."

"I never said that," Pellicano replied, his voice suddenly taking an aggressive tone.

The harsh response took Evan by surprise. "Well, either you're telling me Barry's a liar, or there's some serious misunderstanding here."

Evan couldn't figure it out. Barry had no reason to lie. Pellicano had made an offer and they had come to discuss it. Now he was denying it.

Frustrated by Pellicano's attitude, and Michael's apparent condoning of it, Evan turned to Michael. "You're the only one who can help me now," he said. "I know what you've done to Jordie. He told me everything." Evan then asked his son to confirm that he had, and after the boy nodded affirmatively, Evan waited for Michael's response.

The King of Pop leaned in close, looked Jordie squarely in the eye, and calmly said in a little-boy voice, "I didn't do anything."

For Evan, it was *the* defining moment. "I knew Michael was screwed up, but until that point I wasn't sure where he was coming from. Part of me still believed he was genuinely in love with Jordie and was acting innocently out of a warped mind, without any forethought or cunning.

"But his smile was chilling, like the smile you see on a serial killer or rapist who continually declares his innocence despite mountains of evidence against him. I knew it immediately; Michael Jackson was a child molester! It was suddenly so obvious, June had been fooled, Jordie had been fooled, and I had been fooled. The entire world had been fooled by this pitiful creature with a brilliant but criminal mind."

In the face of Michael's denial, Evan began to read Dr. Abrams letter. "I wanted to show him that it wasn't just me saying it, that a professional psychiatrist had come to the conclusion that sex or no sex Jordie was being harmed by their relationship."

When Evan got to the section of the letter where Dr. Abrams listed the child protective laws that might have been violated, Pellicano cut him off. "Don't bother, I know them by heart," the P.I. said.

"Why would you know these?" Evan asked, not grasping the full significance of Pellicano's answer.

"I've know them for a long time," Pellicano claimed. "So you can stop reading."

"Okay," Evan said, turning to Michael, "then I'll tell you what. If you and Jordie take lie detector tests and it turns out you didn't do anything to him, then I'll get out of your life forever and you can take him on tour."

Michael remained silent, but Pellicano came on like gangbusters. "Michael will never take a lie detector test!" he shouted, jabbing his finger at Evan's face and spitting as he yelled.

"Look," Evan explained. "It's an easy way out. Take the test and . . . "

"I was in army intelligence. I could teach him to beat it in a second!"

"Fine, just take the test and I'm out of your life forever. No one will ever know anything about it."

"I told you," the investigator screamed, his jugular veins engorging with blood, "he's not taking no damn test!"

Jordie huddled in closer to his dad.

"Okay, okay, I heard you. But I don't get it. Why doesn't he just take it? You'll get rid of me like that," Evan proposed, with a snap of his fingers.

A look of indignation appeared on Pellicano's face. He leaned back in his chair, calmed himself, and in a haughty tone said, "It would be insulting."

Ah-ha! Evan thought, the classic response. The one you see in movies when the guilty party refuses the lie detector because it's beneath his dignity. Michael's guilty as hell, and Pellicano knew it all along.

"Then I guess there's nothing more to talk about," Evan announced, protectively wrapping his arm around Jordie as they rose to leave.

Pellicano and Jackson jerked to their feet, amazed that someone would actually have the balls to kiss them off. Evan brought himself and his son face-to-face with the star. "I'll see you in court," he declared, and walked out.

Evan felt victorious. Not because he had won anything, but because he had finally solved the puzzle. Not only had there been sex between his son and Michael, but he now understood Michael's true feelings. He had had a glimpse into the man's heart, and it was not a pretty sight.

✳   ✳   ✳

In December 1993, one month before Jordie's civil lawsuit against the King of Pop was settled out of court, Evan described Michael thusly:

> With Michael you can establish in a few days the kind of good friend relationship it takes years to develop with most people. Or at least that's what you believe. He's the opposite of intimidating. He's accessible and vulnerable. You get the feeling that not only would he never hurt you, but also that he's incapable of hurting you.
>
> It's like finding a bird with a broken wing. In some ways Michael's a little broken. You become protective of him. You want to nurse him back to health. You want to make him happy. But deep down a strange phenomenon is taking place.

In believing that you're safe and in control, you let your guard down and become vulnerable to manipulation without realizing it. His ability to sense who you are and how you can be manipulated is highly refined. By the time you figure out that the helpless sparrow is actually a vulture that can rip the meat off your bones, it's too late.

He goes to great lengths to make you believe he's giving and generous. But he's smart and cunning, like a fox on the hunt. You must remain emotionally remote with Michael to be safe. He means business. He's *all* business.

Nobody controls Michael Jackson. Nobody! He either controls you by manipulating you emotionally or by paying you obscene amounts of money. Either way, you are going to be controlled.

✳ ✳ ✳

Pellicano's version of the Westwood Marquis meeting differs considerably from Evan's. "[T]he father demanded that Jackson set him up as a screenwriter and accused Jackson of molesting his son."[48] When he refused to help Evan with his screenwriting career, Pellicano claims, Evan became belligerent and threatened Michael by saying "You're going to be sorry. This is not the last you're going to hear from me. If I don't get what I want I'm going to go to the press. I'm going to ruin you."[49]

Wow! A smoking gun if there ever was one. So why didn't this famous audio-surveillance expert record the meeting? "I don't want to be in possession of a tape that has my client on it," Pellicano told *Vanity Fair* in January of 1994.

But why not? Michael wouldn't say anything incriminating if he knows he's being taped. Which, according to Pellicano, is what happened anyway. "Jackson did not respond during that meeting."[50]

It seems odd that Pellicano wouldn't tape the meeting. After all, that's what he does. It's his thing. But he couldn't use the tape because it would have shown that his offer of a screenplay deal to help Evan and Jordie

---

[48] Charles P. Wallace & Jim Newton, "Taylor Joins Jackson in Singapore During Ordeal," *Los Angeles Times*, August 29, 1993.

[49] Chuck Phillips & David Farrell, "Tapes Used to Allege Plot to Extort Jackson Released," *Los Angeles Times*, August 31, 1993.

[50] Charles P. Wallace & Jim Newton, "Taylor Joins Jackson in Singapore During Ordeal."

"reestablish their relationship" was the reason Evan came to the meeting in the first place: that it was *the opening offer* in the two weeks of negotiations that followed, and that it came *before* any discussion of money took place. In other words, Pellicano could not reveal that the victim of this so-called extortion attempt made an offer before any demands were made of him.

According to Pellicano and Fields, however, Evan not only threatened Michael at this meeting, there were several other conversations in which Evan and Barry Rothman (individually) tried to extort Michael. Pellicano admitted that he never caught any of these on tape.

Other investigators questioned how Pellicano could have neglected to make recordings that might have corroborated his version of the story.

> Any . . . private investigator that's working a case like that, is going to have some backup tapes," said Don Crutchfield, an investigator with longtime involvement in the film world. It would be the first thing an investigator would do — set up a conversation by putting a tape on the phone. . . . It's beyond me that an investigator wouldn't have those conversations taped.
>
> Legal experts said it appears likely that the tape could be used as evidence in the case, based on California law.[51]

Crutchfield's statement is telling. "It would be the first thing an investigator would do — set up a conversation by putting a tape on the phone." Which is exactly what Dave Schwartz did on July 8, one day after Fields "retained" Pellicano to "perform services."

In retrospect, what's most important about the Westwood Marquis meeting is not what was said, but the mentality that both sides brought to the encounter. Evan came to seek Michael's help in straightening out the mess with June, a problem that never existed before Michael came into their lives. He also came for answers. What was the true nature of Michael and Jordie's relationship? Were they in love? Despite all that had gone down, Evan still believed they were.

"I was caught totally off guard by their hostility. The week before, Pellicano told Monique he wanted to work things out with me 'father to father,' so I figured this was it. I told Jordie before we went to the hotel that

---

[51] Chuck Phillips & David Farrell, "Tapes Used to Allege Plot to Extort Jackson Released."

I was sure everything would be worked out. I expected Michael to be sympathetic toward Jordie."

In an interview for *Vanity Fair* six months after the Westwood Marquis meeting, Pellicano drew attention to the fact that Evan hugged Michael at the start of the meeting. "If I believed somebody molested my kid and I got that close to him, I'd be on death row right now." Supposedly this means that because Evan didn't kill Michael right then and there, he really didn't believe the molestation occurred.

Pellicano, of course, would have us believe Evan had *already* accused Michael of molesting Jordie as part of an extortion attempt, so when Evan hugged him it showed he knew Michael had done no such thing.

But if Evan went there to extort Michael, why would he start off by giving him a big hug? Why would he act friendly? Wouldn't he at least pretend that he believed Michael had molested Jordie and that he was angry? Especially with Michael's audio expert/private investigator present as a witness!

That Evan walked into the meeting and gave Michael a big hug only corroborates that Evan went there with the belief that Michael genuinely cared for Jordie and hadn't done anything intentional to hurt him. After all, the idea that Michael was being accused of intentionally harming the boy — that a "molestation" had occurred — did not originate in Evan's mind. It was Anthony Pellicano and Bert Fields who first used the term.

After telling the *Los Angeles Times* that at the Westwood Marquis meeting Evan threatened to go to the press if he didn't get what he wanted, Pellicano later contradicted himself when he told *Vanity Fair* that by the *conclusion* of the Westwood Marquis meeting Evan had made no attempt to extort Michael. "At this point I never heard any extortion. I never heard any demands. I kept wanting to hear demands."[52] Pellicano would re-contradict himself when he claimed that one month prior to the Westwood Marquis meeting he had listened to Dave's secret tape just for ten minutes "and knew right away it was extortion"[53]

At the Westwood meeting Pellicano acted true to form, aggressive. The best defense is a good offense. Had he waited to find out what Evan was up

---

[52] Maureen Orth, "Nightmare at Neverland," 132.

[53] Mary A. Fischer, "Did Michael Do It?" 220.

to before jumping down his throat, he would have seen that Evan came to understand, not to attack. Or had Michael shown that he cared about Jordie and simply agreed to stop seeing him if Evan felt it was best, Evan would have walked out of the meeting satisfied and the matter might have ended then and there.

At the very least, had they not lied to him, Evan would have stayed and talked further. But the first words out of their mouths, Pellicano's and Michael's, were lies. Once that happened, Evan lost all faith.

After the meeting, Evan and Jordie went directly to Barry's office. Jordie sat in the waiting room, doodling, while the two adults discussed what had transpired at the Westwood Marquis.

Barry was furious that Pellicano had denied making the offer. "These people are unbelievable!" he exclaimed. "How the hell can we negotiate with them?" They talked it over and decided there was no choice but to file for custody.

Just as they reached that conclusion, Pellicano called. He claimed he never denied making the offer and told Barry that Evan was crazy and walked out of the meeting for no reason. Rather than waste time arguing over the phone, Barry invited Pellicano to his office to continue the discussion.

Evan had two goals. First and foremost was the welfare of his son. On the surface Jordie seemed fine, but this wasn't surface stuff. Dr. Abrams had expressed deep concern for the boy and left Evan with the impression that serious damage might already have occurred. Evan hoped for the best but needed to prepare for the worst.

If Jordie needed long-term counseling it could be expensive, and they would have to find a state that did not require psychotherapists to report child abuse to the authorities. That could mean relocating and closing his dental practice. How would he support his family? A worst case scenario to be sure, but possible.

Soured by his experience with Pellicano and Michael — in particular, "Michael looking into Jordie's eyes and denying their intimacy" — Evan's second goal was to punish Michael. "I didn't want him to get off scot-free. But a few million is chump change to him. I figured twenty million was definitely a punishing amount. At the very least it would give him something to think about. If it turned out Jordie was okay and didn't need a lot of counseling, so much the better. He'd be set for life. He deserved it after what Michael did to him.

"And it wasn't just the sex part. Everyone made a big deal about the sex — the press, the cops, the DA. That was important, sure, but it wasn't the main thing for me. It was what Michael did to him to get to that point. He took over his mind and isolated him from his family and friends and everyone he cared for. He made him his own little slave. On the outside it looked like he was showing Jordie the time of his life, but on the inside he was robbing him of his individuality, his soul. That was the real crime, and that's what I wanted Michael to pay for."

But why not go to the police? "I thought about going to the cops. I thought about it a lot. But the more I thought about it the more I realized no good would come of it. It was Jordie's word against Michael's. Maybe it would play against the man on the street, but never against the world's best-loved advocate for children. But it wasn't just that. I was concerned there'd be a storm of publicity and I didn't want to expose Jordie to that kind of pressure. It would embarrass him terribly and quite possibly be more traumatic than what he'd already been through."

It wasn't just after the fact that Evan made these claims. He expressed his fears about a public airing on Dave's secret tape, six weeks before the affair became public. "It's gonna be bigger than all of us put together, and the whole thing's just gonna crash down on everybody and destroy everybody in its sight." His son and himself included.

Evan and Barry reconsidered filing a civil suit against Michael, but that would trigger the mandatory reporting requirement and cause the same public circus as filing a police report. In the end, even if they won the suit, the result would be the same as settling out of court — money.

Convinced Michael would not pay twenty million, Barry tried talking Evan down to five. But Evan was intractable. "Five million was a pay-off, not a punishment." He wanted Michael punished for what he now believed was a blatant molestation.

"Twenty million in trust for Jordie, and that's firm," Evan insisted.[54]

With Pellicano on his way over to negotiate, and Evan not willing to budge on the terms, Barry had to get creative. Since Pellicano had previously mentioned screenwriting, Barry structured his offer around that: Michael would pay Evan five million apiece for four screenplays over a four-year period. Barry figured if the movies were a hit, Michael, as owner and producer, would see a profit from his "investment." If they bombed, it would be one hell of a tax write-off.

Evan hated the deal. "If that's the best we can do," he told Barry, "I'd rather go to court and let the chips fall where they may." Structuring the settlement as a business arrangement — one that Michael might actually benefit from! — was out of the question. And Evan did not want the money for himself — it had to be paid in trust to Jordie.

"Look, Evan," Barry explained, "no one, not even Michael Jackson, is going to hand over twenty million just like that without structuring it properly. What's the difference how we get the money? Our first obligation is to protect and provide for Jordie, not punish Michael."

"Okay, Barry," Evan consented, "you're the lawyer. I'll negotiate only on the amount, but if Pellicano doesn't agree to everything else, I want the custody (against June) filed immediately."

Evan and Jordie left before Pellicano arrived.

When Evan returned the following morning he found Barry "in a state of ecstasy." Pellicano had responded to the deal by saying he thought it was a great idea and would check with the accountants and look over Michael's development deal with Fox Pictures to see how it could be worked out. "I'll

---

54 Several years later Bert Fields testified it was Pellicano who offered the money in trust for Jordie, and that Evan refused, saying he wanted it for himself. Yet if Fields' account was true, it seems odd that neither he nor anyone else on Michael's team leveled this damning claim while the battle was in progress. Fields also seems to have forgotten that back in 1993, when the scandal first broke, Pellicano denied making any offer.

Fields, finally under oath for the first time in this matter, was attempting to plug the holes in his original story. While it took him three years to come up with his version, Evan had relayed his story to the police one week after the events took place, and documented them two months later when he submitted his entire story in writing to Jordie's attorney. Though the document was later stolen and made public by the British tabloids, at the time he wrote it, Evan could not have known it would become public. Further, it was a privileged document between attorney and client that could not be used against him in a court of law. There was no reason for Evan to lie.

get back to you within the week," the P.I. promised, leaving Barry with the impression that it was a done deal.

Evan accepted Barry's interpretation at face value, but doubted Pellicano had any intention of going through with the deal. As he left the office he handed Barry the picture Jordie had drawn while "doodling" in Barry's waiting room the night before.† He also gave Barry a letter with instructions on how to proceed.† Jordie's drawing showed what appeared to be a child jumping off a tall building. Contrary to press reports, the drawing did not represent thoughts of suicide on Jordie's part, rather his fears of going to court and having to tell the world about his sexual experiences with Michael. Fears he constantly relayed to his father.

That same day, August 4, when Pellicano was trying to "help Evan and Jordie reestablish their relationship," June's attorney, Michael Freeman, was drawing up court papers designed to force Evan to give Jordie back to June, and thus to Michael.[55]

– 10 –

AUGUST 6

In an effort to avoid the public spectacle he knew their lives would become, not to mention becoming entangled in an unforgiving legal system, Evan decided to approach June one last time. He knew she would be easier to convince if Jordie were willing to tell her what Michael had done, but the boy was too ashamed. He believed that his mother, like himself, had been duped by Michael, and that she did not know about the sex. In his young and confused mind he felt as if it was *he* who had betrayed her.

Evan thought of telling June what Jordie had admitted, that Michael had touched his penis, but it meant breaking his promise to his son and he feared losing the boy's trust. So he confined his accusation by saying only that he, Evan, was certain Michael had molested their son.

---

[55] The fact that Pellicano had told Barry that his (Pellicano's) intentions were to "help Evan and Jordie reestablish their relationship," is not based solely on Barry's word. There was a letter from Pellicano to Barry containing those very words. (Soon to be discussed in greater detail in this part.)

"It shouldn't have mattered, anyway," Evan believed. "I am his father, and if I'm telling her our child has been molested, that should be enough. Especially when you consider that she knew better than anyone how often they'd been sleeping together."

But June flatly insisted Michael would never do such a thing, and refused Evan's request that she confront the singer about it. Instead, she came back at Evan with the same challenge Dave had presented numerous times during their taped conversation: "Where's your proof? You have no proof."

"Even if she truly doubted there had been any sex," Evan commented, "she should have at least been willing to confront Jordie and Michael. But she wouldn't. She didn't even want to talk about it."

While Evan was trying to reason with June, her estranged yet suddenly ever-present husband Dave, along with her lawyer Michael Freeman, was implementing a sneak attack. That morning, Freeman filed a document in Santa Monica Superior Court seeking an order for Evan to pay June sixty-eight thousand dollars in back child support.

Evan and June's original divorce agreement called for Evan to pay June five hundred dollars a month, an amount he readily admitted was never paid. However, at the time the divorce was signed, Evan, Dave and June agreed that Dave would pay all of Jordie's expenses when the boy was with him and June, and that Evan would pay them when the boy was with him. Dave was very wealthy. He *wanted* it that way. They also agreed that Evan would only pay child support in the event June found herself in need. Both Dave and June have since testified that the foregoing is true.

June further testified that she had never made a request to Evan for payment. That being the case, it seems logical that attorney Freeman would have sent a demand letter to Evan before filing with the court. But he didn't. It's possible that Dave and June withheld the truth from Freeman. But if they didn't, then Freeman's real goal was not child support. It was, as Dave later testified, "leverage in trying to get Jordie back." "It wasn't about the money . . . we thought that's how we could get to Evan, through his pocketbook."

Dave was correct — it wasn't about money. The Jackson camp needed to pressure Evan to back off. Dave testified that he picked Michael

Freeman to represent June because Freeman had previously provided legal services to his car rental business. Small world, though, because it seems Dave's business attorney was pretty chummy with Pellicano.

"I know Mr. Pellicano. I've talked to Mr. Pellicano on numerous occasions," Freeman stated in a phone call he made during Larry King's interview with Pellicano on the night the scandal broke. Two days later Freeman's child-support order became public, and the entire world learned that Evan Chandler was not only an extortionist but also a deadbeat Dad — someone everyone could hate.[56]

Freeman's phone call to Larry King appears to have been set up by Pellicano. A short time before the King interview, Pellicano had informed the media that it was "the boy's mother" who had made the extortion attempt.[57] Freeman then called King to straighten out the media's mistake. Neither Pellicano nor Freeman mentioned that it was Pellicano who had supplied the wrong information. It is hard to believe that Pellicano got Evan and June mixed up. Whether Freeman was in on the apparent setup is unknown.

Freeman not only appeared via telephone on *Larry King Live*, but also in a major hit piece on Evan in a 1994 issue of *GQ Magazine*, both without June's permission. Freeman claims he became disgusted with June and withdrew as her attorney. In reality, by the end of August June no longer wanted or needed his services. She had already conceded to the Department of Children's Services that Michael had mosested her son, and she had signed on with new attorneys.

One wonders who Freeman was really working for? Dave believed that Freeman was manipulated by Pellicano. Maybe so. But Freeman does not appear to be a man easily duped.

---

[56] Jim Newton & Sonia Nazario, "Police Say Seized Tapes Do Not Incriminate Jackson," *Los Angeles Times*, August 27, 1993.

[57] Jeffrey Jolson-Colburn, "Father in Jackson case sought $20 mil film deal." *Hollywood Reporter*, August 26, 1993.

AUGUST 9

Pellicano arrived at Barry's office with a counteroffer to Barry's twenty million dollars demand. Michael would pay one million for three screenplays written by Evan and Jordie: an alleged gesture on Michael's part that would allow father and son to work together and reestablish their relationship. Evan turned it down immediately, for many reasons. A screenplay deal made it sound like the money was for Evan, and he had insisted it be in trust to Jordie. Besides, it wasn't nearly enough to cover a worst-case scenario for the family: moving, leaving his practice, psychiatric expenses, etc. And the amount wasn't punitive to Michael; merely a fly on an elephant's back. It wasn't even coming from Jackson. According to Pellicano, Fox Pictures would pay the money.

While sitting face to face with Pellicano and trying to think of something to say to break what seemed like an insurmountable deadlock, Evan suddenly remembered that Jordie had mentioned needing the computer Michael had bought for him. Jordie said it would help with his schoolwork.

"You know, Anthony," Evan said, "it would go a long way toward helping these negotiations if you could have Gary drop off the computer Michael bought for Jordie."

Pellicano was instantly in Evan's face. "*I* bought that computer!" he proclaimed, "and Jordie will never see it."

"He said it with such a malevolent tone in his voice," Evan recalled. "And we were only talking about a damn computer, for a kid who needed it for school. It was that same nasty demeanor he displayed at the Westwood Marquis." Evan was positive the computer was for Jordie. Michael had told him so when he visited him at the Hideout.[58]

Evan didn't like Pellicano from the start — the man was conniving and abrasive — but this incident convinced him that he was dealing with a basically evil person, an unscrupulous individual who would not only lie and cheat to get what he wanted, but who was "just plain mean."

Evan sprang from his chair and shouted at Barry to "file the papers!" Then he headed for the door.

---

[58] Gary Hearne, Michael's chauffeur, later testified that Michael had sent him to buy the computer for Jordie.

"Wait!" Barry pleaded. But Evan had had enough. "File the papers or you're fired!" he insisted, and marched out.

Pellicano was left red-faced and fuming. "I've never hated anyone as much as I hate him," he told Barry, and stormed out as well.

Desperate to salvage the meeting, Barry tried to keep Pellicano from leaving by appealing to him as a parent. "Look at this, Anthony! Just look at this!" he said, holding up the picture Jordie had drawn. But Pellicano refused to look and assumed Barry was threatening him with a lawsuit. "Go ahead," the P.I. shouted, "file your damn complaint!"

Pellicano caught up with Evan at the elevator. "You haven't seen the last of me!" he screamed in Evan's face. "I'm going to be in your fucking house! I'm going to be in your fucking car! I'm going to be fucking all over you!"

"Fuck off, Anthony!"

As far as Evan was concerned it was over — there were to be no more negotiations. But Barry had no intention of giving up. He waited a day for Evan to calm down, then asked him to reconsider his demand for a custody suit. Evan not only refused, he admonished Barry for not having already filed the papers.

"Evan," Barry warned, "you have no idea how horrible an experience it will be for Jordie to sit on that witness stand. It doesn't matter that he's telling the truth. They'll rip him apart."

No one loathed the idea of dragging Jordie through court more than Evan. But at this point it seemed the least harmful solution. It was more than obvious that no progress was to be made with June or Pellicano, and until Jordie's fate was completely under his control, Evan would rule out no options.

In the end, Evan yielded again to Barry's request for more time. Not so much because he knew Barry's advice was sound, but because of Jordie's heart-wrenching pleas not to make him go to court.

AUGUST 10

Hoping to ease the tension between himself and June, and on the condition that she not badger Jordie with questions, Evan consented to her request to take Jordie to a movie, provided she have him back by ten. June kept her promise, and then called again the following day to ask if she could take Jordie to lunch.

"There was something in her voice that made me wary," Evan said. "It didn't have that conciliatory sound you'd expect to hear when peace is being pursued, like it did the day before. But in the interest of good will, I let him go."

Unknown to Evan, Michael Freeman had instructed June to take her son out of town.[59] So instead of taking Jordie to lunch, June drove straight to Dave's office to hook up with Dave, where together they began pumping the boy for information. What's your dad up to? How much money did he ask for? Did Rothman file for custody?

Jordie was stunned. Never did he expect such behavior from his own mother and stepfather. He quickly caught on that they had no intention of taking him back to his father. "I was scared. I thought they were going to take me back to Michael."

Jordie broke loose from Dave and bolted around the corner out of sight, then found a phone booth and dialed Evan at work. But just as the phone rang, Dave and June drove up and ordered him into the car.

"Touch me and I'll call the cops," Jordie warned. "I want to go back to my dad, now!"

Realizing they would have to physically restrain the boy if they hoped to get away with their plan, and unwilling to go that far, June dropped Dave back at work and headed back to Evan's.[60] When they arrived, June told her son that if Evan were telling the truth she would join forces with them to see Michael punished. Safely inside his father's house, Jordie told Evan what had occurred, and about June's offer to help if she could be convinced.

Evan knew the only chance of accomplishing this was for Jordie to tell June everything, which the boy was still reluctant to do. "I realized for the first time I was going to have break my promise to Jordie and tell June he admitted to being touched. Things were totally out of control and it was the only way to end the insanity."

---

[59] According to Evan, June revealed that it was Freeman who told her to take Jordie. June still had legal custody of Jordie, so this was not a violation of law.

[60] Little Miss Kelly sat in the car, watching her brother's abduction.

The following morning, after sleeping on it for the night, Jordie decided his dad was right, June had to be told. He also knew that he, not Evan, should be the one to tell her. So with his father by his side, Jordie called his mother. "Mom, I want to tell you the truth about what Michael did to me." But before he could get any further, June began to cry.

Evan described her reaction as "strange." "She never actually allowed him to say it. Instead, she immediately became hysterical. Then, in the midst of her anguish, she suddenly stopped crying, regained her composure, and said, 'I'll call you right back.'"

June called Dave, who instructed her to meet with Jordie alone, ostensibly to see what he would say away from his father's influence. June made the request but Evan refused to let the boy out of his sight. "If I thought she really wanted to get to the bottom of things, I would have allowed it, even after their attempt to abduct him. But this time it wasn't just the tone in her voice that gave her away, she came right and told me it really didn't make much difference what Jordie said because she and Dave were positive I had coerced him. No matter how many times I tried communicating with her, she would not listen. Not even to Jordie! Their motives were now totally transparent."

More fearful than ever that "the other side" would grab Jordie and whisk him off to Neverland, Evan called Barry and insisted he file the custody suit. And once again Barry strongly advised against it. He still believed the negotiations with Pellicano could be revived, despite the apparent deadlock.

As they had been doing all week, the two men argued about which course to follow. Evan was convinced no good would come from dealing with the likes of Pellicano, and Barry was equally certain a custody suit would yield the same.

AUGUST 13

Barry and Pellicano met again. This time Pellicano offered one screenplay for $350,000. He pitched it would be quick and easy, and specifically mentioned that the money would come directly out of Michael's pocket, a condition Evan had insisted on.

Barry couldn't believe his ears. Pellicano was completely ignoring the

rules of the game. Barry had started at twenty million, Pellicano had coun-
tered with one million, surely the next number should be somewhere in
between. And strange as it was that Pellicano had lowered his million dollar
offer, it was even crazier that he refused to reinstate it when Barry told him
that he had "busted [his] hump for three days . . . getting Evan hopefully to
agree."

Had Barry known what Pellicano knew, that Michael Freeman had
already set the wheels in motion to take Jordie from his father, he would
have understood Pellicano's hardball tactics. With Jordie back in June's
custody — i.e., on tour and out of the country — Pellicano didn't have to
give up a dime of Michael's money.

AUGUST 17

Late in the afternoon of August 16, Michael Freeman informed Barry
that he had filed a motion for a court order to have Evan return Jordie to
June, and that a hearing was set for the following morning. It was the first
Barry had heard of it.

Accompanying the motion was a declaration from June stating that
Evan had coerced her into signing the change of custody agreement of July
13 (agreeing not to take Jordie out of Los Angeles County without Evan's
consent).† Allegedly, Evan threatened she would never see Jordie again if
she didn't sign.

If Freeman knew that Pellicano had negotiated the agreement and that
Fields had supposedly advised June to sign it, he certainly did not inform
the court about it. The judge would be more inclined to accept June's claim
if he believed that June had been bamboozled into the agreement without
the advice of counsel.

To support his request for a court order, Freeman submitted a declaration
by the well-known and respected Fields that was sure to impress the judge.
Fields began his declaration by informing the court that he had graduated
from Harvard Law School and then spent two years in the Air Force before
starting in private practice.†

Fields described himself as an "an intermediary" who "carried messages"
between June and Evan's attorney, Barry Rothman. Fields avowed that he

did not represent June, but that he called her only to "convey" Evan's request that Jordie be allowed to stay with him for "a brief visit." Fields then stated that June didn't trust Evan, but that Rothman had given his word as a fellow attorney and it was because of that that June decided to let Jordie see his father.

Fields' description of his role was remarkable, as much for what it failed to say than what it did say. Fields had not only given June advice, he failed to advise the court about the true reason for the custody battle over Jordie: allegations of child molestation against his client, Jackson.

In a phone conversation the night before Freeman's request was to be heard in court, Barry counseled Evan that unless he was willing to walk into the courtroom and accuse Michael of molesting Jordie, he didn't have a prayer of winning; June had legal custody and that was all she needed to get Jordie back.

"How long will I have?" Evan asked.

"One, maybe two days."

"What if I refuse to give him back?"

"If you don't give him back the sheriff will come take him. And he may arrest you, too."

Accusing Michael of molestation was a can of worms Evan did not want to open. He doubted anyone would take Jordie's word over Michael's, especially if June took Michael's side. And she'd have to; otherwise she'd be implicating herself. But it was Jordie's fears over the prospect of going to court that weighed heaviest on Evan's mind.

At the same time, Evan knew that as soon as June had Jordie back in her clutches she'd be on a plane to join Michael, who was already out of the country. Evan believed with absolute certainty that if Jordie went on tour with Michael he'd suffer severe psychological damage.

"I'm damned if I do and damned if I don't," Evan lamented to Barry. "What if I take him out of California and hide for a while? Maybe that'll buy you some time to come up with the necessary appeals."

"Appeals!" the attorney exclaimed. "Are you nuts! You'll be a fugitive in the eyes of the law. You'll end up in jail and guarantee June permanent custody. You can forget about any appeals."

Confused and saddened, Evan thanked Barry for all his help and hung up.

"What's the matter, Pops?" Jordie asked. He'd been standing next to his father while he talked to Barry.

"They're going to make you go back tomorrow, Jordie. Barry says we have no choice."

"Uh-uh! No way! I'll run away first."

Buoyed by his son's feistiness, Evan made him a promise. "If that's the way you feel, then I'm with you. But we've got one move left. If it doesn't work, then we'll go."

For the past six weeks the two sides had gone back and forth, each trying to outmaneuver the other in what Evan called "the chess game from hell." Now he found himself checkmated. "They left me no choice. The only move I had left was to kick over the table before they took the king."

Evan dialed the number. "Do you remember me," he asked. "I'm the one who came to your office and told you about my son."

"Yes," Dr. Abrams replied. "I remember very well."

It was the one thing Evan had tried so desperately to avoid. Once he supplied the names, the psychiatrist would have no choice but to file a report with the authorities, who would then assume full control.

"The thought of placing Jordie in the hands of a government agency was frightening," Evan commented. "Almost as frightening as returning him to June and Michael."

Evan took a few seconds to think before embarking into the unknown; then he took a deep breath. "My name is Evan Chandler. My son's name is Jordie Chandler. The adult male is Michael Jackson. Can you help me? *Please!*"

Other than the knowledge that Michael had touched Jordie's penis, Evan had never asked his son about the sex. But Dr. Abrams would, and Evan hoped he would be convinced of the truth and be willing to appear at the court hearing the following morning as an expert witness. "I'm sorry," Dr. Abrams said. "I can't see him today. But don't worry; bring him in first thing in the morning."

Evan and Jordie arrived at the psychiatrist's office at nine the next morning. Dr. Abrams began by advising Jordie that their discussion could become embarrassing and that it was his choice as to whether he wanted his father to remain in the room. Evan shuffled out and took a seat in the waiting room.

An hour later, anxious and bored, Evan idled his way down to the coffee shop in the lobby, ate breakfast and went back upstairs to wait. Another hour and another trip to the coffee shop. Eleven o'clock. Walking the halls. Back downstairs. Around the block. Back to the waiting room. "What the hell are they doing in there?" Evan wondered. "I could have told my whole life story by now."

Ten minutes after noon, Jordie finally emerged. "Hey, Dad, can we get something to eat?" His favorite question.

Evan was startled. He expected Jordie to come out heavy-hearted, but the boy seemed exuberated, almost whimsical. "Are you okay?" Evan asked, wrapping his arms around the boy.

"Yeah, Pops. Let's go, I'm starved."

"He was a different boy," Evan recalled, "and I knew immediately that no matter how long a road might lie ahead, he was going to be okay." Holding back the tears, Evan thanked Dr. Abrams profusely.

"So what do we do now?" he asked.

"You'll have to wait," the doctor replied. "Under the law, I can't tell you anymore."

"Can you at least tell me if you believe him?"

"Oh yes. There's no doubt."

Father and son went to eat, but never talked about the interview. Except once. "You know, Dad," Jordie said, briefly lifting his mug from a plate of French fries, "I'm really glad I talked to Dr. Abrams."

And so was Evan. Because two hours earlier, while Jordie was still relating his lurid tale to the good doctor, the court ordered the boy returned to June within forty-eight hours. Barry's associate, who attended the hearing, assured the judge her client would comply.

Early that afternoon, with the favorable court decision under his belt, Anthony Pellicano called Barry to find out if Evan had accepted the one screenplay deal for $350,000. Barry told him no, but suggested again that Evan might be willing to take the original million dollar offer if Pellicano was willing to renew it. "It's never going to happen," the investigator insisted.

Unbeknownst to Barry, Pellicano was recording the twenty-minute conversation in an effort, as Pellicano later told to the press, "to set them up
with the extortion."[61]†

Months later, Evan made the following comment about Barry busting
his hump to get Evan's blessing on the million dollar screenplay offer.

"Pellicano was such an asshole I knew the negotiations would go nowhere.
I did not want to yield to his terms. Yet each time I insisted upon going to
court, Barry warned me it would be a nightmare for Jordie and my family.

"I was frustrated and exhausted. My sanity was under siege by the pressures of a reality I could never have foreseen: betrayed by the mother of my
child, by his stepfather, who was also a close friend, and by my son as well,
though I knew he was too young to understand what he had done. And at
home, my wife and children were suffering as well. I can't say for sure what
I would have done if Pellicano hadn't been so stubborn. Fortunately, I never
had to agonize over the choice."

Neither Barry nor Evan could understand Pellicano's negotiating tactics.
More than once Evan asked his attorney, "Is it me? Am I missing something
here?" Regardless of what Evan now thought of Michael Jackson, he knew
him to be an intelligent man and could not understand why he would hire
"such an arrogant son of a bitch" to do the job of a diplomat.

As he and Jordie drove home from lunch, Evan called Barry to inform
him of Dr. Abrams' response. Barry, in turn, called Michael Freeman to tell
him that "due to intervening circumstances" Jordie would not be returned
to June as ordered. Later that afternoon he faxed Freeman a letter to that
effect, including the revelation that Jordie had talked to a psychiatrist, a
mandatory reporter.†

✳ ✳ ✳

As the opening act of this twisted tale was drawing to an end, in a land far
away, the curtain was rising on what promised to be one of the most spectacular entertainment events of the decade, Michael Jackson's *Dangerous* tour.
Aptly named, as it might well have been, for a young boy soon to become
known to the entire world as THE THIRTEEN-YEAR-OLD FROM LOS
ANGELES.

---

[61] Charles P. Wallace & Jim Newton, "Taylor Joins Jackson in Singapore During Ordeal."

– 11 –

There was no going back, and little else to do but wait. As darkness fell, Evan, Monique, Jordie and the little ones hunkered in at home, disheartened that the day had passed with no resolution to their problem.

"It was like waiting for the cavalry," Evan recalls. "Every minute felt like an hour. And when they didn't show, I got scared. Like maybe no one gives a damn."

But shortly after nine Evan received a page from his message service to call Ann Rosato, an investigator with the Department of Children's Services (DCS). He and Ann spoke briefly, and an hour later the "troops" finally arrived.

Rosato was friendly but firm and wasted no time getting down to business. In the presence of uniformed LAPD officers, she sequestered Jordie from his family and questioned him for several hours about his relationship with Michael. "Minor was cooperative and communicative and quite open with this caseworker," Rosato stated in her report.

She also wrote that besides relating the details of his sexual experiences with Michael, Jordie told her that his "mother was aware of minor sleeping in same bed and allowed this to continue," and that "he wants to stay with father. Minor feels mother would 'drill' him with questions. Also feels she likes the 'glitzy life' too much to give it up and might allow Mr. Jackson to return to home."

Based on these and other statements, and the fact that she had not yet had the opportunity to interview Evan or June, (it was 2 AM when she finished with Jordie), Ann Rosato decided to place Jordie in protective custody, meaning DCS was now his legal guardian. But because she did not feel the boy was in any danger with Evan, Rosato "placed" him in his father's home, pending further investigation.

When Rosato returned the following day to continue with Jordie, she was accompanied by detectives Bill Dworin and Rosibel Ferrufino from LAPD's Sexually Exploited Child Unit, as well as Los Angeles County Deputy DA William Penzin, and Rani Steinberg from Stuart House.[62]

---

[62] The *Los Angeles Times* described Stuart House as "The nation's first child abuse treatment program to jointly house medical, law enforcement and child protection services to aid prosecutions and reduce victims' trauma." (Henry Weinstein, "Child Sex Abuse Cases Pose Dilemma for Prosecutors," *Los Angeles Times*, September 19, 1993.)

These experts also interviewed Jordie and found the details of his story consistent with those he gave Rosato and Mathis Abrams.

At the same time, Detective Dworin took Evan into a separate room and questioned him about the negotiations with Pellicano.

The following day, on the nineteenth, Rosato conducted two additional interviews: The first was a one-on-one with Evan (he waived his right to have counsel present), in which he related the events leading up to the visit with Mathis Abrams, including the negotiations with Pellicano. Rosato's second interview was with June, who was accompanied by Dave and her attorney, Michael Freeman.

According to Rosato's report, June "stated she was aware that they slept in the same bed but felt that was O.K. as she trusted him (Michael). . . . "She felt father had 'brainwashed' minor, though it was unclear as to what he had brainwashed minor into thinking/doing/saying. . . . Mother also said father had been hinting at things and making innuendoes and she was confused and wanted to hear facts."

So after asking attorney Freeman to step outside, Ann Rosato supplied June with facts. In particular, the specific sexual acts Jordie had described. After hearing them, "Mother stated that if Jordie had said it, it must be true. She did not feel anyone could brainwash him into saying those things and she did not believe he was lying. . . . Mother acknowledged that she loved the attention paid to her by a star. . . . After much discussion, mother admitted she could see now the abnormality of aspects of the relationship. . . . She said she was willing to allow minor to stay at father's indefinitely and not proceed with any custody disputes."

Despite the undisputed facts that over a period of several months June permitted Jordie to sleep alone with Michael at Neverland in Santa Barbara County, the Hideout in Los Angeles, hotels in New York, Las Vegas, Orlando, Monaco, Paris and at least thirty nights in her own home, she claimed ignorance about the sex. It's no wonder Ann Rosato's report concluded: "Minor said he did not want to see Mr. Jackson ever again. He also stated he did not trust his mother completely yet, but was willing to work on the relationship. He seemed to feel better when caseworker told him that he was really in charge of when he wanted to see his mom." DCS's final decision was that Jordie should remain with his father.

The tsunami hit shortly before 5 PM on Monday, August 23, when KNBC-TV in Los Angeles aired the shocking news that the police had raided the Hideout and Neverland. Anthony Pellicano was out of the country, but he knew what was coming down. He called Gary Hearne and instructed him to remove a suitcase from the Hideout and deliver it to his [Pellicano's] apartment." Hearne testified that he delivered the suitcase as instructed, but never looked inside and did not know its contents.[63]

When asked under oath if any lawyer directed him to give instructions to Hearne, or if he knew where the suitcase was, Pellicano refused to answer, invoking instead the attorney-client privilege as an agent of Bert Fields.

At approximately the same time the police were searching Michael's house, Diane Dimond, the reporter for the television show *Hard Copy*, received an anonymous call from someone who claimed to know what the raids were about. "At first I thought the person was a kook," Dimond said months later. "You know, the first of many I expected would try to capitalize on the report and pick up a few quick bucks. But the story was huge so I agreed to meet."

Twenty minutes later, Dimond was sitting across the table from the caller in a Santa Monica restaurant, her eyes glued to a copy of Ann Rosato's report. "I can't pay you for this," Dimond told the stranger. Much to her surprise the mystery caller responded that he didn't want money. The purpose was to have the truth come out, and the caller implored Dimond not to quash the story.

Hindsight, they say, is everything. Yet there were those who understood, even as it was happening, that the Jackson camp's response to the leak — Anthony Pellicano in full battle array — was the worst of all possible worlds. Instead of taking the high road and issuing a simple, dignified statement steadfastly denying any truth to the allegations, Michael, or whoever was orchestrating his response, decided to scream bloody murder.

Certainly it was a monster story and not likely to disappear overnight, no matter what Jackson's response. But no one from the boy's side had yet

---

[63] The contents of the suitcase were never revealed.

made a public statement. If both sides remained silent, the wolfish media would strip the carcass bare and move on to a fresh kill.

Fields and Pellicano already knew Evan was willing to negotiate. Why not pay him off and nip the nightmare in the bud while you've got the opportunity? Especially when you know your man is guilty of sleepiing with little boys, at the least. Not only do you avoid a civil suit, but also, more important, you buy your way around the authorities by removing their star witness. Ten, twenty, thirty million? Money's no object. The deal could be a *fait accompli* within hours. And if it doesn't work, you can always come out swingin' anyway.

Some in the Jackson camp agreed with this strategy. But Fields and Pellicano held to their belief that the best defense is a good offense. So Michael gave Pellicano free rein, and the P.I. hit back hard and fast with a campaign designed to divert public attention from molestation to extortion, from Michael to Evan. And at first, the media played right into his hands.

> The Michael Jackson case, and the sensationalism that surrounds it, raises lots of "red flags." Allegations of sexual abuse, especially when made in a bitter divorce or child custody battle, present significant problems for police, prose- cutors and child-protection authorities. While there are many legitimate cases involving child sexual abuse, others involve bogus claims to use the child as a weapon against the parent during a divorce or to prevent visitation.[64]

> Thanks to Pellicano and Jackson's criminal attorney, Howard Weitzman, the first two days' coverage in the *Los Angeles Times* played up the alleged extortion more than the molestation charges. Only on the third day did the *Times* finally get around to publishing a response from the police as to whether anyone from the Jackson camp had ever reported any extortion attempt to them. No one had. Even then, the paper made only a slight reference to the Department of Children's Services report.

> A lot of people simply did not want to believe that Michael Jackson could molest little boys, and the tepid Establishment-press coverage reflected the public's repugnance and ambivalence."[65]

Who the hell is Evan Chandler? What the world knew of him was only what Anthony Pellicano told them — a liar, an extortionist, a welcher of

---

[64] William G. Steiner, "The Real Shame of Child Molestation Cases," *Los Angeles Times* August 27, 1993.

[65] Maureen Orth, "Nightmare at Neverland," 135.

child support. How can you compete against Michael's twenty years of image building? How do you fight The King of Pop when his "damage control is being carried out in several countries by a cadre of high powered attorneys, private investigators, marketing experts and publicists."[66]

Initial public opinion was overwhelmingly in favor of Michael, and almost immediately its immense power began to slow the wheels of justice, as well as bring tremendous pressure to bear on the individuals — in this case an entire family — who unwittingly found themselves on the wrong side of it.[67]

"It's gonna be bigger than all of us put together, and the whole thing's just gonna crash down on everybody and destroy everybody in its sight," Evan warned Dave seven weeks earlier on the tape. His prediction was becoming reality . . . more horrific than he could ever have imagined.

AUGUST 24

After DCS set June and Dave's minds right, the couple joined forces with Evan, *at his invitation,* to form a united front against the Jackson machine. They met several times at Dave's house in Bel Air between August 22 and 27. Evan had to park several blocks away, don a disguise, and worm his way through the paparazzi to sneak in the back door. (They never caught on.) It was at these meetings that the decision was made to hire prominent Los Angeles attorney Gloria Allred.

On August 26, Evan voluntarily submitted a written statement "under penalty of perjury" to Detective Frederico Sicard of LAPD's Juvenile Division. The statement, which summarized all events leading up to the involvement of the authorities, quickly made its way to the DA's office. Enclosed with the statement were several pertinent documents, as well as a copy of an article appearing in the August 25 edition of *The Hollywood Reporter* in which Allred was quoted as follows. Evan felt Allred's words described his motivations to a tee.

---

[66] David Ferrell & Chuck Philips, "Gloves Come Off in Damage Control by Jackson Camp." *Los Angeles Times,* September 3, 1993.

[67] The DA's response is discussed in Part Two.

> It is not unusual for there to be an effort to resolve a child abuse case by attempting to reach a settlement for therapy, pain and suffering and punitive damages. That may be characterized by some as an extortion attempt, but it is routine. The ($20 million) figure alone is also not indicative of extortion if a child has been sexually abused. For punitive damages, jurors can take into account the net worth of the perpetrator.

Jackson's net worth was reported to be somewhere between three hundred and seven hundred million. Using the lower figure, twenty million would be just one fifteenth (6 percent) of his net worth. Evan and Barry readily admitted to the police that they had asked Pellicano for twenty million dollars, not as part of an extortion attempt, as Pellicano claimed, but in an attempt to settle Joride's civil claims against Michael out of court.

What's interesting about the twenty million dollars figure is that when Evan came up with the number he did not know anything about what Allred was addressing in the above quote, namely, how the law sets damages in such cases. He picked the number because it seemed like an amount that would not only compensate his son — to the extent that money could — but also be high enough to punish Michael. It seemed punitive to Evan, on a commonsense level.

But to the average person the amount was obscene — anyone asking for that much must be an extortionist — and it reinforced Michael's side of the story. Yet, when all was said and done, the amount Michael agreed to pay was reported to be at least twenty million dollars. Evan, in his own naive way, hit the nail square on the head.

✳   ✳   ✳

Had Michael paid the twenty million dollars demanded of him in August, rather than the following January, he might have spent the next ten years as the world's most famous entertainer, instead of the world's most infamous child molester.

PART TWO

THE CENTER RING

– 12 –

BILLIONS OF DOLLARS WERE AT STAKE, not just the future earnings of Michael Jackson himself, but of dozens of individuals and corporations. Sony, Fox, MJJ Productions, Pepsico and who knows how many others all stood to make huge profits off this one man conglomerate. If Sinatra was still going strong in his seventies, why not Jackson? One stock market analyst estimated that Michael's endorsement for Pepsi amounted to nearly one billion dollars a year in sales!

Michael's cadre of PR pros had been hawking the singer's squeaky-clean image for years, manipulating the all-too-willing press with impunity. And for the most part the public bought it, especially the children. So when it came to the extortion allegations, the world was primed to believe any "evidence" that helped maintain the illusion of Michael's purity.

AUGUST 30

At a press conference packed with reporters, Anthony Pellicano and Howard Weitzman (Michael's criminal attorney) played Dave's secret tape for the world, claiming that it was evidence of an extortion attempt by Evan. On the following day the *Los Angeles Times* reported "at no point, however, did the boy's natural father spell out what he might want from Jackson or detail any allegations against Jackson." But the lack of real evidence didn't stop Pellicano. He continued to claim that he had personally witnessed the extortion on several occasions.

When asked why he didn't make tapes of those extortion attempts, Pellicano said he could not have made them legally without advising law enforcement.[68] Two days later, however, he presented a second clandestine tape (of Rothman) to the worldwide media — a tape that was not reported to the police until ten days *after* it was made. No one caught the "inconsistency."

Or any of Pellicano's lies. When Larry King asked why he never reported the extortion to the police, Pellicano replied, "I haven't had an opportunity to talk to them yet." Yet earlier in the interview he told King, "I have been involved in an active investigation for two months relative to an extortion attempt." Two months, and he couldn't find an hour to talk to the police?

Pellicano told Larry King that when the allegations against Michael were first brought to his attention, he "purposely told these people, if you have any allegations to make, bring them to the attention of the DA's office. . . . That's exactly what you're supposed to do. Any law-abiding citizen would do that." Yet Pellicano had just made serious allegations against Evan, *on international TV*, without having reported them to the police. It would be another three days before anyone from the Jackson camp would file a report.

Clearly it was not Pellicano's concern for the law that prevented him from catching the extortion on tape. Nor was it a lack of opportunity; there were several additional phone calls and face-to-face meetings that occurred in the six weeks between Dave's taping of Evan and Pellicano's taping of Rothman. And you can bet the farm that Pellicano was taping everything.

Simply put, Pellicano failed to catch the extortion because there was none. Which explains why Michael's team failed to file an extortion complaint until they were pressured into it by a *Los Angeles Times* article that appeared two days *after* Pellicano's first public accusation against Evan and Barry Rothman.

[68] Chuck Phillips & David Ferrell, "Tapes Used to Allege Plot to Extort Jackson Released."

Details of that alleged extortion, however, have not been reported to police, according to officials in the LAPD's Major Crimes Unit, which is responsible for handling such an investigation. 'Nobody's brought anything to us,' said Capt. William O. Garland, head of the unit.[69]

Embarrassed, Howard Weitzman rushed right down to LAPD headquarters and filed a complaint.

But public opinion, once formed, is difficult to change. The longer the public focused on the blackmailing dentist instead of the child-molesting superstar, the more likely they were to believe that the extortion occurred and the molestation didn't.

And public opinion was the key, the one thing all those billions depended on. So Pellicano came out swingin', and much of the media responded as predicted, like jackals to a fresh kill. Los Angeles based channels 7 and 9 were broadcasting special reports from the street outside the Chandler home, and named "the boy" and his father as the creators of the movie, *Robin Hood: Men in Tights*. Channel 4 showed Evan driving in his car and identified him as a "prominent Westside dentist." Channel 13 provided the parents' names, and assigned reporters, with camera rolling, "to invade the workplaces of both parents."[70]

Pellicano and Weitzman created a swell of favorable public opinion for Jackson, and in so doing brought tremendous pressure on Evan and his family.

No matter that only Jackson's side of the story was being told, many held it as gospel — literally! The following is from a syndicated article written by Eugene Kennedy, whose byline described him as "a freelance writer and a *professor of psychology* at Loyola University in Chicago."

> We could indulge Jackson's bizarreness because his crotch grabbing, seductive stage persona and supposedly simmering sexuality were make-believe. There was nothing behind them; the self was in motion for its own stimulation *with no hint of real longing for anybody else.* Jackson personified safe sex . . . sensuality depersonalized, *sex with the human complications and implications removed,* lust so watered down it could join the flow of a biblical river.

---

[69] Sonia Nazario & Amy Wallace, "International Furor Stirred by Allegations on Jackson," *Los Angeles Times*, August 26, 1993.

[70] Jim Newton & Sonia Nazario, "Police Say Seized Tapes Do Not Incriminate Jackson."

Jackson has been betrayed by as modern a Judas as could be found: a Hollywood dentist who claims the singer/dancer molested his son, the subject of a custody fight with his ex-wife. . .

Is Michael Jackson innocent?

He may well be. After all, others who have suffered for America's sins have often been innocent too." (Italics added.)

A Judas? Suffered for our sins? Did Jesus wear makeup, grab his crotch and sleep with little boys, too?

You don't need a degree in psychology (obviously!) to know that none of us is devoid of "a real longing" for others, and though we may bury emotions deep in our subconscious, we can never remove "the human complications or implications" from sex.

More absurd than the flawed psychology was that here was a (supposed) man of science publicly pronouncing a verdict without one shred of objective, confirmable evidence. If a professional could buy the hype, just think what the general public would do.

Evan had no idea how prophetic his words would be when Dave captured them on tape: "It's going to be bigger than all of us put together, and the whole thing is going to crash down on everybody, and destroy everybody in sight." Hardly the words of an extortionist looking forward to big bucks!

If, as the press reported, Evan *never* mentioned money or made any demands on the tape, what did he say? There are thirteen separate quotes in which Evan states that his goal was to sit down and talk to June and Michael about Jordie, nine quotes in which he laments the break up of his family due to Michael's influence; and twenty-one quotes in which he talks about the harm Michael and June have done to Jordie and how concerned he is with the boy's well-being.

The following are excerpts selected from various portions of the official court transcript of the tape.

Page 64

EVAN: . . . and she [June] made those decisions to the harm of her son, despite the fact that, yeah, maybe she's insecure, maybe she's macho on the surface, and maybe you [Dave] fucked her over. Maybe you did. Maybe you didn't. Nobody's gonna give a shit about that. I know what you're saying. And I agree with you, and I think that had you two had a really good [tape irregularity], maybe she wouldn't have had to do what she did. And I know what you're saying, and it breaks my heart, but I truly believe my son is being harmed greatly and that his life — he could be fucked up for the rest of his life [tape irregularity].

Page 97

EVAN: I'm telling you this: That as bad as my life is, I'm willing to let it get a lot worse and sacrifice whatever it is — and I don't even consider it a sacrifice — give up whatever it is so that my son won't be damaged. You're not willing to do that. You fall apart just to save one of your kids [tape irregularity] away from my practice, from my family, from my wife, from Cody, from everybody else, do whatever I have to do.

DAVE: And you think that'll save Jordie? I mean, don't you think there's a happy medium?

EVAN No. You're not gonna save him. June's not gonna save him. Who's gonna save him? It's gotta be me.

DAVE: I mean, do you really think he has . . . You don't think it's just gonna run its course? I mean, you know more than I know, so I'm at a disadvantage.

EVAN: Well, then, I will tell you without question. It's gone way too far. Jordie is never going to be the same person he was. It's never — by the time it runs its course — if it does, he will be so damaged he'll never recover.

Page 39

EVAN: Let me put it to you this way, Dave. Nobody in this world was allowed to come between this family of June, me and Jordie. That was the heart [tape irregularity] be the opposite. That's evil. That's one reason why he's evil. I spoke to him about it, Dave. I even told him that [tape irregularity] the family.

DAVE: When did you talk to him?

EVAN: Months ago. When I first met him I told him that. That's the law. That's the first thing he knew. Nobody's allowed to do that. Now there's no family anymore. I mean, Jordie's — Jordie's my life. Period.

DAVE: How does this help it?

EVAN: It doesn't. It doesn't. I don't know how it'll help it. It can't hurt it anymore. It's — I have — that's why I have nothing to lose. I made this really clear to them. If they're all there we could all sit and talk. If they're not there they're taking it out of my hands, and there won't be any talking anymore. They have a chance. They have a chance to talk it out in a calm, peaceful manner. Even you said you can be there. You could be there. I'm not going to do anything with you there. Michael can come with twenty bodyguards, and all with guns if he wants to. He can even come there with his [tape irregularity]. I don't care. All I'm saying is everybody who's a party to this (inaudible) sit down and talk about it.

DAVE: Well, I don't disagree with that.

EVAN: If they don't want to be there, then they have made it to the point where I can't talk to them about it, so I have to force them to the table.

DAVE: Well, no. I don't disagree with everyone sitting down and talking about it.

EVAN: Well, that's what I'm calling . . . that's what I called him about.

DAVE: You mean, that was the message on the machine?

EVAN: Yeah. That was the message on the machine. It said they'd better be there, because on the other times I tried to tell them that I needed to talk to them, all I got was "Go fuck yourself. We're not talking to you." So now I had to let them know and make sure that they know they'd [tape irregularity] they're gonna get hurt by it, so (inaudible) . . . I had to make [tape irregularity] if they don't sit down and talk to me they're gonna get hurt. They can't keep telling me to go fuck myself anymore. They have to talk. I want to talk to them. I don't want to hurt anybody. They're forcing me to do it. They're forcing me to do it by refusing to sit down and talk to me. That's all I ask for. "You sit down and you talk to me [tape irregularity] side of the story, I'll listen to yours, we all sit down and see how it could be resolved.

Page 7

DAVE: But, you know, here's the whole thing. We can't, you know, I can't put her [June] down [if] that's all she's doing is hanging out. It's not so horrible.

EVAN: That what?

DAVE: That, you know, I mean, she's into hanging out. Hanging out is okay.

EVAN: Hanging out's kind of a benign thing. She's not hanging out anymore. When she stopped hanging out and became actively destructive in Jordie's life is when I stepped in and when I decided I have to do something about it. I tried to talk to her about it, Dave, on several occasions.

DAVE: Well, we know she's hard to talk to.

EVAN: Well, if you could . . . if you could . . . yes. I mean, that's unquestionable. She is impossible to talk to. And I've never really . . . I mean, I've gotten angry with her many times and [tape irregularity] long as you've stepped in, the issue has never involved potentially harming Jordie for the rest of his life. There have been issues over Jordie before that I've backed down on because you asked me to or whatever the reason was, and I've never been . . . I've never been that set on pursuing it until now because I truly believe this will damage him for the rest of his life. And she will not . . . and I've told her that, and I've tried to talk to her about that and she's not willing to talk to me about it. She doesn't even want to hear what might be harming him. She doesn't want to even know — she doesn't want to hear any words. "Get out of my face. Don't even mention that." That's not an issue for her. I mean, what kind of person is that? If . . . I stopped taking that personally.

DAVE: Well, we all have different ways of coping.

EVAN: You see, as an adult, coping's no excuse. That's like driving drunk and saying, "I'm sorry, but I didn't realize there was a law against driving drunk," and you just ran on the sidewalk. The fact is you're a responsible adult. You're supposed to have some sense and judgment, and that's how it's going to go down.

Page 214

EVAN: I cared at the time. I mean, I was totally shocked that she would respond that way to me. I couldn't believe it. Okay? So I know that I have tried in every way. I've appealed to her in every way I know how. I've appealed to her intelligence, I've appealed to her emotions, and so I've done every — I've gotten on the ground and I've groveled in front of her. I've gone so far as to tell her that her son is in danger. None of it made a difference, none of it, and so what else am I supposed to do to get their attention?

But several times on the tape Evan did threaten to ruin Michael if he didn't get what he wanted, and those are the quotes Pellicano took out of context and played for the world. Yet in over two hundred pages of transcript there is not one mention of wanting money. So what *did* Evan want and how was he going to ruin Michael if he didn't get it?

The answer is simple. The tape was made at a point in time when Evan had not been permitted to see his son for over one month because June and Michael would not allow it. *Evan wanted his son back*. And though he feared what might happen if the allegations against Michael became public, he was willing to file a custody action against June containing allegations that could ruin even a superstar.

SEPTEMBER 1

Knowing only what the Jackson PR machine was feeding them, the public initially bought the extortion charge. But when neither the authorities nor the media found the tape to be proof that any crime had been committed, Michael's camp was forced to launch a second salvo to prevent this skepticism from trickling down to the masses.

So once again, at a grand press conference televised to the world, Howard Weitzman attempted to bolster the claim that an extortion attempt had occurred by presenting the secretly recorded "smoking gun" conversation between Pellicano and Rothman.

And once again the press found no extortion.

> The two men never directly state the reasons for their . . . negotiations. . . . Neither Pellicano nor . . . the father's lawyer specifically mentions the alleged sexual molestation, nor is blackmail discussed. . . . Rothman does not make any specific threats . . . [71]

No threats, no demands. Just *negotiations*.

But the fact that there was no extortion on this second tape didn't matter either. By smearing the character of Evan and his attorney, Michael's team accomplished their real goal of diverting public attention from the child as victim to Michael as victim. "In recent days, the extortion allegations and their denials have come to dominate the controversy surrounding the investigation," the *Times* reported.[72]

Oddly enough, no one, not even the investigative reporters from the *Times,* seemed to notice the absurd contradictions in Pellicano's statements. Here is his legal justification for recording Rothman:

> Pellicano said he refused that offer, and on the next day he told the father's lawyer that he would pay the father $350,000 in a film development deal. "I was trying to set him up with the extortion," Pellicano said. "I wanted to see if he would take it."[73]

---

[71] Amy Wallace & Jim Newton, "Jackson Aides Go Back on the Offensive," *Los Angeles Times*, September 2, 1993.

[72] Ibid.

[73] Charles P. Wallace & Jim Newton, "Taylor Joins Jackson in Singapore During Ordeal."

Five days later Pellicano told the *Times*,

> They just kept trying to get money from us, and when *we wouldn't pay*, some-
> one called (a child protective agency).[74]

Pellicano gave the same conflicting explanations on *Larry King Live*. When asked why he did not report the extortion to the police until two days *after* the story became public, Pellicano said:

> It had to go full circle. When and if they were to accept money, I would have
> had law enforcement in on this.[75]

Yet just moments earlier he told King, "A demand for twenty million dollars was made and presented. It was flatly and consistently refused." How could Pellicano make it go "full circle" and "set him up with extortion," if he "flatly and consistently" refused to pay? It's absurd.

In fact, after rejecting Rothman's initial request for twenty million dollars, Pellicano came back with the two additional offers, the first for one million and the second for three hundred and fifty thousand. This is hardly what one would call "flatly refused." And as for "trying to set him up" and make it "go full circle," when Rothman tried to accept the million dollars offer, Pellicano withdrew it!

Pellicano contradicted himself so often and so foolishly in the opening weeks of the controversy, that Jordie's attorney, Larry Feldman, couldn't wait to get him on the witness stand. "I'm going to tear his ass off," Feldman rejoiced. "I don't have to get him to say anything. All I have to do is read his own statements back!"

The Jackson camp also claimed that poor Michael unwittingly became entwined in a custody battle between Evan and June. Yet Evan, June and Dave swore under oath that none of these problems existed prior to Michael's entry in their lives, and that he was the cause of them.

Whether or not Bert Fields believed that Michael was sexually involved with Jordie, he knew from the start that Evan was making that claim. Fields

---

[74] Jean Merl & Shawn Hubler, "Michael Jackson is Subject of LAPD Inquiry", *Los Angeles Times*, August 24, 1993.

[75] Anthony Pellicano, interview by Larry King, *Larry King Live*, CNN, August 24, 1993.

made that statement to *Vanity Fair*.[76] In addition, Fields was involved in the change of custody agreements and in arranging the visitation. What conclusion could he have come to other than the custody dispute was a direct result of Michael's relationship with Jordie? Michael Freeman's motion, with Fields' declaration attached, would force the return of Jordie to June. And without Jordie to back him up — the boy would be on tour with Michael — Evan's claim of child abuse, if he dared make it, would be received as nothing more than the ranting of a fool.

Considering the downside of forcing Evan to go to authorities to prevent returning his son to Michael, why didn't Pellicano settle the dispute when he had the chance? On tape, Rothman can be heard telling Pellicano that he had busted his hump to get Evan to agree. Yet Pellicano withdrew it. Why?

And when the scandal became public, why did Jackson's people scream bloody murder about an extortion they could not prove in a court of law? Sure, it was an obvious attempt to control public opinion and get their opponent to back down — the trusty "best defense" strategy. And a grandiose attempt it was. But it soon became obvious that it wasn't working and that a legal battle was imminent.

So why didn't Fields and Pellicano retreat from the headlines and work out a deal behind the scenes? In early September, just two weeks after the scandal broke, Feldman and Weitzman agreed to a media truce so they could work out a private settlement. But Pellicano and Fields successfully counseled Michael against it. Why?

On the morning of August 17, 1993, as he negotiated with Barry Rothman, Anthony Pellicano had in his possession a copy of the psychiatrist's report with the names omitted. He held in his hand the future of the most famous entertainer in human history. Yet the tape is replete with examples of Pellicano refusing to compromise on what would amount to chump change to Jackson. Why take the chance of Michael's name ending up on that report and triggering an investigation?

"It's that or it's nothing," Pellicano told Rothman on the tape. "[Evan's]

---

[76] Maureen Orth, "Nighmare at Neverland," 131.

got nothing and if he wants nothing he's got nothing." That Evan and Rothman even considered negotiating a multi-million dollar screenplay deal turned out to be a huge mistake. The perception was devastating. Can you imagine how bad it would have looked had Evan actually accepted such a deal and put his name to paper? Pellicano was so close, yet he blew it. Why?

"I believe I am the best in the world," Pellicano once claimed.[77] "I involve myself in cases that take tremendous amounts of thought — Sherlock Holmes-type things."[78]

Lofty company indeed. The best! No doubt the man actually thought that much of himself. And why not? His clients included Kevin Costner, Roseanne Arnold, Sylvester Stallone, James Woods, Ed McMahon, and of course, the biggest name of all, Michael Jackson. "And make no mistake," *People Magazine* wrote, "Pellicano is Hollywood's top-of-the-line troubleshooter."

Certainly the man was good at what he did. But it was not superior intelligence or world-class investigative skills that brought Pellicano to the top. Far from it. What made him so valuable to those who had something to hide was his willingness to do whatever it takes to suppress the truth.

Immersed in his own hype and robotically programmed to use the Mafioso methods that had brought him to the top, Pellicano simply could not entertain the thought that a mere dentist might defeat him at his own game. Yet had he stopped for moment to think, as the great Holmes surely would have, Pellicano might have noticed that this situation was not following the pattern his other cases had. Had he taken the time to assess his opponent, he would have noticed that each time he tried his formula approach of aggressive intimidation, it pushed a button in Evan that made him "ratchet things to the next level" rather than cower and acquiesce, as the vast majority of Pellicano's opponents did when confronted by his criminality.

On August 17, with June in possession of a court order that would enable her to give Jordie back to Michael, Evan had nothing left to lose. Michael, on the other hand, with his name on the verge of appearing in a DCS report

---

[77] "Private Eye Keeps Watch Over Stars," *USA Today*, December 26, 1991.

[78] Bill Hewitt, Lyndon Stambler, John Hannah & Leah Eskin, "Trouble Shooter," *People Magazine*, September 20, 1993.

and possibly plastered all over the media, had everything to lose. So why did Pellicano screw up so badly?

Hunter S. Thompson once described corrupt politicians as drug addicts who will "lie and cheat and steal" and "sacrifice anything and anybody to feed their cruel and stupid habit"[79] The shoe fits here as well. Evan Chandler has never said a word about these events in any public forum, despite years of relentless media attacks against him. It was not he who destroyed Michael Jackson. It was arrogance, the "cruel and stupid" arrogance of Anthony Pellicano.

✳   ✳   ✳

In 2003, during a raid on The Pellicano Investigative Agency, federal authorities found illegal hand grenades and plastic explosives in Pellicano's private safe. The search was part of an investigation into death threats made against a *Los Angeles Times* reporter.

The reporter had received a series of threats attempting to thwart her investigation into possible links between a well-known actor and the mafia. The last of these threats came in the form of a dead fish with a rose in its mouth left on the reporter's car, and a bullet through her car window, accompanied by a note warning her to stop the investigation.

Ironically, it was in a secretly recorded conversation made by the FBI that an ex-convict drug dealer admitted being hired by Pellicano to make the threats. In January 2004, Anthony Pellicano was sentenced to thirty months in prison for possession of the explosives.[80]

An intensive FBI investigation into Pellicano's illegal wiretapping activities is in full swing. Bert Fields is "a major focus" of the investigation.[81]

Michael Freeman was convicted of bankruptcy fraud in 1997 and sentenced to thirty months in prison. He resigned from the California State Bar to avoid being formally disbarred.[82]

---

[79] Hunter Thompson, *Rolling Stone,* July 1994.

[80] David Rosenzweig, "Pellicano Is Sentenced to Thirty Months," *Los Angeles Times,* January 24, 2004.

[81] Henry Weinstein, Chuck Philips & Greg Krikorian, "Celebrity Lawyer Fields Is Subject of Wiretap Probe," *Los Angeles Times,* November 12, 2003; Richard Winton, "Reflections on 2003; Law Enforcement," *Los Angeles Times* December 27, 2003.

[82] Jose Cardenas, "Man Sentenced for Hiding Assets in Bankruptcy Case," *Los Angeles Times*, March 6, 1997.

– 13 –

SEPTEMBER 1 *(continued)*

Evan had consulted with criminal attorney Richard Hirsch, who advised him that the allegations of extortion and molestation would probably amount to "a wash" because the DA would decline to press either charge. Hirsch believed that it was a good deal for Evan and Jordie and that he should accept it. But Evan's instincts told him otherwise, so he sought a second opinion.

With little to eat and no sleep for two nights, Evan paced back and forth as he relayed the basic facts to noted criminal attorney Arthur Baren. Evan concluded with his personal concerns for the future.

> I want you to understand, I have no fear of an extortion charge. I have no fear of going to jail. I have one fear only, and that is that there's going to be a deal made and I'm not willing to cut a deal. I would rather be charged with extortion than have to make a deal for them to drop the Jackson case. That's what I'm afraid is going to happen and that's why I'm here right now.

> Now you have to understand this. My motive for wanting to go ahead with this is because my son wants this to go forward, he wants to protect other kids in the future and because I promised him if he told me the truth that nobody would ridicule him — that in the end he would be a hero. And he has to learn at this point in his life to stand up to anybody who tries to push him around.

> He believed me when I told him that, and if the DA doesn't take the case he's not going to believe it anymore. I don't know what the psychological effects will be of that — of being betrayed by the government, by society. So I don't care what happens to me. I want this case to go forward. Gloria Allred is in the DA's office right now arguing for this case to go forward regardless of my involvement.

Baren listened attentively. Then, for the first time since the nightmare began, provided Evan with his first clear understanding of the forces at work.

> [DA] Lauren Weis is under a lot of pressure, trying to do her job and having to worry about what is politically appropriate with all these politicians loving Michael Jackson to death. And she's also under pressure in trying to predict the media.

But Baren believed that irrespective of those pressures, Deputy District Attorney Weis would "do the right thing." Especially since the decision whether or not to prosecute Jackson lay more in the hands of Stuart House than in the DA's office. As for the prediction of a wash, Baren advised:

> The big danger for both you and your son is that this whole thing will disappear. Your lives will be ruined and you'll never get a chance to be vindicated in a court of law. The wash is the worst thing you could have.

Baren understood that Evan and Jordie were already marked men, demonized by many for their evil attack on a god. He also knew there was no way that Evan, with his limited resources, could counter Michael's media onslaught, and that given enough time Michael would triumph in the public forum. Evan's only hope, Baren believed, was in the legal arena. "I don't think anybody in legal circles believes the extortion," Baren added. "That's not an issue. The real issue here is whether Michael Jackson molested your son."

Evan emerged from his consultation with Baren convinced that agreeing to "a wash" was dead wrong.

That afternoon, accompanied by Gloria Allred, Jordie gave a sworn statement to Lauren Weis. "I'd already told my story to Dr. Abrams, the cops and DCS, so I wasn't so nervous this time," Jordie remembered of the experience. "Lauren was really nice. I think she knew I was telling the truth."

He was right. Like everyone else who heard his story, Lauren Weis came out of the session convinced it was true, and told Gloria so. "That's why I took the case," Gloria replied, "because I know he is too."

That evening, June and Dave met with Gloria and her partner, Nathan Goldberg, to work out the wording of Gloria's press conference scheduled for the following afternoon.

At the close of this whirlwind day, Evan and Rothman met at Rothman's office to take stock. In the midst of their conversation Rothman received an urgent call from his brother, an attorney practicing nearby in The Valley. "He wants me to call him back on a pay phone," Rothman told Evan. "Wait for me here."

When Rothman returned he was in shock. Apparently Bert Fields had published an article in a law journal accusing Rothman of unethical conduct in the Michael Jackson case. And if that wasn't enough, Rothman's brother had also heard a rumor that LAPD Chief Willie Williams threatened to "extract a pound of flesh" from Michael's accusers.

"I thought Barry was going to die," Evan said. "He was having difficulty breathing and told me he was having chest pains."

Heart attack or not, the experience scared the bejeezus out of Rothman. After that night he implored Evan and the other attorneys involved to make the whole thing go away.

Barry Rothman was not the only one experiencing a change of heart. Though still undecided about the role his mother had played in all of this, Jordie was now crystal clear that his father had saved him from an ugly fate, and that instead of being praised by the media and the public, Evan had been vilified. The injustice angered the boy to the point where his fear of public exposure had transformed into a desire to do whatever it took to clear his father's name.

– 14 –

SEPTEMBER 2

Evan arrived at his office just before 8 AM. Following his usual routine, he parked in the garage across the street, entered the building through the rear door and began walking toward the elevator at the far end of the lobby. BLAM! He was struck on the back of the head.

The blow hurt like hell, but he maintained his balance, wheeled around and smashed his attacker in the head with a heavy briefcase. The assailant staggered backwards, and then came at Evan again.

As Evan attempt to flee, a second man appeared, video camera rolling, and blocked Evan's way by striking him in the face with the lens. Evan swung at the camera and sent it careening across the marble floor, then escaped into the waiting elevator.

Safely locked in his office, Evan called the police to tell them about the attack and about the death threats pouring in on his office answering machine. Then, head-in-hands, he crumpled into a chair and cried.

I had not heard my brother cry since we were kids. But now he was sobbing like a baby. I hung up the phone, stuffed a few items in a backpack and drove the ninety miles from Santa Barbara to L.A.

We sat in Evan's office and talked about how crazy the whole thing was. The guys in the lobby were probably just a team of freelance journalists trying to get a few pictures to hawk to the tabloids. But combined with the vehement death threats, the attack brought home the fact — and the fear — that the media frenzy had stirred people to a point that could very well trigger a real lunatic. One who would give no warning.

Were we being paranoid? No, we decided. Paranoia is unreasonable fear. Michael was too well loved to play the odds. "Look what they did to John Lennon," I reminded Evan. "And all he did was refuse to sign a damn album. You've taken god and accused him of being the devil."

And then there was Anthony Pellicano, the devil incarnate as far as we were concerned. How far would he go to squash this? We had no idea. But from now on we would watch our backs.

Barry Rothman called at noon to say he had hired a criminal attorney named Robert Shapiro to defend him in case the DA filed an extortion charge. Evan had never heard of the man, but Barry assured him he was one of the best. "And he doesn't think Gloria Allred is the right attorney to handle the molestation case," Rothman added. "He's got someone else in mind, Larry Feldman."

"What a minute," Evan protested. "You gotta run that by me one more time. Who the hell is Larry Feldman? And why should I listen to this Shapiro guy anyway? He's your lawyer, not mine." It took a bit of convincing, but Evan finally agreed to a conference call with Feldman.

In true lawyer fashion, Feldman started off with a disclaimer. "Look, I'm happy to talk to Barry, and if Barry wants you on the line, Evan, that's okay with me. Ethically, I can't start giving you opinions. I don't want Gloria Allred to sue me for interfering with her client. What's she planning on doing at this press conference anyway?"

"She's going to make a statement just to focus the attention on Jordie being the issue," Evan answered, "and molestation being the issue, and moving it away from extortion. That he's very courageous and just wants his life back. But no specifics."

Feldman's strategy was diametrically opposed to Allred's. A civil attorney by trade, his goal was to sue for money, not push for a criminal prosecution.

"First Gloria will make a statement, then Weitzman or Pellicano. Then you'll have to make another statement, and then they'll have to. That's what the press wants and that's what keeps the pressure on the DA. As long as you're in that environment, Michael Jackson can't pay even if he wanted to because there's too much heat and it would be an admission of guilt."

"That makes sense, Larry," Evan replied. "But you know what's going on here is that there's a campaign against Barry and myself and it's affecting our lives. It seems that all you can do when you're being slaughtered by the media is get the truth out and hope it makes a difference."

"I understand how you feel," Larry said. "But do you think because Gloria Allred makes a statement, true or not, it's going to change anybody's views? They'll print her story, and then print the other side's version, just like they do every time. No. You have to have a goal. And if the goal is to have it go away, and for your son to have some money and get his life back in order, it seems to me that having Gloria Allred making a public statement is not going to get you closer to that goal.

"The harsh reality is litigation, what you prove in court. No one remembers what they read. I mean, it's nice to have people sympathetic to what you're going through, but Jackson's people are not going to stop taking shots at you in the media just because Gloria says your son's a great kid and wants his life back. That's not what's going to stop this."

"Maybe not," Evan responded, "but my first attorney's advice was to say nothing and Gloria's advice was you've got to say something. No one else gave us any other advice. And saying nothing did us no good at all. They just kept barraging the media and it's destroying our lives. That's the reason that we got Gloria, because silence didn't do any good."

"Still," Feldman counseled, "I think silence is the right advice."

"But doing nothing and saying nothing got me punched out this morning, and it's ruining Barry's practice and my practice."

"Nevertheless, my gut feeling is that Gil Garcetti doesn't want to be forced into this molestation thing. And you can be sure Jackson won't press the extortion issue if his case goes away.[83] He can't take the exposure. But your son — if this pressure keeps up the DA's gonna have to file something and the kid's gonna get torn apart. No, Evan, everybody wants the criminal thing to go away."

"Let me ask you something then, Larry. It could have all gone away before it ever got this far. Michael's people could have stopped it. What makes you think it will all go away now?"

"Because Michael Jackson is not going to have his deposition taken. Up till now you've been dealing with Pellicano, but your lawyer, whoever it is, isn't going to deal with some investigator. I can tell you that!" As if Pellicano was some sort of bug to be squashed and kicked aside.

Feldman's credentials were impeccable: past president of the Los Angeles Trial Lawyers Association *and* the Los Angeles Bar Association, as well as having been voted Trial Lawyer of the Year by his peers. Not that Evan put much stock in awards, but Feldman's advice made sense. The way to end this nightmare was to have Michael pay up and shut up, or force the truth out of him in a court of law.

And Rothman's new lawyer was no slouch either. According to Feldman, Robert Shapiro had a reputation as a top-of-the-line criminal attorney. "Some consider him the best in L.A.," Feldman said.

Feldman, Shapiro, Hirsch, Weitzman & Weis, (Oy vey!), all were part of a neat little "old boy" network, just the ticket for getting this nightmare over and done with — quietly. Gloria Allred, Rothman told Evan, was out of the loop. She played the game in the media, not behind the scenes. That might work against an ordinary rock star, but not against an icon like Michael Jackson.

"I feel a lot more comfortable now," Evan told Rothman, after Feldman was off the line. "Maybe they'll be more cooperative with Feldman and Shapiro at their throats."

Much to her credit, Gloria did a great job at the press conference. She stuck to the approved text and never let the reporters brow beat her into saying more.

At 4 PM, two hours after speaking with Rothman and Feldman, Evan and I

[83] Gil Garcetti was the Los Angeles County District Attorney in 1993.

were still at his desk discussing the pros and cons of the various strategies when the receptionist poked her head through the door to announce a phone call.

Evan had left instructions that he would take patient, family and attorney calls only. Hundreds of people had been trying to reach him: every talk show host, TV talking head, newspaper reporter, gossip columnist and whomever else you can think of, from a dozen different countries.

"Who is it?" Evan asked, "a patient?"

"No," the receptionist answered. "She says she's an ex-employee of Michael Jackson's and wants to help." Evan grabbed the phone as if it were God himself on the line.

The caller was reticent to reveal her name; she had "past experiences with Anthony Pellicano" and didn't know whom to trust. It took several minutes to convince her it was the real Dr. Chandler she was talking to, not one of Pellicano's people. And she had placed the call!

Though frightened, she felt "compelled to help you and your son prevent Michael from molesting more children." "I, too, have a son, and my heart goes out to your little boy."

Alison Fox had worked as a secretary at Neverland, a job that brought her in daily contact not only with those who were closest to Michael, but often with the star himself. She had no doubt he was guilty.[84]

Mindful of Feldman's warning not talk to anyone — tainting the witness, he called it — Evan asked Alison to turn her information over to the police. But she refused to get directly involved, fearing some form of reprisal from Pellicano if her name got out. She would meet only with Evan, and only if he promised to "take it all the way." "Michael has to be stopped," she insisted, "and I don't want to stick my neck out if you're going to give up."

Alison suggested meeting the following day but Evan was concerned that Pellicano might get to her by then and "convince" her to keep silent. With a little coddling, she agreed to meet at 5 PM that afternoon in the lobby of Warner Records in Burbank. It was further agreed that she and Evan would each bring a second to act as a witnesses.

We had forty minutes to get from Beverly Hills to Burbank, in rush hour.

---

[84] To protect her privacy, Alison's real name has not been used.

So we decided to avoid the freeways and stick to the surface streets. Evan drove, I navigated, alternating between checking the map and watching for a tail. A dozen miraculously undetected moving violations later, we arrived at the Warner building at 4:55.

Alison led us across the street to a small garden where we sat conversing in hushed tones, often reverting to meaningless chit-chat whenever a stranger strolled by. The first half hour was a feeling-out process, getting to know and trust one another. Then, for nearly two hours, we listened as this scared but compassionate woman told her story.

And oh what a story it was! A treasure trove of information about several young boys who had been "with Michael," about the roles their parents played, details of the relationships, details of how the children were procured and who did the procuring, and on and on about the inner workings of Neverland.[85]

According to Alison, Pellicano paid her a visit shortly after she left Michael's employ, and he "quizzed" her about whether she thought Michael had a problem with little boys. She took it as a warning to keep her mouth shut. After that, two men sat in a blue van outside her house for a few days, overtly watching her come and go. "I feared for my safety and my son's safety," Alison told us.

Among the information Alison gave us were two key names. Miko Brando, Marlon's son, and Norma Staikos, Michael's chief of staff at Neverland. Miko was very close to Michael, Alison said. "If anybody knows about Michael, it's Miko."

Amongst her other duties, Staikos was in charge of the children's groups that visited the ranch. She would invite back only those children that Michael took an interest in — always little boys. Norma was also in charge of the parents, seeing to it that they were kept entertained while their children went off alone with Michael.[86]

---

[85] Most of what Alison revealed was subsequently verified by the police and/or by Feldman's private investigator.

[86] When the s--t hit the fan, Norma Staikos left U.S. jurisdiction for her native Greece the day before she was scheduled to be deposed. (Maureen Orth, "Nightmare at Neverland." 137.) She returned to appear before the Santa Barbara Grand Jury after the settlement. (Victoria Inzunza, "Jury Relished Glimpse of Pop Lifestyle," *Santa Barbara News Press*, September 23, 1994.)

When the rendezvous ended, Alison suggested we meet again at her house. She trusted Evan now and wanted to give him something she felt would be helpful to the police, a rolodex containing the names, addresses and phone numbers of Michael's friends, business associates and key employees. It would save the cops a lot of time tracking them down.

"I want you to understand," Alison said, repeating what she had told Evan over the phone, "I like Michael, I really do. But he's got to be stopped." She also reminded Evan of his promises to see things through to the end and not to reveal her name. Evan reaffirmed both and thanked her sincerely on behalf of Jordie and himself.

We left at staggered intervals and in separate directions.

Evan and I could hardly believe our good fortune. We were convinced that once the cops got their hands on that rolodex they'd round up everyone and make them talk. It was only a matter of time.

"We cracked the case!" Evan declared, high-fiving me as we took off for home.

"Can you fuckin' believe it!" I said. "The cops are gonna have a field day with this stuff."

Looking back, I've got to laugh. We thought we were hotshot sleuths. Too many Charlie Chan movies, I guess. We were totally ignorant about what makes the wheels of justice spin. Or more to the point, not spin. Alison called two days later, mad as hell. The police had questioned her that morning. "You sold me out!" she screamed. Click. There would be no rolodex.[87]

SEPTEMBER 3

Evan and I had gone out earlier in the day to talk to attorney Richard Hirsch about the inner workings of the DA's office. We had several more stops to make but decided to go back to the house first to look in on the kids. They were complete shut-ins. Prisoners in their own home.

"We should leave now," Evan said, after we had been home for awhile. We had an appointment with another informant who promised to give us information about Pellicano. We were to meet in a restaurant on San

---

[87] We never found out how the police got to Alison so quickly.

Vicente Boulevard and we wanted to get to there before he did so we could pick the table. It had to be private so no one could hear us, and situated so we could sit with our backs to the wall.

The death threats were increasing at an alarming rate. Hardly an hour went by without some lunatic calling to announce his intentions to kill or maim Evan, Jordie and the entire family. We trusted no one.

I pulled the window shade back a tad to check the street. A dozen or more reporters had been lurking outside most of the day, but for some reason they were gone when we returned from the attorney's office. I figured they just got bored. Or maybe there was a juicy accident somewhere and they all rushed over to film the blood. Now they were back. Mostly tabloids. The Brits are the worst; they respect nothing.

"There's about ten or twelve of them," I reported, "and the blue van is still there." A dark blue van with tinted windows had been parked up the block for several days. It was the same make, model and color as one I'd seen in Burbank during our meeting with Alison. "I'd like to get a look inside. You can see through those tinted windows if you get close enough."

"Yeah," Evan snickered, "if there's reporters inside they'll get a close-up and it'll be all over the front page. Everybody'll think it's me."

"So what," I said, "can you imagine how embarrassed they'll be when they find out it wasn't?"

"Great, so the crazies will shoot you instead of me."

The possibility had crossed my mind. All of our lives people had mistaken us for one another. Same height and weight, same hair color, similar features, you could tell right off we were brothers. After listening to the string of death threats the prospect of taking a bullet in the head didn't seem so remote.

A star of Michael's magnitude has hundreds if not thousands of obsessed fans. We had to assume that there was at least one nuts enough to be violent. "We're coming to Los Angeles to take your blood," one particularly nasty Wacko Jacko fan threatened. "Your blood, your fucking whore of an ex-wife's blood, and your shitty little son's blood."

We buckled ourselves in and followed procedure: start the car, put her in reverse, hit the garage door opener, then back out while the door's moving.

The car had to be in motion by the time the door was fully opened, otherwise some tabloid schmuck would stand behind it so you couldn't drive, while his buddy snapped pictures through the side windows.

"Here, you better take this," Evan said, as we headed toward our appointment.

"What is it?"

"It's a gun, stupid."

"Wise ass."

"It's a thirty-eight. Be careful, there's one in the chamber. That lever next to your thumb is the safety."

I knew jack about guns. Never even held one much less fired it. And as far as I knew, Evan hadn't either. The one he was stuffing in his jacket was jet black and looked like one of those German Lugers I'd seen in old war movies.

"What kind is that?"

"Nine millimeter."

"Do you know how to use it?"

"Yeah, you shoot the other guy before he shoots you."

Just the day before I was sitting by the sea in Santa Barbara enjoying a leisurely breakfast. Now here I was in L.A., riding around with a loaded pistol tucked in my waist. What was it John Lennon said on his final album: "Life's what's happening to you while you're busy making other plans."

With the weekend came a semblance of peace. Even the herd of reporters grazing outside the house had dwindled to one or two stragglers.

Holed up at home, we didn't feel so much like targets, constantly watching our backs. Once in a while, out of habit, I'd peer through the curtains or check the yard, especially when the dog barked. But it was much safer than being out and about. Being shut in was hardest on the kids. They just wanted to go out and play.

Though safe inside, the affair still dominated every facet of life. There was no way to escape it and no point trying. The affect on the kids, the press coverage, public opinion, death threats, safety issues, use of weapons, the police investigation, the DA's attitude, advice from attorneys, Pellicano, Fields, Michael — the list was endless.

Over the weekend, a series of meetings was set up for the coming week.

On Tuesday, June and Dave were to meet Larry Feldman for the first time to hear his strategy — though, in the meantime, everyone agreed to go forward with Gloria Allred. A meeting with Gloria and her partner was already scheduled for Monday afternoon. And Rothman's lawyer, Bob Shapiro, felt it would be helpful to go over some basic concepts of legal procedure before the conference with Feldman, so a meeting was set with Bob for Monday morning.

– 15 –

SEPTEMBER 6

They met at Shapiro's office in Century City: Evan, Monique, Jordie and Richard Hirsch. Evan believed that Jordie should attend as many discussions as possible. After all, it was his life they were talking about. "I wanted him to see how the game is played and how each player operates, so he would never again be duped." But most of all, Evan wanted Jordie "to learn to stand up for himself, even in the face of overwhelming adversity."

Bob sat them down, got everyone coffee or tea, and made small talk with Jordie about school and the like just to make him feel comfortable, then got down to the heart of it.

"This is perhaps the worst situation any family could be in," Shapiro began. "If the world didn't know about it, and it was only a private family matter, it wouldn't be so bad. But when it becomes not only a matter of national knowledge, but international knowledge, where you're being victimized to the highest degree, and then somebody turns this matter around and tries to turn you into the guilty party, it's beyond a nightmare."

Shapiro wasn't telling Evan and Jordie anything they didn't already know, but it was comforting that he understood what they were going through.

"So what can we do about it?" Evan asked.

"There are lots of options," the attorney suggested. "What you need to do first, is to get all the information you can about what each course of action holds for each one of you, especially Jordie, as the victim. He's the most important person."

Turning directly toward Jordie, Shapiro continued. "It's going to be his decision as a thirteen-year-old, along with his family, as to what is best for him. First, what is best emotionally, because you've been through a traumatic experience that was not your fault. One that was brought on by an older person who manipulated you — and a lot of other young boys in this case — and can cause deep scars and a lot of guilt and remorse.

"This is similar, psychologically, to a woman who's been raped: somebody close who takes advantage of you, somebody who's in power. I've talked briefly with the district attorney and I've talked with the lawyers for Michael Jackson, and I will tell you that I have, without even talking to you, no doubt that your allegations are true."

"On what do you base that opinion?" Evan asked.

"On my experience. On the profile of pedophiles that I am familiar with after twenty-five years of practice, and on my personal knowledge of Michael Jackson. Based on one, outside, independent report, which I believe has verified another victim. Based on the conclusions of Lauren Weis whom I have known for twenty years, whom I greatly respect. And based upon the reports of the psychiatrist. Just based upon the way this whole scenario has gone down; the knowledge of Pellicano and how he operates, what a scumbag he is."

"You're right about everything," Evan declared, happy to have such a strong and well-connected ally.

Shapiro went on to explain that the first thing the family needed to do was to set goals. Did they want a civil trial, a criminal trial, an out of court settlement? Did they want it all to just go away? Whatever they wanted, he assured them, their lawyers could provide, because it was their side, not Jackson's, that was holding all the aces.

"Can I write this down?" Evan asked. "So Jordie and I can review it?"

"Absolutely. You can record it if you want," Shapiro answered. "Now let's get started. As you know, the district attorney is investigating the molestation charge. There are two questions here. First, was a crime committed? I believe the district attorney is already convinced that there was a crime. Second. Can he prove it beyond a reasonable doubt and to a moral certainty? That's the criteria. Most criminal trials of this nature do not involve any corroboration. It amounts to a one on one, like a rape case."

"So what you're saying," Monique concluded, "is that unless we have corroborating evidence, it comes down to Jordie's credibility."

"Most likely."

"I think there's an overview here," Richard added. "That the district attorney, who is a politically elected official, is not going to take a chance on this case unless he's sure he's going to benefit. There are molestation cases going on in town right now that are one-on-ones and they'll get filed. This case is different."

"Absolutely," Bob agreed. "If you were all completely anonymous people we would be able to get the district attorney to prosecute this case immediately. I say that unequivocally under this state of the evidence.

"Now, let's say the prosecutor says, 'This is too hot a case. I mean, look at all the problems: Michael Jackson is a famous person, he's got a lot of powerful and famous friends, I'm up for re-election, people have their careers on the line, I'm not going to take a shot at this. I'm going to put it in the hands of the Grand Jury.'

"Ninety-nine percent of the time that a district attorney asks the Grand Jury for an indictment, he gets it. So, temporarily at least, the DA can avoid the tremendous political backlash by letting the Grand Jury make the decision. But eventually it comes back because he has to prosecute it.

"So even if the DA rejects this case, we have the Grand Jury. We can't compel the Grand Jury to hear this, but certainly public opinion can rise to such a degree that Jordie should be heard, and it would be very difficult for Gil Garcetti to refuse sending the matter to the Grand Jury.

"So let me tell you where the DA's office is at. They have a child they firmly believe is a victim of molestation. They also have a very high profile defendant who will deny it. And they have, floating around before this matter came to the courts, two unusual things that took place. Number one, an opinion was sought anonymously from a psychiatrist about what happened. And number two, there were negotiations for money. That's a very negative thing in a criminal case."

"Maybe not so negative if you understand the context in which it occurred," Evan defended.

"You can put spins on anything," Shapiro said. "All I'm saying is, generally, in the context of a criminal prosecution, it's a very negative thing. The

other thing is that the Grand Jury would have to hear exculpatory information. That would mean Evan would have to testify, and then Pellicano would
testify. So they would end up hearing both sides of it and may or may not
return an indictment."

"Of course," Richard explained, "they might even return an indictment
against you, Evan."

"It'll never happen," Evan responded. "There's no evidence and there
never will be."

The aside comment of Richard Hirsch regarding the political nature of
the DA's office should not be overlooked. As Shapiro stated (as well as every
other attorney, DCS investigator, police officer and social worker familiar
with the case), if the perpetrator was anyone other than Michael Jackson,
the DA would have already arrested and charged him.

From an evidence point of view this case was no different than the vast
majority of sex crimes against children. They are "one-on-ones."
Corroborating evidence is helpful, but often not available, so the likelihood
of a conviction depends solely on the credibility of the victim's testimony.
And according to Shapiro, the DA believed that Jordie's testimony might be
the best they'd ever had from a child victim. There is no doubt that by mid-
September the authorities had more evidence against Michael than they
had revealed. Many child molesters had been convicted on less.[88]

So why, at this point, wasn't Michael charged?

The DA had recently lost (or at least hadn't won) several high profile
cases: Rodney King, Damien Williams (the Reginald Denny beating), the
first Menendez Brothers trial. Videotapes and all, they still lost. With the
competency of his office in serious doubt, it would have been political suicide
for Gil Garcetti to indict The King of Pop without an open and shut case, a
sure win. Which meant having at least one more victim willing to testify.

But Garcetti was a symptom of the disease, not the cause. The cause is
the man in the mirror. Jack and Jill Citizen do not want their superstars
treated like everyone else. And Michael was the most super of them all.

---

[88] What Jordie's lawyers didn't know at the time was that the police had discovered child
pornography "often found in the homes of pedophiles" during their search of Michael's
home. (Maureen Orth, "The Jackson Jive," *Vanity Fair*, June 25, 1995, 114.)

They wanted him at the presidential inauguration. They wanted him doing halftime at the Super Bowl. And they were ready, willing and able to ignore his "idiosyncrasies."[89]

Yet if a pancaked, lipsticked, eye-lined, crotch-grabbin' nobody lived on Joe Citizen's block and admitted sleeping in bed with the neighborhood boys, a jury would have locked him up, or the neighbors would have strung him up, pretty darn quick.

But the citizenry does not apply the same standard of proof to Michael Jackson as they do to themselves. And therein lies the rub. No one is more aware than a big city DA that of all the forces at work in a high-profile case, public opinion is by far the most influential. So like it or not, Garcetti's reluctance to charge Michael was to a great extent a reflection of the collective prejudice of his constituents.

Evan and Jordie left Shapiro's office at eleven-thirty, grabbed a quick bite, and hopped over to the Loew's Santa Monica Hotel for a strategy meeting with Gloria Allred and her partner, Nathan Goldberg. The participants — Jordie, Evan, Monique, June and Dave — settled around a huge conference table and quickly got down to business.

"So tell me," Evan asked, "do you think the DA will file?"

"It's completely at his discretion," Nathan answered. "If he feels that public sympathy is with not filing, then it's more than likely he won't. But that's one of our goals. We want to create the kind of climate in the community that will neutralize some of the effects of what Jackson is doing."

"How do you think it would affect the DA if they don't find another kid?" Dave asked.

"In most cases, if the district attorney has a child who's credible, who makes sense and tells a straight story, then that's enough to support a criminal prosecution. But in this particular case, because of who it is, there's going to be a ton of pressure on him not to file.

"Make no mistake about it," Nathan went on, "a child's testimony alone, if believed by a jury, is sufficient to convict. They don't need anything else. They don't have to have one piece of corroborating evidence. But none of that happens if they don't file. So that's the first step in the process."

"How many jurors are there?" Evan asked.

---

[89] Curiously, when Roseanne grabbed her crotch once as a comic gesture mimicking baseball players, many were outraged. But when Michael did it repeatedly, few complained.

"Twelve."

"And what's the requirement for a conviction?"

"Unanimous, in a criminal case."

"Twelve out of twelve?"

"Right."

"And nine out of twelve in a civil case?"

"Right."

"And in the criminal it's beyond a shadow of a doubt?"

"No," Nathan explained, "beyond a reasonable doubt. But those are just words; that's the legal standard the jury is instructed to meet. What it really boils down to is does the jury believe this happened."

"So we just want to get the message out," Gloria said, "that Jordie wants to have his day in court and have the truth come out. That is really the entire message. Who can argue with that? I think we should get this message out every single way we can. I should be on everything and get that message out, certainly on national television."

"So the whole purpose is putting pressure on the DA to file?" Monique asked.

"Yes, and to get other witnesses to come forward. Those are two major goals that we have."

"And," Nathan pointed out, "what you're also trying to do in terms of preserving all options is that ultimately, if there's a civil case filed, you want to have a climate where that's possible. Right now we have a climate where people are saying this is an extortion attempt. Hitting the media hard will change that around."

"Can we discuss the legal options?" June asked.

"Sure," Gloria said. "I'm going to get into the legal options soon. But first I want to see if we have a consensus about this, because there's a window of opportunity now to shape public opinion. If you wait too long to make a decision, public opinion may have gelled to the point where you can't unglue it. Once they've made up their minds, they don't want to be confused."

"Does anyone have an opinion about what she said so far?" Evan put forth to the group.

"What I'd like to do first," June said, "is hear Gloria out before we even run around the table. How do you feel about it, Jordie?"

"I think she should keep going."

"Alright," Gloria began again, "let's look at the legal options. One we had talked about was the civil suit against Michael Jackson, and I said that it's not wise to file right now because Jordie has time to do that. But I want you to remember that that is one of the options, and it can be filed whether or not the district attorney decides to prosecute."

"I'm not so sure about that," Monique challenged. "I mean, what will public opinion be if the DA never files?"

"That's a very important question," Gloria admitted. "That's very important. And that's one of the reasons why we want to be sure that we have public opinion in the best possible way supportive of Jordie. My guess is, if there's no criminal trial, you're going to want to go ahead with the civil lawsuit so that he does have his day in court."

"Okay," Monique pressed, attorney-to-attorney, "you can certainly try to position yourself. But in my view it's going to be very hard to predict how the public will react if the DA doesn't file, especially when you're dealing with someone like Michael Jackson."

"That's why we have to deal with it very sensitively and we have to be right on target," Gloria defended. "We want Jordie to have his day in court, and if the DA isn't going to provide it then we will. It's the timing that's so important."

"That's right," Nathan agreed. "And there's another option, a suit against the county for the leaked DCS report. Not just for the money. Filing against the county gives us the opportunity to initiate the discovery process. We would have the ability to get certain information from the county as to who did what, who said what, and stuff like that. It also gives us subpoena power which we don't yet have."

In a nutshell, Gloria's strategy was to hit the media hard and fast in hopes of creating a groundswell of public opinion that would pressure the DA to indict Michael.

Evan didn't like it, whipping up the media like that. He had had enough of his family being in the crosshairs. As a mother, Monique abhorred the effect the fishbowl was having on their children. And as an attorney she rejected Gloria's argument that a failure to garner enough public support for a criminal indictment, or failure to convict Michael if he was indicted, would not have a profoundly negative effect on a civil suit.

– 16 –

SEPTEMBER 7

The group met again, this time at Larry Feldman's office in Santa Monica. Evan, Jordie, Monique, June, Dave, and Barry Rothman listened while the team of attorneys advised their clients on where to go from here.

Present as legal counsel were Bob Shapiro, technically representing Barry Rothman against possible extortion and State Bar proceedings, but acting more as an advisor to the Chandler's; Richard Hirsch, representing Evan against possible extortion charges; and Larry Feldman, not yet but soon to be representing Jordie against Michael.

Since it was clear to everyone that Gloria's strategy was to force a criminal proceeding against Michael, Bob Shapiro began by explaining what would happen if criminal charges were brought.

"It is my opinion that in a case of this magnitude, even though the law offers protection for juveniles, there will be leaks. And the way they do the leaks is, they go to Europe, and then the press here picks up what's reported in Europe. That's how they get around the laws protecting children.

"Jordie would have to testify in public before the jury, and be subject to virtually unlimited cross-examination, as would anyone else involved in this case. And as I've already described to Jordie, we call the witness stand the most uncomfortable chair in the world.

"For a child to sit out there alone and be cross-examined by a defense attorney is a traumatic experience, something you have to look down the road and see what kind of scars it's going to leave, whether you're vindicated or not. Because even if you are vindicated you were still a participant. And though you were psychologically coerced into doing this, it's an act that a lot of people might find embarrassing, especially young boys.[90]

"The problem with a criminal trial is twofold: not only does Jordie and everybody else go through a traumatic experience, but at the end of the day,

---

[90] Bob was right. The vast majority of Jordie's schoolmates treated him with respect, but some were cruel. Had there been a criminal trial, the world would have experienced MJ a year before OJ. And Jordie would have been in the center of it. Not a fun place to be.

if there's no conviction, your civil case is shot. There's no chance of anybody getting a civil recovery."

Shapiro's last point had been on Evan's mind for some time. "Bob, I just want to emphasize one thing that hit me hard the other day. All it takes to have no conviction is one of the twelve jurors to say 'I have a doubt.' That's it. He's off scot-free."

"Yes, I eventually was going to bring that up."

"And I'd like to raise one other issue," Evan added. "What are the possibilities of Pellicano getting to the family members of one of those jurors and offering them a million dollars to say 'I have a doubt.' Is that a possibility?"

"Sure, anything's possible, but let's stick with . . .

"But it is a possibility?"

"Well, basically, if you have one person that hangs up the jury . . . "

"He's free!"

"Yeah, that's pretty much the end of it. But let's say there is a conviction. That's a home run if your idea is to put Michael Jackson in jail, because he *will* go to jail. And it's also a home run for Larry and the civil lawyers because then the only civil issue is damages — the molestation has already been proven in a criminal court.

"If there's a hung jury, sure, it could be retried, but time goes on. The real risk is if there's an acquittal. In that case, prevailing at a civil suit afterwards becomes a real uphill battle.

"Now the alternative is for you to bring a civil suit first. And the first thing we would do is schedule a deposition of Michael Jackson, placing him in an extremely uncomfortable position because everything he says could be used against him in a criminal case. And if he takes the Fifth Amendment to avoid that, it can be used against him in your civil case. So immediately, he's in a real bad spot.[91]

"But there's a third alternative. If we went to the other side and said, 'Listen, a trial for Michael Jackson is a disaster, he can't win. Because even if he's acquitted, when the public hears what this boy has to say, you will

---

[91] In a criminal trial, the jury is instructed that they must not view taking the Fifth Amendment as an admission of guilt, though everyone sees it as that anyway. In a civil trial, the jury is instructed that they must view it as an admission of liability.

have no endorsements, you will have no contracts, you are virtually finished. If we say that, it is my belief we have control of the situation, we have power.

However, if this matter is pushed too far and somebody starts screaming there should be a Grand Jury or the DA is not handling this correctly, then we lose all control. Garcetti will have to go to the Grand Jury, even if he doesn't want to. And if the Grand Jury returns an indictment on a case the DA can't win, especially against a superstar, then you're all screwed.

"So my suggestion is to keep control. We can always, if you want to, press the issue and have the DA bring criminal charges. And we can certainly, without much effort, get the Grand Jury to have an investigation. All you have to do is just say a few things in the *LA Times* and there's no way the district attorney can say 'I'm not going to the Grand Jury.' It'll look like he's whitewashing. He's a political animal; he'll have to do it.

"Now, the other side realizes all this. So let's say I'm a lawyer for Michael Jackson. What am I thinking? I'm thinking, 'Oh my God, if this matter goes before a Grand Jury, Michael Jackson will be finished if he's indicted. If Jordie sues civilly and wins, we're still in an awful position. The best thing I can do is settle out of court.'"

"So my advice is to take the next thirty days and keep control. Let Jordie be the power in this case. That, to me, is a sensible approach. If it doesn't work we've lost nothing, because we have all our other options available."

"Let me interject one thing," Richard said. "We've spoken to the district attorney several times, twice in the last two weeks, and I don't think they're likely to bring criminal charges unless the police come up with some form of corroboration. So this opportunity Bob's talking about may disappear when and if the DA announces he's not filing against Michael. We'll lose our leverage. So if you decide you want to settle, now would be an opportune time to start negotiating."

"Coincidentally," Evan pointed out, "I just saw the news before I came over here. The DA said she would not be making a decision whether to charge Michael for at least another month. So as you said, we have to utilize this window to our advantage."

"What scares me," Bob went on, "is that once you start rattling the drums: making press conferences, impugning the reputation of the district attorney, saying in the papers that Michael Jackson's a pedophile, then it's a lose-lose situation for everybody. Because everybody's in the public limelight, everybody's dirty laundry is aired. Jordie will be crucified on the witness stand and I don't know if he could survive it. And when all is said and done, if we don't have a criminal conviction or a civil recovery, it's a horror beyond imagination. So that's why I was very very concerned with the aggressive stance of Gloria Allred.

"My forte is dealing with the media. I've handled a lot of high-profile publicity cases and I believe the media is an essential part of a civil or criminal case. Manipulating it is essential. But in this case you have to stop everything, because Richard and I can now call Howard Weitzman and have Pellicano stop, have everything stop. In fact, we've already done that. We have a truce. It's temporary, but we do have a truce. And it was almost broken when Gloria Allred made her statement."

"All that sounds fine," June said. "But what I want to know is, what's best for Jordie? I mean, I don't know what he wants."

"Okay," Bob replied. "Let's ask Jordie. Jordie, talk to your mother. What are your thoughts?"

"I think it's a big decision that's going to affect me for . . . . It's too big, you can't just make it on the spot."

"Tell us, Jordie," Dave asked, "how would you feel now if it all just sort of calmed down and there was a settlement. It just evaporated. Would you like that?"

"Yeah, I'd like that a lot."

Meanwhile, the man everyone had come to hear had been content to sit silently on the sidelines while Shapiro laid out the basic philosophy of the legal team. Now that the discussion had come round to the concerns of the victim, Larry Feldman decided to make his presence felt.

"Okay, let me speak a while, because I probably have a lot more to say about representing children than anyone in this room. I've represented them over and over again in civil cases — kids that have been abused, brain damaged, paraplegics. Kids are kids. Your son, when the day is over, is going to have to live his life. And it isn't worth putting him through what the lawyers are going to do to him.

"Whether it's civil or criminal, it is a horrendous, horrendous experience. So if he were my son — and I have a son his age — I would want it as normal as I could possibly get it, as fast as I could get it.

"The media doesn't care about him, Michael Jackson doesn't care about him, and Howard Weitzman doesn't care about him. If Michael gets sued, whether it's Weitzman or an insurance company lawyer or ten lawyers, they're going to get the price down. They don't care. Their job is to win the case for their client. They're going to do whatever it takes.

"The minute the courts get a hold of any matter, whether it's civil, criminal, domestic, you name it, you lose control. My wife does nothing but this, defending parents of children in abuse cases. That's all she does. And know this, it's just horrendous what the courts can do to kids. They may think they're acting in the kid's best interest. They may think they're doing right. But you know, they have ten minutes to give to this situation, they don't worry about what's going to happen five years from now when the media has drawn all this attention and Jordie's left with his life to live.

"So I don't have an opinion as to whether Michael Jackson's sitting there with a big check or not. I sort of have a view that once the criminal case starts, you can forget it, there's no way it can get it resolved.

"The most important thing is that you've got to get your priorities in order. As far as playing the game in the media, all of us lawyers know that it doesn't matter what's said today. It may matter what's said a week before the trial — that may mean something. But the bottom line is this, what do you want for your child? Do you want to make your child healthy and secure?

"Sure, the best for Jordie is that Michael Jackson goes to criminal court and pleads guilty. Then Jordie gets money and his life is secure. But Michael Jackson isn't going to do that. That's not what's going to happen because any one person can say they didn't prove it beyond a reasonable doubt. I'll bet if you took some kind of a poll that most people . . ."

"There was a poll taken," Monique offered.

"And the results?"

"Eighty-seven percent not guilty."

"Yeah. Not guilty. If it was any other human being but Michael Jackson, you'd get a different result."

"They don't want to believe it!" Dave exclaimed.

"No," Larry agreed, "they don't want to believe it."

"Can I say something here," Evan broke in, "just to sum up what you guys are saying. There are really only two goals. The goal is either get a lot of money for Jordie and make his life comfortable, or get Michael Jackson. Is that right or wrong?"

"I don't know why you wouldn't want to get him a lot of money," Larry said. "I mean, why wouldn't you want to have him supported for the rest of his life? That's certainly one goal."

"Then what you're saying," Evan went on, "is that the probability of Jordie's life being pretty good is a lot better if we focus on getting money than if we focus on putting Michael in jail — which is, according to what you lawyers are saying, very difficult."

"And if you send Michael to jail," Larry asked, "what do you do to your son in the process?"

"Exactly!" June exclaimed. "That's what I was going to say."

"You'll have Michael in jail," Larry cautioned, "and Jordie in his own emotional prison for the rest of his life."

"Is it safe to conclude, then," Evan asked, turning from Larry to June, "that you and I and Dave and all of us want what's best for Jordie?"

"Of course!" June replied. "Who doesn't?"

"Nobody!" from Hirsch.

"Nobody!" from Feldman.

"Okay then," Shapiro said, "this is a team effort, everybody has the same goals: to get rid of the nonsense that this was an extortion and to make Jordie whole. To get back, in some way, what was taken from him."

"We have a unique situation here," Hirsch added. "Bob and I have known Howard Weitzman for at least twenty-seven years. Howard and I had an office together for many years. We've had cases together and Bob has had cases with him as well. He's one of my dearest and oldest friends, which has nothing to do with my approach to the case. If I have to take him head-on I'd do it, and he knows I'd do it.

"Lauren Weis also happens to be a good friend of mine. She's a personal friend and she trusts us. We're not playing both ends against the middle here, we have entree to both sides in this case, which is very unique. And if something is going to get done we have the ability to make it happen before it gets into all-out war.

"If you want to start lobbing mortars and have war break out, that can happen. But as Bob and Larry pointed out, it easily gets out of control and whatever happens, happens. So what we're here to decide is whether or not you want to try to settle this thing because it's in the best interest of your family, or stay the course you've got."

"Well," June answered, "I have no idea where Jordie's coming from. The last time I asked he said he'd like to see Michael in jail. I'm backing him up. If he doesn't want a trial, that's okay with me. If he wants to get Michael in jail, that's okay, too. I'm backing him up."

"We've already addressed that, June," Evan responded. "Let's not go over the same old stuff."

"June, look," Monique explained in plain English, "here's the dilemma. We all want to fry this sucker. We all want to throw his ass in jail. The problem is, it's going to traumatize the shit out of Jordie and Evan and traumatize the shit out of you, too, because you two are not clean, I'll be honest with you.

"And this kid is going to go through hell. The fucking paparazzi have been camping outside our house for days. You can't even go outside, you have to sneak around and all that stuff. I don't want the family to go through that. I mean, is it worth it in the end? For what? The guy's going to fucking get off anyway!"

"Jordie, why don't you talk to Mom," Evan suggested. "Do you mind, June? Do you mind if he talks right out here in front of everyone? Because we have to make a decision before it gets out of control."

Jordie didn't wait for his mother to answer. "Well, Mom, what I found out yesterday was, in court, it isn't as easy as I thought it would be. That's the information I got yesterday. So now I have a different opinion from what I told you before."

"Jordie, I back you up all the way, Sweetie. Whatever you want to do in your heart is what I want to do. Okay. You just let me know what you want to do."

"Why don't you tell Mom what you told me yesterday," Evan reminded his son, "when Bob said, 'Give me five minutes and I'll make you cry right here and now.'"

"Yeah, I was afraid of that because Bob is on our side, you know. And if he can make me cry, imagine what Howard Wietzman can do for a lot more than just five minutes, when the public and the jury and the judge are all watching, when his whole motive is to destroy me and keep Michael alive. I wouldn't enjoy that, you know."

"So what we're really talking about here, June," Evan said, "is how does Jordie get on with his life and how is his adult life going to be. We all agree that we want him to be happy. So what's going to achieve that goal best, going to trial and facing years of trauma for everybody? Nobody will have a decent, normal life. And Michael's probably going to be found not guilty anyway.

"And so that's why I've asked these guys to talk to you, because when they explained to me what they explained to you a few minutes ago, I saw a whole different scenario played out. And in Jordie's best interest, I just don't see the value of going to a criminal trial. It's a vengeful thing against Michael, it isn't in Jordie's best interest."

"He can't even go to school!" Monique added.

"He can't go to school and he may need years of therapy," Evan continued. "I just want to tell you, June, this is how life's going to be."

"He has to stay at home," Monique explained further. "He can't go out and play with his friends, he can't go roller blading."

"But that's only if there's a long criminal trial," Dave said. "If you make a settlement, Jordie gets his life back and the whole thing's over. See, June and I heard Jordie wanted to go the whole way, so that's sort of how we got in on it. But now, I totally agree. I don't have to listen to anyone else."

"Can I just see Jordie outside for five minutes by himself?" June asked. "Is that okay?"

"Sure," Evan said. "Do whatever you want."

June took Jordie outside, away from the pressure of the crowd, and what she probably still believed was the coercive influence of his father. They returned shortly, and nothing further was said about which course to follow.

SEPTEMBER 8

The group met once again, this time at Larry Feldman's office to officially hire him as Jordie's attorney. Larry wasted no time getting down to business. "What I need is thirty million for Jordie, a million for Mom, and a million for Dad."

That triggered a lengthy discussion over numbers, and how to go about finessing money out of Michael's attorneys.

"Look," Larry offered, "after some twenty-five years or so in lawsuits I can tell you, you have to reel them in slowly. You throw them the line and get some nibbles. Once you get them in the settlement mode, things happen. When they can see a way out, when they can *taste* it, obstacles will disappear."

"You know that works conversely, also," Evan pointed out. "We're thinking thirty million dollars, but after this goes on for a month, you're down to ten."

"And they might be thinking twenty million to start," Dave added.

"You're in the major leagues here," Larry assured them. "Don't worry about that."

"No, Larry," Evan explained, "what I mean is that the idea that this whole nightmare could possibly be over makes you think, well, okay, I'll take that much less just to get it over with. It works conversely, too."

"Oh absolutely, you're right," Larry agreed. "It works both sides."

"Wait a minute," June cut in. "Where did you get the idea Michael would like to settle? I don't think he does."

"His lawyer told us," Richard Hirsch answered.

"Really?" June was skeptical.

"Yes," Richard assured her. "He said, 'You make this go away and we'll all make a lot of money.'"

"He said that to you?"

"Yeah."

"That's exactly what he said," Dave confirmed.

"He said that to you, too, Dave?" Evan asked.

"No. Pellicano said it to Michael Freeman and Freeman called me." [92]

"So you don't think Pellicano will be an obstacle?" Evan asked Dave.

---

[92] According to Dave, Freeman called him and tried to work out a deal on the side.

"No, I don't think so"

"Pellicano is definitely an obstacle," Shapiro cut in.

"I agree," June said.

"But Pellicano is going to be taken out of this," Shapiro continued. "I talked to Howard Weitzman this morning."

"Oh, he will!" June reacted, not believing for a minute that Pellicano could be so easily pushed aside.

"Yes," Bob said. "I told Howard we were meeting with all of you today, and that the condition of our employment is that we deal with him and Bert Fields only, not Pellicano. And he agreed."

"Does Weitzman or Bert Fields have direct access to Michael?" Evan asked.

"Oh, very much so," June answered. After hanging around with Michael for a year, she knew who had his ear.

"I am not going to deal with an investigator," Larry asserted. "I have *never* dealt with an investigator."

"I wouldn't put it past Pellicano to sabotage this whole thing behind Howard and Bert's back," June said, having had more contact with Pellicano than any of them. Nobody disputed her observation.

"The thing I'm concerned with here," Evan continued, "is that Pellicano is going to want to play the big hero and tell Michael he can do it for much less. Or whatever else he can come up with."

By the conclusion of the meeting, June and Dave, like Evan before them, had no doubts about switching from Gloria Allred to Larry Feldman. The choice came down to either waging an all-out media campaign to pressure the DA to seek a Grand Jury indictment, or conducting subtle, behind-the-scenes negotiations toward a quick, quiet and highly profitable settlement. Avoiding the trauma that a lengthy criminal or civil lawsuit would bring to the entire family, especially Jordie, was a no-brainer.

The pressure from public exposure had already soared beyond anyone's imagination. It was, as Monique had put it (pardon her French), "A fucking nightmare!" With Gloria Allred fanning the flames it would get even worse. No one needed that.

Allred meant well; no one doubted her sincerity and concern. And had the defendant been other than Michael Jackson, her strategy might have been more appealing. But Larry and Bob's insights made a lot of sense. Getting a conviction against Michael would be near impossible without a second victim.

It may be said that Gloria was more concerned with the larger issue of child abuse, and that bringing the truth to light via a criminal trial was a nobler goal than getting a lot of money and sweeping the entire affair under the rug. But as Evan commented months later, "The overriding consideration in every decision had to be what was best for Jordie, and Larry's way was more consistent with that goal. Doing anything that might bring additional fear and anxiety was the last thing Jordie needed. Or any of us."

Eliminating the horror of worldwide exposure from a protracted trial was not only the best thing for Jordie, it was best for Michael as well. The money it would cost him to settle with his accuser was incidental. Keeping his career intact was what really mattered. Shapiro knew all this from the start. By steering Evan and June toward Larry Feldman and away from Gloria Allred, he was doing everyone a mitzvah, including Michael Jackson.

As the meeting came to a close, all that was left was to sign the retainer agreement with Larry. Anticipating a huge settlement, Dave assumed that Larry would take less than the standard 25 percent rather than pass up the opportunity, so he began negotiating for a smaller fee.

Larry politely explained that his fee was not out of the ordinary and tried to impart to Dave some idea of the amount of work involved should the case go to trial. But Dave was intractable. He became loud and pushy, demanding that Larry negotiate. Dave was also pissed off at all of the lawyers because they told him that if there was settlement he could not be included.

Larry remained calm. He informed Dave, once again, that because he was neither Jordie's natural or adoptive father he had no legal claims that could be included in Jordie's complaint. But Dave became increasingly belligerent each time the lawyers explained why it was not possible. He didn't give a damn about legalities and kept demanding money. Four million dollars, to be exact. The same amount, according to June, that he attempted to borrow from Michael.

"You fucking son of a bitch!" Evan finally snapped. "If it wasn't for you none of this would have happened. Shut the fuck up!"

"Fuck you! I've supported Jordie for ten years. I've been through hell. I'm losing money every day at work. I have as much right to the money as you and June."

"You greedy bastard! How can you be arguing over money we don't even have yet. We're talking about what's best for Jordie and all you can think of is how much you're gonna get. That's all you give a shit about. You stabbed me in the back, you fucking asshole!"

"Go fuck yourself!"

"Fuck you!"

Though recent events had already exposed Dave's true colors, Evan never suspected they could "shine" this dark. Until now he had consciously subdued his resentment, but in the heat of this verbal battle he sprang from his seat and slapped Dave in the face. Several of the lawyers stepped between the two men and separated them.

While Larry and June babysat Dave, Bob Shapiro and Richard Hirsch ushered Evan into an adjoining office. Dave was way out of line, no one disputed that, but they needed everyone to remain united; dissention among the ranks was a weakness the other side was sure to exploit.

There was no telling what Dave might do in his present state. The lawyers were concerned that the press would catch him running amuck and shooting off his mouth, so they prevailed on Evan to swallow his pride and apologize to Dave.

With tempers now abated, Evan and June, as guardians for Jordie, signed the retainer with Feldman, who then notified Gloria Allred. Out of professional courtesy, Larry left it to Gloria to explain the switch any way she saw fit. Hence her sudden announcement that she was withdrawing from the case.

The stage was now set and the actors were in place. Everyone believed a quick settlement would be negotiated — clearly the best alternative for Michael as well — and the final curtain would soon fall on this entire, freakish mess.

Unfortunately, Anthony Pellicano and Bert Fields were following a different script.

✳ ✳ ✳

That afternoon, Jordie and I had lunch at a local deli. It was not my intent to question him about his relationship with Michael — I was there as his uncle, not as a writer — but every once in a while he'd broach the subject.

"I should have known in the very beginning, when he was hugging [that little boy in the limo] like that."

"Well, how could you know, you're only a kid. Even the adults didn't know. . . . Was he kissing him, too?"

"Yeah."

"On the mouth?"

"No. On the cheeks and stuff."

"Do you think he touched other kids?"

"Oh yeah, I wasn't the first kid. He's good at it. He's an actor. He knows how to play the kid thing to get what he wants."

"What did he say to you?"

"Stuff like, we'd be pals forever and we'd never have to grow up. It was just a line."

"But you couldn't have known that at the time."

"No. It [the sex] felt wrong, but I didn't want to hurt his feelings."

"Like being pulled in two directions at once?"

"Yeah."

"How do you feel about him now?"

Jordie thought about it for a while, then said, "I don't hate him, but he for sure knew what he was doing. I guess he's really sick."

"How come you didn't want to go with Dave the other day? Remember, when you and I were sitting on the front lawn and he showed up and asked if you wanted to do something with him?"

"Because I hate him. He doesn't really like kids — they're just an ornament. Even Kelly. He only married my mom so he could have a babe to show off."

"Do you think your mom knew what was going on?"

"I don't know. Maybe she should have — you know, what's that thing about everything not being gold?"

"You mean all that glitters isn't gold?"

"Yeah. Maybe she should have seen that. But Michael was so good at it, maybe she just didn't figure it out."

– 17 –

SEPTEMBER 13

Evan, June, Dave and Richard Hirsch met at Larry's office to discuss the complaint soon to be filed against Michael on Jordie's behalf. Larry had drawn up two versions. They differed only in that "the lurid one" listed the specific sexual acts. "As a lawyer," Larry counseled, "there's no question which one I'd recommend, that's the lurid one. But it could be embarrassing for him [Jordie]. It's more of a parental decision."

"Once this thing gets filed," Richard Hirsch explained, "the press is going to be all over this office like flies on . . . on fly paper. It's going to start the whole press machine again. So we have to decide whether to have a press conference with Larry making a statement at the time the complaint gets filed, or have them come here to the office and make a statement here."

Evan and June were stunned. A week ago they had left Gloria Allred because Larry, Bob and Richard convinced them to stay out of the media. Now they were trying to decide where to hold a press conference!

"If I don't say anything," Larry explained, "if I just file this, there's a press person at the courthouse that runs the titles down and they'll pick it up. That's all they do is check these filings on a daily basis. So the press is in it, that's not an issue now. It's how to respond."

"No!" Evan protested. "It is an issue. Because until now you and everybody else has been telling me we want to stay out of the press and let the DA do their investigation."

"Oh no, no! Wait a minute, Evan. Hasn't anyone told you? Richard found out that there isn't going to be a criminal complaint filed for at least ninety days, maybe more."

"So what? Did they say they're not filing at all?"

"They don't know right now. They still have a lot of leads to follow."

"Okay, so why is that a factor?"

"Because," Richard answered, "if this thing continues as it has, with all these charges and counter-charges appearing in the press, then . . ."

"But we don't care about that," Evan broke in. "We only care what the

DA and the police think."

"Look guys," Larry reminded them. This case is *not* going to settle. There's no choice now. There's going to be a lawsuit. It's going to go public."

Evan agreed. "It's definitely not going to settle. I told you yesterday it wasn't going to happen."

"There's still a slim chance," Larry said. "There's this black attorney who called me and said that he met with Michael's security people in Moscow before Bert got there, and the bottom line is they don't intend to settle. Richard and I met with Weitzman on Thursday and the two of us are convinced there's no deal to be made.

"Howard called me back later that day wanting to know why the big rush to file a complaint. I said, 'Howard, I don't think there's a rush if we're all talking about the same thing. If we are, then give me some sign that we're going to talk seriously — not with Pellicano but with real people — and then there is no rush. Just give me something that I can take back to these parents so I can tell them why they should wait. You've never said a word, you've said nothing. So what you're telling me is that you have no authority. You're telling me that nobody wants to meet.'"

"And there's no response. That was Thursday evening. We had a deal with Howard that he was not to respond in the paper to any of this. It was to be a hush-hush thing. Saturday he's in the paper. It was a breach of our agreement."

"What are you referring to, Larry?" Evan asked.

"Where Weitzman said maybe Gloria withdrew because she didn't believe the kid. I fuckin' reamed him! They're jerkin' us here."

"Meanwhile," Richard reminded them, "it's going to be at least three months before the DA decides to do anything, plenty of time for Pellicano to get to the witnesses who can testify against them."

"See, that's the trouble," Larry explained. "Pellicano's out there interviewing while we're sitting here on our butts. We have no subpoena power unless we file."

"Neither does the DA," June added, "And they don't want to do anything."

"Sure," Richard agreed. "The DA would rather put it off as long as possible. They won't file against a guy like this without an air-tight case."

"Let's turn it around the other way," Evan proposed. "If we do file, how could that harm the DA's case?"

"I think it will help the DA," Larry surmised. "I think it will help because we will develop evidence that will lead to one of two things. Either Michael will take the fifth, and the whole world will see him do it, or he will have to submit to a deposition."

Evan did not want to cross the DA. "Richard, you know Lauren well. How do you think she'd take it?"

"She probably won't like it. If I were a DA, I'd prefer that the victim never sues. It keeps them lily white. But you can't wait until the criminal case is over because you only have a certain amount of time to make a decision or you let it get stale. Your son was damaged. You were damaged. Everybody was hurt in this case. Why shouldn't you get money for some of these things? You'd be fools if you didn't."

"They're not going to deal," Larry said. "So we have to hit 'em and hit 'em hard. My belief is we will win this case. We have a much, much greater chance to win civilly than the DA does criminally."

"Based on what? Evan asked."

"Based on they have to prove it beyond a reasonable doubt, and they don't have the process of discovery."

"They don't!"

"Well, they can get search warrants, but they can't take depositions. They can ask but they can't compel. So here's the problem. If months from now the DA makes a statement saying they're not going to file, and then we file a lawsuit after that, we look like money-grubbing lowlifes. You can forget it!"

"And besides," Richard continued, "Lauren is not going to decline to prosecute because you filed civilly. If they want to charge him with a crime they're going to do it whether you file or not. But the way it's looking now, unless they come up with some bombshell, or some other kids come forward, this case is not going to get filed. I don't even think right now that the chances are fifty-fifty."

"But you know Lauren believes Jordie?"

"She absolutely believes him. And every therapist believes him."

"Is Lauren a mother?"

"She believes him, Evan! But that's not enough."

"No," Evan expounded, "the point I was raising was that you're going to get admissions from other children under oath; both the children and their parents are not going to be able to lie consistently to protect Michael. Jordie and I have been through it. If we weren't telling the truth there's no way we could have stuck to the same story over and over again."

"Yeah, but Pellicano's already taken care of that," Richard reminded him.

"So what! This is different. Pellicano pays them off or scares the shit out of them and they say nothing happened. That's not under oath. Let me give you an example. Tommy Jones's parents are a postman and a secretary who live in an apartment and end up with a huge house and a Lexus for each parent. Explain that? Where does the money come from?"

"We'll be a little bit more subtle than that," Larry mused.

"Yeah, but what I'm saying is that when you pursue that line of questioning, they can't consistently lie. So if you give these depositions to Lauren at some point, will she refuse to go ahead because we pissed her off? Could there be any personal reason for the DA not to take it?"

"The DA cannot overlook a major crime simply because she doesn't like us anymore," Richard responded. "Especially one committed by a major personality who may be out committing additional crimes."

"I'm just wondering what the downside is?" Evan added. "How could it hurt us? I've always heard that if the DA goes first and they win, it's the best that can happen for us."

"Sure, that would be great," Larry answered. "But the chances are so slim."

"Okay, then let's say the DA does file this in three months. What if we file this right after that? Then we're committed and she's committed."

"No," Larry explained, "because then you've accomplished everything that we have today, except you've wasted three months while we're just sittin' here and the other side is working against you."

With that, Evan was convinced. "Okay, so how does the chronology go? Let's say you file this tomorrow."

"Thirty days or so later, they'll have to file a response."

"Do you think they'll deny it?"

"Sure. I expect them to. But at least they'll know I'm dead serious and we're not playing any games. If they're smart they'll come right to the table."

"They're going to fight," June said. "I'm sure of it."

"Right, or they'll fight us tooth and nail," Larry conceded. "If they do, within ten to twenty days I'll notice Michael's deposition, and we'll have a fight in court as to whether they're going to bring him in or not, or whether he's going to take the fifth. I can't think of anything better than having Michael Jackson, in public, taking the Fifth Amendment."

"What are his other choices?" Evan asked. "Can you go abroad to do it?"

"He has only two options. We can go anyplace in the world to depose him, or he can take the fifth."

"But," Richard explained, "with the criminal investigation pending, he really can't take the fifth."

"He just might!" Larry exclaimed. "But think about the headline: MICHAEL JACKSON TAKES FIFTH AMENDMENT. Now tell me how good your civil case looks! . . . and your criminal! That's it. He's finished! Everyone knows only guilty people take the fifth. Think about it. A superstar says, 'I didn't have sex with this child,' but is afraid to say it under oath. You think the public is going to believe him? I love it! They can't hope to win!

"You know," Larry continued, "Bob and Richard supposedly had this great relationship with Howard, but they got fucked, the guy screwed 'em. And Richard Hirsch is too credible. You're not going to get any better than Richard as far as integrity. And he was sitting right there with Shapiro when Weitzman said they were going to settle."

"I hate to even think this," Dave mentioned, "but maybe Weitzman just wants to drag this on to make more money."

"I don't know," Larry responded. "Could be Howard lied to Richard and Bob, or whoever was telling Howard lied to him. Either way, I believe we've got to file right now."

"And we believe you," Evan said, "because you're going to work your ass off."

"Right! I mean it's better for me to take the easy way. Do you think I need this?"

"So why are you so optimistic when you haven't really spoken to any of the principals involved?" Evan asked.

"Because I've read the DCS report, and I believe that no kid could make that up. There have now been four professionals who've seen him, and every one has concluded that he's telling the truth."[93]

"Bert Fields is going to love this," Evan said, relishing the thought of anything that would make Fields or Pellicano miserable.

"He deserves it," Richard agreed.

"Yeah, he sure does," Larry said. "He could have met with us on Friday and started something going. He just shined us on and left the country."

"So what else is new?" June injected, remembering when Bert refused to return her calls after things got too hot.

"If I were Michael Jackson," Richard offered. "I wouldn't be very happy with Bert Fields, who had a day to talk to the people who may do me great harm and just shined them on. He didn't even say 'Look, I'm going to go over there and I'll talk to you when I get back.' He just left us in the lurch."

"We begged Howard," Larry went on. "We said, 'Howard, you gotta tell us something. These people are here and we have held them off from wringing your lousy neck!'"

"Yeah," Richard continued. "And when we tell him this, he says he wants us to meet with Bert and Anthony. I nearly hit the table!"

"He told you that?" Evan asked, incredulous that Michael's chief attorney, one so well respected, had to seek approval from the likes of Anthony Pellicano.

"Yes!" Richard answered, barely able to believe it himself. "Then he calls back and says we'll have a conference call with Pellicano. Can you fuckin' believe that?"

"So tell me," Larry asked, "why Michael Jackson, who's so innocent, needs a guy who's 'going to make you afraid of the dark.' What kind of stand-up person has that kind of a henchman?"[94]

"Yeah, well catch this," Evan said. "The police said to me today they found evidence of a wiretap on my house. And they said it's very important

---

[93] Larry was referring only to psychiatrists and therapists. Jordie was also interviewed by the DA and several detectives, including those from the LAPD's sexually exploited child unit. These detectives are better than therapists when it comes to questioning an alleged victim. Everyone who interviewed Jordie was positive that Michael had molested him.

[94] Feldman was referring to a statement Pellicano had made about himself to the *Los Angeles Times* two days earlier. (Shawn Hubler & James Bates, "Streetwise Gunshoe to the Stars," *Los Angeles Times*, September 11, 1993.)

that I remember if Pellicano ever said he would tap my phone. So I started to think back, when did I first get paranoid about Pellicano taping everything? And it seems like . . . the day I heard his name!"

Everyone laughs, but Evan is serious. "Hey! The guy's dangerous. Everyone knows he's a surveillance expert. The cops want to nail him real bad."

"They'll go after him more than Michael," Larry said. "But they'll need more than they've got to make it stick."

"He'll do anything," June said, turning toward Evan. "You know what he told us about you, to find out what you're doing? He said all he had to do is pay your neighbor five thousand dollars to sit by the window and watch your house. He told us he was going to put a twenty-four-hour watch on your house."

"I'm sure he did," Evan answered. "When you guys [June and Dave] went to Bert Fields the day Dave and I had that argument, the first thing Bert said was to meet him at Pellicano's office. He doesn't say come to my office, tell me the story, let me find out what's going on. He says meet me at Pellicano's office. And now Pellicano has admitted in an interview that he's the guy that lawyers hire when they know that they can't protect their client without dragging them through the mud and the courts.

"Remember when I first came to your office, Richard, how scared I was. I mean, I've never known fear like that. And I knew in my heart I was right. Imagine the fear that's in Michael's heart right now, because he knows he's lying. When you have that kind of fear you surround yourself with people who tell you that if you do this and do that it will all be okay. You lose your rational thinking. Pellicano is promising Michael the world. That's why Howard has to go back to Pellicano, because Michael put him in charge."

"Oh yeah!" Larry agreed. "It's crazy. I told you my response when Howard called me and said, 'If you won't meet with Pellicano, how about a conference call.' I told him, Howard, let me put it this way. If we were in the middle of a deserted island, and it was just Pellicano and me, and he was totally naked, I wouldn't meet with him. Now is that clear enough? Do you get it? I'm not meeting with Pellicano now, on the phone, in person, anyplace, anywhere, anytime.'"

"You all seem to find it strange that they're not trying to settle this and protect Michael," Evan said.

"I don't think they know what they're doing," Richard offered. "I think they're out of control."

"I think they know they can't prevent it now," Evan said. "The truth is about to come out and there's nothing Howard or Bert or Anthony or anyone else can do to stop it. So they're going to milk it for whatever they can get."

"Howard Weitzman hinted that he knows that," Larry said. "I think Evan hit it right on the button. The problem is so big right now that it can't be stopped."

"By the way," Dave interjected, "the police called me today. They wanted to talk to Kelly about the time in the hotel in New York, when Michael broke the lamp in front of Kelly and Jordie. He had a temper tantrum."

Larry's evidence-gathering ears perked up. "In New York? In a hotel?"

June related the story of how one night, when she returned to the hotel after an evening out with some old friends, she found two lamps shattered on the floor and the rest of the room trashed. Jordie and Michael told her Michael had been practicing karate kicks and got carried away.

But when June went to check on Kelly, who had been lying awake in bed in the adjoining room, the little girl told her mother that Michael had lost his temper and was yelling at Jordie and breaking things. Yet the next morning, after a little rehearsing from Michael and Jordie, Kelly changed her story and corroborated Michael's.

It wasn't until months later, after the molestation became public, that Jordie told his mother the truth. As it turned out, Kelly's original account was correct. While June was out, Michael became enraged when he learned that June's brother, a New Yorker who had come to visit at the hotel, found out that Michael and Jordie were sleeping together.

"That's what pisses me off most," Evan explained. "More important than the sex was the brainwashing. This kid had been changed so much that nobody really knew anything about him anymore. Michael was so slick he made Jordie slick. He fooled us all."

"Right," Larry said. "Let's save that for the courtroom and get back to business. The only thing that will change all this is if Cochran calls."

"Who's that?" Evan asked.

"The black lawyer I was telling you about. Johnnie Cochran is a very wheelin' dealin' lawyer in town. A great guy. A very, very solid, honest guy."

"Do you think you can work out a deal?"

"That's why I say there's still a slim chance. This guy is a major player in the black community."

The remainder of the meeting was devoted to working out the details of the complaint and how Larry would handle the media. Evan and June signed the document and that was it. Larry would file the complaint the following day.

It was later discovered that Howard Weitzman hadn't lied; he honestly wanted to make a deal with Feldman. But he was overruled. Whether Fields and Pellicano truly believed they could win this thing in (or out) of court, or whether they had concerns other than Michael's best interest, only they can say. Either way, The King of Pop got royally screwed.

– 18 –

OCTOBER 8

It was midday and Evan and I were sitting in the den discussing recent events when the phone rang. Attached to the phone was a recording machine installed by the police to catch death threats. It was set to begin rolling with the first ring.

Evan rarely answered the phone. At his office there was staff to do it. At home, I screened most calls. But this time Evan was sitting next to it and answered out of reflex.

"My name is Kirsten Danzig," the caller said, in a heavily accented but understandable voice. I'm calling from Germany. I wanted to speak with Dr. Chandler."

"Why?"

"Because my son, too, was molested by Michael Jackson."

"Did he touch his penis?" Evan asked — the crucial question.

"Yes," Kirsten answered. "And he tried to kiss him."

Kirsten relayed how she and her eight-year-old son had met Jackson in

Munich, and that at Michael's request she let her son go alone with him for a few hours.

"My son was changed," Kirsten said, sobbing. "He's not the son I've born. . . . He told me, 'Mommy he touched me but it was not a touch from a mother or a father, he touched me very strange.' And then he showed me where he touched him. You know, I felt so bad and I feel guilty, I feel so guilty! I left him alone."

Evan and Kirsten talked at length about the long-term effects of such an experience for a child and the need for them to get immediate help. Evan offered to buy her and her son airline tickets to the United States to come talk to Feldman and the DA. Kirsten said she would consider it, but a therapist advised her that the trauma of going public would be devastating for her son, so she decided not to come forward. (Therefore her real name has not been used.)

Feldman was not concerned. His case was more than solid without her.

– 19 –

OCTOBER 17

While Feldman and his clients were waiting for Michael's response to the complaint, they conducted frequent strategy sessions designed to keep the many facets of the case focused in the same direction.

Among them were the other lawsuits to be considered after the molestation case was concluded. Certainly Evan (and probably June as well) had an excellent case against LA County for the tremendous damage he and his family suffered due to the leaked DCS report. According to the attorneys, that was an open and shut case worth millions.[95]

On top of that, Evan (and Barry Rothman) believed they had a powerful case against Anthony Pellicano for libel and slander. Because Pellicano was acting as an agent of Bert Fields', a favorable judgment might reach deep into Fields' and Michael's pockets.

---

[95] Although it would have been a slamdunk (most likely settled out of court), the Chandler's decided not to sue Los Angeles County.

As for the renegade in the group, Dave's anger over the lawyers' refusal to include him in the anticipated settlement grew by leaps and bounds as the weeks went by. Eventually, he broke ranks and demanded one thousand dollars an hour, with a five-hour minimum, for his continued cooperation. He also retained his own attorney to explore ways of partaking in the anticipated spoils.

Evan was concerned that Dave might do something to screw things up. He was also disappointed with Dave for breaking up the family again, now that they had all worked so hard to piece it back together. Certainly their relationship would never be the same, but Evan was willing to let bygones be bygones — if not for the adults' sake, then at least for the kids. He called Dave at work to patch things up and bring him back into the fold. The two had a lengthy and revealing conversation, but it was all for naught. "I'm on my own," Dave insisted. "I'm going for the throat."

Apparently Dave's attorney advised him to be patient, because he soon returned to the group and never said a word about wanting money. Until after the settlement, that is, when he sued Michael and Evan (separately) for the most absurd reasons imaginable.[96]

I had known Dave Schwartz for nearly a decade. Over the years my family and I visited with him and June many times, and he always treated us well (though on most occasions he would only pop in for a short dinner and return to work). In some ways I respected him. He worked hard, and though quite wealthy he was never ostentatious. He liked driving old cars and wearing faded jeans and a sweatshirt.

It wasn't that Dave was cheap. Thrifty, yes, but his shoes didn't squeak. Quite simply, Dave Schwartz did not enjoy spending money nearly as much as he did making it. And he was always out making it, seven days a week, devoting precious little time to his kids.

Though I never talked directly to Dave about the events surrounding this scandal, I did talk to June in early December, six weeks before the settlement. Not only does this conversation provide an "insider's" view of Anthony Pellicano and Bert Field's involvement, it delves deep into the

---

96 Coming up in Part Three.

psyche of Michael Jackson himself.

"You know," June began, "Larry wants to settle. I mean, that's the ultimate of what he wants to do. He told me that all he cares about is getting money for Jordie. But I told Larry how awful it would be if I had to keep my mouth shut afterward. I told him, 'do you know how my life has changed? How I have to go see shrinks, have sleepless nights, and don't have my son anymore? And I should say everything is fine now!'

"Let me tell you one thing, there's no person more important here than Jordie, for him not to suffer. But for me to say, 'Oh well, forget it,' I mean, there's no closure for me. Not that it's just about me, but it's what Michael did to him that affects me, and all of us."

I asked June if the staff at Neverland knew what was going on.

"No. Uh-uh. Once his bedroom door is closed, nobody knows. He had lots of boys and lots of friends but it could have been sleepovers — no big deal, nothing. Parents are over and it looks like it's okay.

"If you don't know what's going on in the bedroom, just like I didn't . . . Oh sure, you're saying, 'June should know, how come June didn't know? There's her bedroom, there's Jordie's bedroom, how come she didn't know?' I mean, once that door is closed you don't know what's going on. Maybe they're watching TV. Maybe they're playing video games or talking, you know.

"And Jordie's saying, 'But, Mom, there's nothing going on.' And I'm saying, 'Okay, you're my son, I believe you.' And Michael's looking at me and saying the same thing.

"There are only two staff allowed in the bedroom. One . . . well, we'll see what she has to say. I mean, she can definitely say she saw them in the bed; that they slept in the bed. But she can never say she saw them in an act. I mean, there might be a guard or someone who saw something, you know, like Michael sticking his hands down some kid's pants.

"But most of those people up there are nice people. They're full of integrity. They're great. They were really nice people who thought that it was great to work up in this beautiful ranch where it's peaceful and nice. But I don't think they saw anything. There might have been gossip, like, 'What's going on? How come there isn't a girl here? Where's his date?'

"But now, knowing us — mostly Kelly and me, because Jordie would hang out with Michael so much — now that we've actually said something, now it all comes into place.

"But it took one person to break it open, because everybody allowed it. Kids allowed it, parents said it was okay, people all over who came to Neverland knew where the kids slept. They'd have sleepovers, they'd be in Michael's bedroom. Nobody thought anything of it until Jordie said, 'Yeah, but I was molested.' And then everybody goes, 'Oh wow! Wait. That's what he's all about.'

"He looks weird, but you don't know what anyone's sexual thing is until you're in the bedroom. Really, you don't."

I asked June about Norma Staikos, Neverland's chief of staff.

"Oh, yeah, Norma knows where the boys are sleeping."

I suggested to June that Fields and Pellicano must have known.

"That's right! But they're not going to tell anybody. That's where they have to draw the line . . . that nobody ever talks about this again.

"Michael became very close to us as a family. Okay. That's like saying a brother or a cousin . . . like saying a cousin did this to his other cousin. But yet, that cousin was in my house! And he affected me and Kelly. I mean he was definitely part of our lives. He said 'June, don't worry, I'll take care of you, I love you.' I have a letter to bring to Larry now. I'll show you."

While June went for the letter I asked if Michael was nice to her.

"Unbelievably nice! The best guy. If he just didn't do that it would be perfect."

I asked June if she thought Michael's niceness was premeditated?

"Yes! Yes! He's a predator. He knew exactly what to say, what to do, how to do it. Look what he wrote." (She shows me an original note from Michael to Jordie.)

Jordie, you're not only my cousin but also my best friend. I can't stop loving your mother and sister. I have found true love in all of you. If more people were like us the world would change instantly. I have such golden dreams for you. I want you to be a giant in the industry. You are my new inspiration. I love you. Doo doo head. Applehead. Disneyland soon.

Love, doo doo.

Call soon, bye, doo doo head. Tell Mom I love her.

"See what I mean? It was all about love, honesty. You know, just hope . . . that he loved kids. And I love people who love kids. And he was exactly what I thought he was, loving children, but understanding that you didn't have to scream at them. That you could be kind, loving, good. That you didn't have to be a strict disciplinarian. Let them have fun, you know.

"And I said to Michael, 'I know you love kids.' I was seeing him through *his* rose-colored glasses. That he was a gentle human being that wouldn't harm a child. Look what you see on TV — he's surrounded by children.

"And he said, 'I'm thinking of adopting this orphanage.' And I said, 'Great! I'd love that, to have kids around? Why not! I'd love that!' And he would say all these things to me."

I asked June if she now thought it was all just a ruse on Michael's part.

"Yeah! You got it! So can you imagine how I feel? That's why I can't sleep at night. I mean, it occurs to me: Oh, that's why he said all that, so he can have Jordie and not to be altruistic at all. It was just a selfish means to get what he wanted.

"It might get closed for Jordie if we settle, but it won't be closed for me. Not in my heart. In my heart I can't keep silent. My life isn't going to be better with my son if we settle.

"I said, 'Larrry, you don't understand. My son doesn't even want to come home and sleep in his own bed now. Even if we changed around his room to look completely different, the memories are in this house. Don't you think it's changed my life, from a mother with two kids and now my son doesn't even want to hang out here? Can you imagine your son not wanting to come to your house, and to keep that going?'

"That's what I have to deal with. It's like a broken record. I can't sleep at night. I can't stop thinking about it. So there's no closure. My life is different.

"At least Evan has Jordie. I mean, it's the toughest thing on a Mom — it's very hard. I'm happy he's getting to stay with Evan, to be with his father. I think it's important at this point in his life to be with his dad. But I'd like him to feel like, wow, I could come here, too. Plus, there's anger. I mean, even though he's not admitting it yet, it's going to come out against me in the future, because looking back, I should have stopped it, you know.

"He saw how to use Evan, how to turn Evan against me, how to turn me against Evan, how to turn Jordie against his family. All of that! He knew exactly how to zero in, charge at his bait and do exactly what he had to do to get us to believe him. Look how we were all duped by an icon that we put up on this pedestal as a man who loves children. And look how he duped us all, how he's exactly the opposite — using children for his sexual desires. He should be burned at the stake."

"What about Michael being the victim of child abuse himself?" I asked.

"That's right! I believe he was. I believe he needs help and I feel sorry for him. But I hate him because he used my family. But I definitely think he needs help. And if I want to think in a godly way, I hope he gets help. But I understand it's very hard to cure pedophilia.

"But that's not my problem. I don't care about him anymore because he fucked me over and he fucked my son. I would like to sit in a room with him and try to kill him. That's why it's almost better that I didn't know, because then I would have to kill him and then I'd be up for murder and my kids wouldn't have me. If I had known, I would have plotted to be alone and then shot him, because there's no justice in the courts. He might be vindicated, or be in jail for four years, and then he's out again. I wouldn't wait. I'd do my own justice."

"What about the public, don't they have some responsibility in this, too?" I asked June.

"Absolutely they do! And I'm just as responsible. I said, 'look what he's done for kids, he'd never do that.' Who the fuck am I to say that? I don't know what he's all about. And I should have. But I didn't. Everybody thinks they know him. What, did they speak to him today? I thought I knew him and I was in the same house with him!

"Superstars really believe they're above the law — the law's not for them. You see, he's treated like a little prince, like a child mogul, and all the adults are just waiting for him. I mean, if he sneezes . . . That's what Michael used to say: 'I can't tell anybody I have a headache because fifty people will bring me bottles of aspirin.'

"And here I thought he'll be here and it will be just a normal life in this little house in Santa Monica. And he'll know what it's like to live normally and we're not going to treat him like a superstar. He just used us. And here

I thought I was just being the mother and he would be part of the family. He would be nice to us and we would be nice to him."

As I listened to June talk, it was difficult not to believe she meant every word. I'd known her for twenty years, and though our lifestyles were vastly different, there was one thing about which we held similar views, children. They were, without a doubt, the most meaningful part of her life.

I'm certain June never consciously said to herself, I know Michael is having sex with my son but I'm going to let it continue even though it's harming him. Yet I am equally certain, as is everyone else who has studied the situation, that it must have crossed June's mind, several times, that Jordie and Michael were sexually involved.

I believe she *chose* to look the other way by rationalizing the obvious as a gay thing. After all, Jordie slept with Michael thirty nights in her own home, nearly all their weekends at Neverland, and on all their trips to Las Vegas, New York, Florida and Europe. It couldn't be more obvious.

June's rationalization probably went something like this: Well, okay, they spend every night together behind closed doors, but Michael says it's not happening, and Jordie says it's not happening, and I actually haven't seen it happening, therefore it isn't happening. This is basically what she said in the above conversation. And it might be a more palatable excuse had June confronted Jordie and Michael periodically throughout the relationship. But according to Jordie, she broached the subject only once, in Las Vegas in April 1993, the first time he slept in Michael's bed, after watching *The Exorcist.* Despite Jordie's explanation that he was scared after the movie and stayed in Michael's room, June admonished her son and told him never to do it again.

What reason, other than being concerned about Michael's intentions, could June have had for ordering her son not to sleep in the star's room? Clearly June may have suspected hanky-panky from the start.

"Mother was suspicious of abuse," the DCS emergency response report stated, "but was persuaded by the perpetrator to allow the relationship to continue. . . . Mother admitted she liked the attention paid to her by a star."

To ease her conscience, June may have rationalized the relationship as a gay thing. "So he's gay. So who cares," Evan claims she told him. But that still wouldn't justify allowing her son to sleep with Michael, which explains why June never used that excuse on the record.

June mentioned to me that giving her deposition would be easy because she was "coming from the truth." She sounded convincing, as if she was truly ignorant of the goings on between her son and Michael.

What June knew and when she knew it, only she can say for certain. But is there any doubt that Michael presented a great temptation: permanent financial security, limitless shopping sprees, endless travel, lavish accommodations, cavorting with the rich and famous, blissful freedom from a stifling marriage? What a story! The eccentric yet benevolent zillionaire rescues the cherubic child and his adoring mother from the evil stepfather. A fairytale-come-true. Disneyesque.

Except for one slight detail.

– 20 –

By mid-October the Chandler's could be reasonably assured of walking out of their front door without having a camera staring them in the face. Which meant that Jordie was able to play in the front yard or across the street at a friend's house. To look at him, he seemed without a care, running and laughing like any other kid. But to those who knew him well, there was much inner conflict.

In Jordie's small circle of friends there were boys *and* girls, but as of yet, *la difference* seemed to be of no interest to him. Then one day his friend's eleven-year-old cousin came to play — a dark, slim beauty with big brown eyes. Jordie was smitten. And apparently the feeling was mutual. She returned the next day, and then the next, and soon they were spending much of their days together.

"He would do stuff," Evan explained. "Like throw a stick to show her how macho he was. And then she'd remark how far he'd thrown it and act impressed. Sometimes they'd go off on their own, just a few houses away, and sit on the lawn and talk. The other kids would giggle and make fun of them. What a relief!"

"What do you think of her?" Evan asked his son, after watching the relationship blossom for several weeks. "I want to kiss her," Jordie replied. "But we might get in trouble with her mother. She's too young." And he was right. Not too young to kiss, perhaps, but too young to establish a more intimate bond — which I'm sure is what he had in mind.

Being the gentleman that he is, Jordie controlled his desires and learned an important lesson, for his patience was soon rewarded. A day or so later a new, older girl appeared on the block. "Hey, Pops," Jordie exclaimed, "look at her, she's beautiful!" And that she was. A sweet kid, too. They "dated" for over a year.

OCTOBER 30

Evan and Larry met at Larry's office to discuss Bert Fields' answer to the complaint.

"Alright," Larry began. "Here's what's happened. Remember I told you that if we ever got Michael to take the fifth, this case would be over, that the public perception would dramatically change?"

"Yeah," Evan answered, "I remember."

"Well, I want you to think back in your life. You've never seen a megastar take the fifth, no matter what was going on. Of all the stars that have been in trouble, from Sinatra to sports figures, nobody ever takes the fifth when you're in the public limelight. Even politicians don't take the fifth. They'll say they didn't do it and they'll lie, but they never take the Fifth Amendment.

"So, yesterday afternoon I come back to my office and on my desk is an answer to the complaint. In twenty-five years of law practice I have never seen an answer like this. This is written totally for the press. They've filed a countermotion in which not only does Michael Jackson say he will take the Fifth Amendment, he says this case can't go forward for at least six years! It needs to be stayed [postponed] for six years so his criminal rights are protected, because that's how long the statute of limitations is for child molestation. People are absolutely astonished."

"About what?" Evan asked, unimpressed.

"By him asking for the Fifth Amendment and saying there should be a six-year hiatus."

"Is there any precedent for that?"

"Never."

"So where do we go from here?"

"On Monday we'll file a motion to compel his testimony, because he won't show up as planned, and a motion for priorities."

"Because Jordie's under fourteen?"

"Right. And if Weitzman or Fields had a fucking brain in their heads and knew anything about how to litigate, they would have delayed this till Jordie's fourteenth birthday. Because then we'd be fucked, because I wouldn't get this motion."

"What makes you so sure you'll get it?"

"Oh, it's an absolute right. Jordie is entitled to a trial within one hundred and twenty days. There's absolutely nothing anybody can do to stop it. I mean, I don't know if there's a case where that right has come up against the Fifth Amendment, but there's no question it's our statutory right. There's no discretion, the judge *has* to do it. He *has* to find us a courtroom. We're gonna argue to the court that we want a trial date by January tenth.[97]

"They're out of control, Evan. They don't know what the hell they're doin'. If they were smart they would have fucked around with me on jurisdiction and kept delaying this as much as they could to prevent themselves from having to answer. And they only had to fuck around for a couple of months!"

"Then why did they choose to go ahead with this?"

"I don't think they know what they're doin'. They're kid's moves! But we'll know in three weeks if we get our motion. The worst is if they're granted a stay, then we go to the court of appeals. You think the Supreme Court is going to let this criminal stop this case for six years! No fucking way!

"They're desperate because I've hit 'em. Every time they turned up the volume I turned it up more, and now they can't control it because we got the chauffeur's and Pellicano's depositions coming up."

"The chauffeur's nothin', Pellicano's nothin'," Evan argued. "In the subpoena you sent Pellicano, they'll only send back what they want you to

---

[97] A victim of sex abuse under the age of fourteen has a right to a trial within 120 days of filing his complaint.

have. Pellicano is a practiced criminal who will tell you only what he wants you to hear."[98]

"You don't understand, Evan. We don't want to turn Pellicano into our witness — if we get that, it's a plus — we want to neutralize him."

"By doing what?"

"By deposing him and making him produce his records. Because from the day we ask, anything he's already done they've either got to produce or forget about using it at trial."

"So he's already subpoenaed?"

"Oh yeah . . . well, I mean, I know what they're gonna do, they've already said. They're going to ask that all these depos get stayed. And I'm not going to agree and they'll file some kind of protective order."

"Nobody's gonna show up," Evan insisted. "And they'll file those stays for other children and their families as well, right?"

"Everything's stayed for six years if they win this motion. That would be unbelievable! But if it works, it works. I mean, there's nothing we can do about it."

"Wow! That would be insane if it worked. Do you have . . .? Okay, let's not even talk about it."

"Right. Let's not worry about the worst possible scenario."

"Tell me something, Larry. How can they continually deny everything and then in the same breath he takes the fifth? What does that mean to the public?"

"You tell me. Everybody I've tried it out on thought it was the most outrageous stunt they've ever heard. Here's this big star who hires this goon to go out and publicize terrible things about a little boy and his father, and when it comes time to say it under oath he's afraid.

"He's lying and he's afraid to have the truth come out. He wants to stop it for six years! Lawsuits are a great equalizer, Evan. They can play all the little games they want but ultimately they're going to deal with me, and we're going to deal on the same, level playing field.

"Now, that's one thing. Second thing is, everybody believes this little boy needs closure — that he has to get it behind him. For six years he has to live

---

[98] A subpoena to produce all documents and tapes.

with this around his neck? Till he's nineteen? Give me a break! If anybody had any doubts . . . look, mega-stars don't take the fifth. It's that simple. The public will perceive this as Michael being guilty as sin. If he's so innocent, why not tell it under oath, right? So here's what I'm gonna do. I'm gonna file a motion to compel Michael's deposition, and we're going to lay in some more facts about the molestation in that motion."

"But even if Michael takes the fifth, the trial can still go ahead without him, right?"

"Well, it could. But this motion is being done for a different reason. Right now, public perception is still in favor of Michael. Don't quote me, I'm not an expert, but I think that will change by Friday of this week. We are going to let out some facts that we haven't let out yet. That this was not a grope in the back seat, it was a relationship that went on for months, and that every expert in child molestation that has seen him has said it's the clearest case possible.

"Just two days ago Fields was writing me these fucking letters arguing about what day Michael Jackson's deposition was going to be taken, and now they're saying you can't have him for six years and he ain't gonna testify!"

"Gee, whadya know," Evan chuckled, "they didn't keep their word. Maybe they're so desperate they might come to you with an offer if they thought they could get rid of the criminal."

"Yeah, that's true. I would if I were them. They've got nothing to lose at this point."

"But is Lauren still going ahead?"

"I haven't talked to Lauren since I told her what they did. See, Howard Weitzman wrote her a long letter to let her know that Pellicano's going to have to go out and do hard investigation because Feldman has been extremely aggressive in his discovery."

"He's freeing Pellicano up. He's covering himself so he can justify why he's seeing all those little boys."

"Right."

"So you have to interview these boys before they do."

"Well, maybe. But in any event, Lauren got this letter."

"So what was her reaction to it?"

"Evan, it is absolutely astounding. I think they're scared and they don't have a move that's any good. I don't think they ever believed I was going to go this tough and this hard. I think they thought that this was a bluff. It's the only way I can explain what they've done, because it's so amateurish."

"I have a theory on all this, Larry. I'm not a lawyer, but by the way Bert behaved with June and Dave, didn't he violated some ethics code or something, and now he's concerned about losing his license, or even having criminal charges brought against him? Why else would Fields litigate this in the first place? As brilliant as he may be, this is far from his field of expertise. How can he let the truth get out to another law firm? That's what I think."

"You may be right, Evan. We're certainly going to mention Fields role in this tomorrow when we file. The important thing is that we got 'em on the run, and we're gonna keep hittin', hittin', hittin' harder, harder, harder, and get this over with. Not so much for the money, but for your kid's sake."

"It would be devastating for him, Larry, to drag this on six more years."

"Absolutely devastating. So we're gonna hit 'em in these motions. And we're gonna tie Mr. Fields right up in all of this, starting by attaching the declaration he filed to take Jordie away from you, so the world will see this little creep.

"Then, about ten days from now, we're going to file our opposition to their motion for the stay. We're going to get a declaration from Stuart House saying that it is imperative for Jordie's mental health that this case have closure, and that if you delay this case for six years it would have terrible consequences for this boy. It's not like they're going to get anybody on the other side to claim that delaying the trial for six years won't hurt Jordie."

"Yeah, right, it's obvious."

"We've fucked 'em, Evan! Just think about it. This man, who claims to be the lover of all children, has to explain to the world how the fuck he can argue, 'I am innocent, these people are extortionists,' but will not come and testify under oath. Who is going to believe this asshole! The audacity of this man, hiring a goon like Pellicano to call Jordie a liar, yet he refuses to come testify under oath about what occurred!"

"He's afraid."

"You bet he is! He's so damn afraid he doesn't want his chauffeur, or

Pellicano, or La Toya, or all the little children he's had relationships with to testify. He doesn't want *anyone* to testify for six years! Is this an innocent man? In twenty-five years of practicing law I have never, ever, heard of a person doing this. And I believe in the Fifth Amendment. I think a person has a right, especially guilty people."

"Doesn't that screw their whole case, Larry, if he takes the fifth?"

"It's fuckin' gonna kill 'it! Oh, I mean Fields can always withdraw the motion and decide what to do next — whether he's going to let Jackson testify or not. We can't force him to testify if he wants to take the fifth. But so what, you know. So fucking what!

"Now, here's what I want you to think about, okay. Should we go out to the public on this issue?"

"You mean so the public doesn't just find out he took the fifth because it's a public document."

"Yeah, to comment on how bad this is, and really get everybody upset."

"What's the end purpose of doing that?"

"To influence the public. The public perception of you and your children is important no matter what money there is."

"For our safety."

"Right, that's one thing. And ultimately to pressure Jackson to finish this sucker. We have to show he can't survive this; that he has to get on another tack."

"I'm just wondering, Larry, does it look to you that they still intend to go into the courtroom and litigate this?"

"Does it look like it to you?"

"No."

"Right. Listen to this, Evan. Maureen Orth is writing this big *Vanity Fair* article.[99] And when she went out to see Fields he said, we're going to litigate this case hard and heavy, we've got nothing to hide. Now he wants a six-year stay! She's fuckin' gonna see this and flip . . . and Diane Dimond too, you know, who's really your closest ally.

"So, we need to decide if I'm going to do a couple of sophisticated interviews: 'Mr. Chandler isn't afraid to testify, he hasn't hidden, he's willing to

---

[99] Marueen Orth, "Nightmare at Neverland."

tell all, why aren't they willing?'"

"I'd love to get up there myself!"

"I know!"

"I'd love it, Larry. And once you take his depo close up, and the make-up starts cracking on his face, people will see how weird he really is."

"Right. Sure. I mean, I've always said, up till a few days ago, that I can't believe Michael Jackson is going to take the Fifth Amendment. I cannot fucking believe that he would ever take the fifth! I mean, how can a fucking superstar, whose whole career is on the line, take the Fifth Amendment?"

"Only because of the public perception."

"Of course! Right! Only because of who he is, not if he was some schmuck. There's no lawyer that wouldn't tell him to take the fifth if he were a nobody. But how can he do it! I mean, you have to be practical. Look what it's doing to his career. I was convinced on Wednesday that their strategy was now going to be to produce him. They were going to litigate the shit out of this case and worry about it down the line, because if they didn't win it Michael's career was going down the tubes anyway. And since they couldn't see a way out of this right now, the thing to do was just litigate it hard — litigate like you're innocent. And that made some sense to me, stand up there and say, 'I didn't do it.'"

"Did you have some communication from Bert on that?"

"Well yeah! There's these fucking letters going back and forth. So that's what I thought those guys were doing, see, because that's what it seemed that their every move was about —him saying, 'Fuck it, let's go litigate it.' But now, what he's saying is . . ."

"I'm desperate."

"Yeah. He's saying you got me and I can't control it anymore. We've checkmated him!"

"So what we're really looking for is the court's answer, right, which we'll get on November nineteenth? So nothing really happens between now and then, we just sit around and wait?"

"Basically, and file papers. I don't know what the court will decide, but I think they'll let us go forward and take the depos. They're not putting anything over on us, Evan. We're going forward!"

In the (six) letters Larry mentioned, faxed between October 25 and 28, he and Fields' law firm bantered back and forth about depositions. Larry requested that Michael be deposed sometime in November, and stated that he would go anywhere in the world, at the star's convenience, to depose him. Fields suggested January, because Michael was on tour and wouldn't be available until then.

In his last letter to Larry, dated October 28, Fields talked about arranging ". . . mutually convenient deposition dates . . . for your clients," meaning Jordie, Evan and June. But the next day Fields filed his motion for a six-year stay.

Feldman was so pissed off that he included Fields' letters in his next motion and pointed out to the judge how untrustworthy Fields was. "An attorney who is acting in good faith does not offer to produce a defendant for his deposition in January 1994, and then four days later file a motion to stay all discovery and the trial for the next six years."

Larry went even further:

> Plaintiff's [Jordie's] father discovered the sexual abuse and intervened to stop the relationship between plaintiff and Michael Jackson. Defendant Jackson refused to acquiesce to the request of plaintiff's father that he terminate the relationship. Rather, defendant Michael Jackson involved his counsel, Bertram Fields and his private investigator, Anthony J. Pellicano. Both Fields and Pellicano were used by defendant Jackson in an attempt to prevent the father from obtaining custody of plaintiff. Indeed, Bertram Fields filed a declaration in support of a motion to compel the father to surrender plaintiff.

Feldman was preparing to put Fields and Pellicano on the witness stand and "tie them up." At the very least, Fields would no longer be able to represent Michael.

– 21 –

NOVEMBER 8

Larry met with Evan and June to talk about pursuing an out of court settlement.

"One thing that is always on my mind," Larry explained, "is trying to figure out a way to win without Jordie having the pain of going through this a million times. We're squeezing them hard, and they're going to start squeezing back. They're going to take Jordie's depo — for days probably. They're going to have him examined by a shrink. And then there's the potential trial. And I gotta put him through some more stuff, too, to get him ready. There's no other way."

"So what you're saying," Evan asked, "is that if there is a chance to settle, this would be a good time to do it. Right?"

"Yeah. Because look, on the twenty-third of November, when the judge decides these motions in our favor, it will force Jackson to respond; either take the fifth or not. So there is a window of time now before he has to commit himself. Their lawyering is pathetic."

"So are you saying that if Michael takes the fifth, in return the judge will grant him the motion?"

"No, Evan. He won't even consider granting it until *after* Michael takes the fifth. And then he might not grant it anyway. I wouldn't, if I were a judge."

"Holy shit, Lar!" Evan said, finally grasping the dire straits his opponent was in. "So is there any reason to consider approaching them for a settlement other than Jordie's welfare? Any legal reasons?"

"We shouldn't ask for anything," June declared. "We should just run them down! He's already lost in the public's eye. Even Pepsi has dropped his endorsement."

"No, not yet," Evan disagreed. "He hasn't lost in the public eye. And besides, anything can happen. You can prevail in the trial and be awarded lots of money, and then they can say he only has three thousand dollars and declare bankruptcy. You get nothing. You win and lose at the same time. What are the possibilities of that, Larry?"

"I've never known a person who has as much money as he allegedly has, who can hide that much. Maybe he could. I mean, I haven't got to that stage of what Michael Jackson owns or doesn't own."

"I'm just thinking," Evan continued, "is it worth considering this early on that you can go through the whole thing for nothing?"

"Nope. Everything's great. You got a killer motion for a trial, you got jurisdiction, you got a judge who couldn't be better, you got Bert Fields stickin' his foot in his mouth. Hell, even his buddy Liz Smith is writing about how his image is going down the tubes."

"So Jordie's emotional welfare is the only reason to consider approaching them? Period. That's it."

"Well, it's always better to get the money today than tomorrow. But I'm not even certain there's anybody over there that'll listen. I mean, I assume they're smart enough to pick up the goddamn phone and say, 'Hey, let's talk.'"

"That's right. Wouldn't you think they would have approached you? Wouldn't you if you were them?"

"Well, I don't know what they know. I can't figure out what it is, other than the possibility of criminal charges. But I don't think the DA wants to file. I don't want them to say that yet, because it'll take tremendous pressure off Michael.

"I mean, sometime in all this we're going to have to take on the DA, and I don't know how else to take him on. I mean, I know what to say. They can't win a case; they can't win Rodney King, they can't win Damien Williams, they got it on tape and they still can't win! How the hell are they going to win this one! I'll have to take them on if that's what it comes down to. I mean, even though Garcetti's a friend, I'd have to do it. But I don't want to. That's why we got out front so we don't have to deal with it. Because they either file and lose, which kills us, or they announce they won't file and that hurts us too.

"Now if they file and win, that's the best. But they can't win a case. They can't win a damn case! Even if they had him on video they'd lose! But they're trying. I think they are in good faith conducting an investigation."

"Evan," June asked, changing the subject. "How is Jordie about this? Because I know he wants this badly."

"He doesn't think about it much. He'll be scared when he goes to court, just like you and I will be."

"Does he watch it on television?" Larry asked.

"No. We never do. We don't give a shit. Jordie's into his girlfriend. That's all he cares about. I don't even think about it day to day because it's so speculative, you know, the news and their comments. I'm only interested in the facts and what actually happens. Quite frankly, I'm beginning to think that Jordie will be the least affected by all this. He seems very strong. He'll be very scared if it goes to court, but that's probably the main emotion he'll feel."

"That's going to be a lot!" Larry reminded him.

✳ ✳ ✳

On November 12, Bert Fields announced that Michael had cancelled the *Dangerous* tour and entered a drug treatment program somewhere in Europe. On November 23, his doctors announced his condition was "greatly improved," but that his recovery would take another six to eight weeks. The big question, of course: Would he ever return?

NOVEMBER 23

Fields and Weitzman argued their case before Superior Court Judge David Rothman. In a nutshell, their reasoning went something like this: Michael really wants to testify at a civil trial so he can prove his innocence, but his testimony could be used against him at a future criminal trial, so he'll have to take the fifth if there is a civil trial.

Judge Rothman, knowing nonsense when he heard it, ruled that Jordie's right to a trial within one hundred twenty days superseded any rights Michael might have regarding a criminal prosecution. He also ruled that the discovery process should go forward, and set a trial date for March 21, 1994.

Faced with the choice of being deposed or taking the fifth and facing a public relations nightmare, it was not surprising that the day after the judge's decision, Michael's attorneys abruptly cancelled all scheduled depositions of Evan, June and Jordie. Howard Weitzman also informed Larry that Anthony Pellicano, whose deposition Larry had scheduled for the following Wednesday, would testify that he possessed no tapes of either Evan or Barry Rothman.

So much for their extortion defense.

When Larry called Evan with the news, he reacted with his usual skepticism. "Well, it's a good thing we know them to be such honest people."

"No, no, Evan." Larry assured him, "they wouldn't dare lie about this.

We're going to have it under oath that there is no tape. Weitzman is even thinking of agreeing not to call Pellicano as a witness. That's how bad he thinks he is. And Fields is basically out of the case."

"What! Who's on the case?"

"Weitzman."

"No, I mean on the civil."

"Weitzman."

"No shit, Lar! How do you feel about that?"

"We're doin' fine. So your depos are off for now. Everybody can relax."

Evan sensed something in Larry's voice "There's something you can't tell me on the telephone, right?" Nobody trusted Anthony Pellicano and his little wiretapping fingers.

"Uh . . . well . . . yeah, that's true."

"Okayyy. . ."

"Nothing earth shattering, Evan. But I'm going up to see *the* person."[100]

"Great!"

"And they do not have that person. That person has now given us two new things, major developments. This person is terrific!"

"You're worried about losing her?"

"Yeah, that's why I'm going there on my holiday. Ha! I'm a pilgrim!"

"Hey listen, Lar, if I could go in your place I'd be happy to do it."

"Ha! Ha! Ha! If you'd let me drill on . . ."

"No way! I wouldn't let you touch my teeth."

"You said it, Pal! I know what I'm good at and what I'm not. So look, come by on Monday and we'll talk."

"Good luck, Lar, and Happy Thanksgiving. I hope you'll be successful after all this effort."

"Oh, we're going to be successful all right. I can smell it!"

"Wonderful. Hey, Larry, one more thing. Remember you always told me that I have the right to be present in depositions as Jordie's guardian?"

---

[100] Blanca Francia, a maid at Michael's home, testified that she had seen Michael and several boys (individually) in bed naked, and Michael in the shower with a young boy. (Jim Newton & Miguel Bustillo, "Maid Tells of Nude Jackson, Boys," *Los Angeles Times*, December 14, 1993.) She also stated that she would occasionally pick up the children's clothing off the floor in the morning for the laundry, including their underwear.

"Yeah."

"Do you think it would be of any benefit if I went in there during Pellicano's depo?"

"Yeah, I think it might. Try to leave that day open. It's the fourteenth . . . unless they take him out."

"They probably will, right?"

"I don't know if they will. I wouldn't, if I were them. They could always decide that later on. Let him tell his stupid story for now. I'm going to tear his ass off anyway! (Evan cracked up.) I'm going to chew him up in front of a jury. Shit, I don't even have to work! All I gotta do is quote what he's already said in *People* and the *L.A. Times.* I don't need anything more. I wish you could have been in court, you'd have been proud of your lawyer."

"I wish I could have been there, too. But I don't dare go — my picture would be blasted all over the news. But I would like to be at the depo just to say hello to my old friend Tony."

"Antoine."

"Ha! Is that what you call him now, Antoine?"

"Yeah. Call me tomorrow."

NOVEMBER 25, THANKSGIVING

Late in the afternoon, after everyone had consumed their holiday repast, Larry Feldman called Evan with news they could all be thankful for. "Hey, Evan, you gotta hear this one. Howard Weitzman demoted Fields again. They definitely don't want your deposition, or June's deposition. They don't want to preserve anything. If they're gonna make a deal they don't want anything on the record about Jackson."

"No shit! Larry, these guys are in a real mess."

"Yeah, they fucked this up unbelievably. What could be better? But I'm going forward. We're going to push on. So far there ain't a button I've missed. The only thing we gotta do is keep the criminal behind us. I don't want them going first."

Larry had said it before, but it hadn't registered in Evan's brain till now. "You mean if they indict, the criminal case *automatically* goes before us?"

"Yeah."

"Jesus Christ!"

"Right! So we don't want that."

"How would you feel if the DA let you try their case?"

"Oh, I'd love it! That'd be the best."

"Would they let you do it?"

"I don't think so."

"Don't you have Jordie's testimony to trade on?"

"Yeah, but I want to use it so they'll stay behind me. Then they won't have to deal with this either."

"It's to their advantage to stay behind you, right?"

"Right, to their political advantage. And now these fucking guards are on *Hard Copy.*"[101]

"Is it good for us what they said?"

"Yeah, it's great for us. But it fucks it up that they're getting paid. They're stupid. They don't think of the way it looks. They have good things to say, but why the hell their lawyers would let them do that is beyond me. Anyway, enough of all that. Tell me something, Evan. Is Jordie happy? Is he aware of where we are right now?"

"Everybody asks me that question, Larry. He was a lot happier a couple of weeks ago than he is now. I'm beginning to see the effects of time dragging on."

"I'm sure of that. . . . Oh, yeah, Lauren Weis told me today that this disease Michael says he's got, vitiligo, that it's capable of changing anywhere you look, so that anything Jordie says is irrelevant. It can change very quickly with this disease."

"Shit, these guys seem to have an answer for everything."

"No, that's good for us!"

"Why?"

"Because if he's right, he's right. And if he's wrong, we've got an explanation!"

"Ha!"

"Yeah, it's a no-loser for us."

---

[101] Several of Michael's security guards sued the star, claiming they were wrongfully terminated because they knew too much.

"That's very good."

"Good? It's terrific! You stick with the teeth, kid. I'm stickin' with the law."

Legally, everything was going swimmingly. But there was always one issue that kept an ominous cloud hanging over everyone's head.

"Now look," Larry continued, "about these death threats. I don't know what the hell to do, but this has got to stop."

"I don't think there's anything that can be done. I just wrote you those letters to get your advice as to whether or not you want them documented in a police report."

"Yeah, we want it documented. There's a report that's gonna hit the news today. One of these guards was shot at. Listen, Evan, don't let Jordie out at night."

"You know, the fact is, Larry, if they want to get him they'll get him any hour, any time. And about the tapes, they're really frightening because you can feel the venom in their voices. They're really very frightening people."

"I think we should definitely report it."

"You know it's just that those calls came in first, and then these three events occurred. And maybe they're totally unrelated and I'm scared. But last time, when I got attacked in the lobby of my office and I made a police report, it was in the paper and everybody knew about it. And what I'm afraid of now is that there'll be some lunatic who'll decide that he'll be the one to take me down. So I only feel it would be worthwhile making a report if you think it's going to help your case."

"I'd make the report, Evan. Hopefully it won't leak out. But keep him inside at night."

"Yeah, okay. So you definitely think I should make a police report?"

"I don't know. It's good for the public to know what you're going through. What I am afraid of is that it'll intimidate witnesses from coming forward."

"Yeah. I'm sure they won't stop at intimidation. They have too much at stake."

"I don't know — it's hard to tell. Technically, I think you should report it. That's my gut. It would be hard to argue why you didn't report it if I wanted to go public with it later."

"Well, okay, the gunshots are one thing. Should I forget the incident about the bottle being thrown over?"

"Why forget that? Hey, listen, if people are doing this, let them go arrest them."

"They'll never find them anyway."

"Well, they may and they may not. And if our boy (Pellicano) has anything to do with it, wouldn't you like the police to nail this guy? I mean, if he is involved, there's going to be ten people between him and the act. But wouldn't it be nice? I'd report it, Evan."

"Alright, Lar, I'll call the cops in the morning. But you know, after the shots came over the fence, I took Jordie to the Beverly Hills Gun Club and taught him how to shoot a gun."

"I wouldn't tell them that part."

"No. But I mean, in this case there's a certain logic to teaching your child how to protect himself. I can't be around him every minute. I worry for him."

"I understand."

"Especially when I'm not around. I don't know how else to teach him to be able to defend himself when the assailants have guns."

"Shit! Evan. What a fucking mess."

"Yeah."

Defeating Michael, in or out of court, was now a given and no longer of primary concern. Staying alive, on the other hand . . .

Having your life threatened on a near daily basis is bad enough. But there's an irony to it that the victim of a single threat does not have to face. For one thing, the experience has no closure. Even the victims of a single violent act, horrible as it is, can begin the healing process.

Part of that healing process involves the understanding and sympathy of others. They may never have been beaten up, but almost everyone has had a sudden painful injury, like smashing fingers in a car door, and has some idea of what you're going through. But living each day, month after month, with the fear that your fingers will be smashed in the door at any moment, or that at any moment you may be attacked and beaten to a pulp, á la Rodney King, is an experience that few can relate to.

Eventually people become desensitized to your plight. You begin to look a bit paranoid, because you act paranoid, and though you're really not paranoid you begin to wonder if maybe you are paranoid, until they threaten again to spill your son's blood, then you know you're not paranoid, except now you act more paranoid. And in the end, even if you are paranoid, that still doesn't mean someone isn't out there waiting to kill you, your wife and your kids.

After three months of this the cops suggested placing a "trap" on Evan's phone. A trap is basically the modern version of a trace, except it's instantaneous. The phone company gets a read-out of where the call is calling from (caller ID), turns it over to the cops, and the caller is busted.

Wow! That's great news, we told ourselves. We'll catch one of these sick bastards and make an example of them. Too bad the cops didn't tell us about this months ago. But hey, what the heck, it'll all be over soon.

Close, but no cigar.

For one thing, the phone company can operate only within a given jurisdiction, in this case, the greater L.A. area. But most of the calls picked up by the trap came from overseas, and an international sting operation over a bunch of irate rock fans making "prank" calls is not exactly on the top of Interpol's list. Unless, of course, you've already been murdered.

Even within the jurisdiction, public phones are the most common point of origin. But unless the caller makes more than one call and continues to use the same booth, which is unlikely, it's a waste of manpower for cops to stake out the booth. Unless, of course, you've already been murdered. Then the expense can be justified. Though it's unlikely the caller will continue to threaten you once you're dead.

In other words, although dozens of death threats came in after it was installed, the phone trap was useless. Whether it was the 1993 technology, the laws (no Homeland Security Act), the lack of manpower, or a combination of the above, nothing came of it. Not one, single, solitary thing. It was a major letdown.

DECEMBER 8

In a stunning display of courage and honesty, LaToya Jackson, speaking to the world from Israel, avowed that she could no longer "be a silent collaborator of his (Michael's) crimes against small, innocent children. . . . If I remain silent, then that means that I feel the guilt and humiliation that these children are feeling, and I think it's very wrong."

The *Los Angeles Times* reported this was the first "hint" from a member of the Jackson family that "her brother is guilty of sexually molesting young boys and of paying off their families to keep them quiet."[102]

To the Chandler's this was a godsend. LaToya knew Michael better than anyone who had come forward. Other than a videotape or an admission by Michael himself, it was the best corroboration they could ask for.

Ten years later LaToya retracted her statements by claiming that she made them under the influence of her then husband and manager. If this claim is true, the degree of mind control required to coerce her into making such false claims against her own brother must have been immense. What in LaToya's past would make her that vulnerable to such an abusive man? Perhaps the same forces that affected Michael.

– 22 –

DECEMBER 14

Back in September, Jordie had given a detailed description of Michael's penis and testicles to the DA. Feldman was aware of this, but had yet to discuss it with his young client. If the description matched the police photos it was one more giant straw on the camel's back that was Michael's defense. And the poor beast was already swayback.

On the other hand, it had been medically established that the markings of vitiligo were subject to change. So if Jordie's description was wrong, Larry would be able to say the markings had shifted over the months. Either way, Larry's case was solid as a rock and he didn't need it. But since the DA was making a big deal over it, Larry had to be sure what, exactly, Jordie had seen.

Before getting down to the business at hand, Larry informed Evan that the other side had decided to withdraw Anthony Pellicano from their witness list. Or at least, that's what they told him. "I think they're so full of shit," Larry commented. "I mean, they just don't know what the hell they're doing; they're on both sides of everything. Wait till the press gets this!"

---

[102] Jim Newton, "Jackson's Sister Says She Believes He Is a Molester," *Los Angeles Times*, December 9, 1993.

To Evan, the news was not surprising. He knew better than anyone that Pellicano's story was a pack of lies, and there was no way the investigator would hold up under the cross-examination of an expert like Feldman. Instead, Evan's mind was on the gag order he believed the judge had issued. Swimming against the tide of public opinion had been exhausting for him, now the tide was turning and he wanted to be sure it continued. It was Michael's turn to drown for awhile. But if Larry couldn't talk to the media . . . ?

"There is no gag order," Larry assured him, explaining that the judge was considering it and would make a final decision by the end of the week. Until then, both sides had voluntarily agreed to keep silent. "There's a major story in the *Times* today about what the maid saw," Larry continued, just to let Evan know that information was still getting out to the public, gag order or not.

Evan had one other major concern. "Hey, Larry, let me just tell you what I heard in the car on the way over here. It was a talk show call-in type thing and this guy says, 'How can Michael be guilty when he just flies in and they don't arrest him, while all this time everybody's saying he's going to get arrested as soon as he lands.[103] The police haven't made a move, the DA hasn't made a move, so it looks like he's pretty innocent to me.' This is what the guy said on 640 (KFI-AM in LA). So what I'm asking is, did the DA do something really stupid?"

"No, Evan," Larry said. "Keep your eye on the ball. We're concerned about our case, not the DA's."

"But I keep remembering you telling me how important public opinion is."

"Sure, but we can't control the entire world. You can't have it both ways. The problem is, if they indict, the judge will stop me. I assume that you'd rather have me talking for Jordie instead of the DA."

"That's a reasonable assumption," Evan snickered.

"We're done, My Boy. We fuckin' got 'em! I got the chauffeur dead! Gary Hearne was terrific for us. We got enough out of each maid that they can't say anything bad. They're all neutralized. If anything, it's positive. It's all positive. It's not like the chauffeur, but everybody, even that asshole Pellicano is positive. Big deal, he's bullshit! He's going to take the Fifth Amendment, they've told me this. He ain't gonna testify. That's why they

---

[103] Michael flew into Santa Barbara on December 10, 1993.

want this gag order, 'cause they can't take the fifth and then let me go out and say he took it.

"And this maid, Blanca. It's the best thing we got on the discovery part of the case. And it's in the *Times!* I'm telling you, Evan, we're not going to get much better."

"Well, Larry, my concern was public opinion. That was the issue you raised to me, that it was important. And now people are starting to think that he's not guilty again because he's back and the cops aren't doing anything. You don't want the momentum to fall back the other way."

"Are you crazy! Read the *Times!* And don't worry about a gag order. The maid's story is out there. And that letter that June gave me. Doo-doo head, Applehead, I mean, what do you think Michael would say if he knew. What do you think the press would say if they had that letter — though there's no sex in the letter — about calling himself doo-doo head. Doo-doo head. Applehead. I love you, Jordie. You're my inspiration."

"Well, he was his inspiration, for the wrong thing."

"He's a thirty-five-year-old man for Christ's sake!"

"Yeah. He's very sick."

The *Los Angeles Times* reported, as Larry had been saying for a week, that a deal had been negotiated between the DA and Michael's attorneys: Michael could return to the U.S. without being arrested if he voluntarily submitted to a strip search.[104] "His drug treatment was supposed to take six to eight weeks," Larry remarked. "It's been less than three. Amazing how quickly he recovered once a deal was made."

It was a good deal for both sides. Michael *had* to come back. Living in exile, a fugitive from justice, was not a life Michael Jackson could endure, no matter how luxurious that exile might be. He lived to perform. It was all he had, the only life he'd ever known. He must face the music if he had any hopes of making music again. But to return only to be handcuffed and hauled off to jail, no matter how luxurious that jail might be, was also something Michael could not endure. Nor could his career.

The deal also took pressure off the DA. If they arrested Michael they'd

---

104 Jim Newton, "Lawyers Meet to Discuss Jackson's Return to the U.S.," *Los Angeles Times*, December 11, 1993.

have to charge him, but their case was nowhere near ready. (If it ever would be.) At the same time, allowing the singer to return unconditionally would be a sign of weakness on the DA's part. Hence, the strip-search. Embarrassing as it was for Michael, he was home. And the DA now had in his possession a powerful bargaining chip to use against this intensely private man — pictures of his genitals.

The talk show host Evan had heard on the radio was not privy to this information and apparently took Michael's "un-arresting" return as a sign of innocence. But public speculation was of little concern to Feldman. What really mattered was that the DA did not preempt the civil trial with a criminal trial, one that was certain to end in a hung jury, at best, and all but destroy Jordie's case.

The strip-search deal solved that problem. And as an extra added bonus, now that Michael was on U.S. soil he would *have* to submit to a deposition or take the fifth. Or better yet, pay gobs of money to make the whole thing disappear.

The DA might soon have pictures of Michael's *cajones*, but Larry Feldman now held them firmly in his grasp. And it was time to put the squeeze on.

Jordie was about to begin his description when the meeting was interrupted by Larry's secretary. A phone call had just come in from a prominent attorney who had been struck by a car and wanted Larry to represent him. Evan recognized the name immediately. "Wow! That's big, Larry!" Evan assumed Larry would take the case.

"What do you think," Larry responded, "should I take him or give him to Fields? Fields has dropped out, so . . ."

"What! He dropped out?"

"That's what I was told today. He wrote a letter dropping out. So we could give it to Bert, he'll have room. And he's never lost a case."

"Now we know why," Evan chuckled. "When he knows he can't win he drops out. But that's just for show. Michael fired him, right?"

"That's what I think. But who knows? Maybe he did quit. What I can't understand is, if they did fire him, why it took so damn long."

"Pellicano," Evan answered. "Why else? He's so fucking egotistical he convinced Michael he could get him out of this. Instead, he was digging his grave."

"Yeah. Who knows? Anyway, let's get down to it. Okay, Jordie, here's what I gotta ask you my friend. What does Michael look like, physically, because they're going to examine him?

It took several hours for Jordie to provide a description that Feldman could understand. There were numerous distinctive markings and discolorations on Michael's privates, and it was difficult for the boy to explain exactly where they were located, what size they were, and what shape they took.

The problem was not Jordie's memory: he had seen Michael's genitalia so many times and from every possible angle that he had a precise mental picture. The problem was trying to explain the details. But they pressed on and eventually arrived at a description that turned out to be an accurate match to the photographs taken by the Santa Barbara authorities a few days later.[105]

– 23 –

DECEMBER 20

Michael Jackson had achieved the crossover dream: he had transcended classification by race and was admired equally by everyone. And it was because of that admiration that everyone, including the media, had ceased regarding him as a man of color. In that regard, he was decades, perhaps centuries ahead of his time.

Of all the hoopla surrounding the child abuse allegations, none seemed more absurd than the involvement of the NAACP. "Our primary concern is that Michael Jackson is being tried and convicted in the press. We're not going to stand by any longer and let that happen," said Shannon Reeves, West Coast director of the NAACP.[106]

Officially the NAACP wasn't taking a position on the molestation

---

[105] After Michael denied the match in a 1995 interview with Diane Sawyer, Santa Barbara District Attorney Tom Sneddon told *Vanity Fair* that Micheal's "statement on TV is untrue and incorrect and not consistent with the evidence in this case." (Maureen Orth, "The Jackson Jive," *Vanity Fair*, Sepetmber 1995, 116.)

[106] Jim Newton, "NAACP Questions Media Coverage of Jackson Case," *Los Angeles Times*, December 21, 1993.

allegations, that wasn't their beef. It was the lopsided press coverage given to well-known blacks they objected to. But even if there was some truth to that accusation, the choice of Michael Jackson as the typical example of media prejudice toward blacks, well-known or otherwise, was . . . Jeez Louise, it was nuts! And ironically, when you think about it, it was insulting to Michael as well. The NAACP was denying him one of his greatest achievements, that he had made the world see him for "the content of his character, not the color of his skin."[107]

No one was more responsible than Michael's own wise men for whipping up the press. It was they who dominated the media in the opening weeks; press conferences, interviews, so-called smoking gun tapes. No one's tongue wagged more than Anthony Pellicano's. But the NAACP didn't get it, or chose to ignore it.

In any event, if the tone of the media coverage was so overwhelmingly negative as to rankle the NAACP, it was only because by the end of December, when the NAACP made its claim, the majority of the evidence that presented itself was suggestive of Michael's guilt.

Many people came forward and made statements that were not favorable to Michael. The press did not make them up — they simply reported them. Had Diana Ross, Brooke Shields, Quincy Jones, Oprah Winfrey, or any of Michael's friends and fellow entertainers come forward to support him, the media would have reported that, too. Liz Taylor and certain members of the Jackson family were his staunchest allies and the media gave them all the print and airtime they wanted. Liz Smith, a well-known newspaper columnist, was an outspoken supporter of Michael.

Besides, what other conclusion could the press come to when Michael's answer to Jordie's complaint was to ask for a six-year stay until the criminal statute of limitations expired? Or when Bert Fields complained that his client was being forced into taking the Fifth Amendment?

When Mark Furhman took the fifth about his use of the "N" word, Johnnie Cochran stood on the courthouse steps and told the world, "What more [proof] does anyone out there need?" In other words, invoking the

---

[107] Had the NAACP done its homework, they would have discovered that Jordie Chandler has a considerable amount of "black blood" flowing through his veins.

Fifth Amendment is tantamount to an admission of guilt.

The December 21 *Los Angeles Times* also reported that "NAACP lead-
ers are concerned that police were not respecting the rights of children
whom they interviewed as part of their investigation." This criticism mim-
icked complaints by Jackson's attorneys, but an NAACP spokesman said
that the letter was not drafted at their request. Curiously, the NAACP did
not complain about Pellicano's interrogation of Jordie, which was also
public information.

Instead, the NAACP complained of "curbside justice."[108] But where was
the NAACP's outrage when the Chandler family was being tried and convicted in the press by Michael's paid henchmen? In the NAACP's own words,
"Does the degree of concern depend upon the status of the accused?"[109]

To those old enough to remember, the NAACP is synonymous with
names like Rosa Parks, Medgar Evers and James Meredith. It rekindles
images of the march on Montgomery, of cops and dogs attacking innocent
people, of Dr. King sharing his dream with an entire nation. But the
NAACP's role in the Jackson affair — a pox on an otherwise long and right-
eous struggle — will be remembered by no one. Thank God.

In an article about the O.J. Simpson case, Harry S. Ashmore, Pulitzer
Prize-winning author and respected civil rights activist, wrote the following
words on the politics of race. They fit the Jackson case like a sequined glove.

> [This is] the case of a certified member of the privileged class, who has
> removed himself as far as it is possible to get from the under-privileged neigh-
> borhood where he grew up. O.J. Simpson's [substitute Michael Jackson's]
> status as a multimillionaire has allowed him to live in a walled estate with a
> Rolls Royce in the driveway, to play golf at exclusive country clubs, to mingle
> freely with the CEOs of leading corporations, and to enjoy the special treat-
> ment top-drawer establishments reserve for the in-group.
>
> But by the time he made his second court appearance, his defense team, made

---

[108] Reverend Cecil L. Murray, pastor of the First African Methodist Episcopal Church
urged the press to use caution. "Curbside justice is no worse than flashbulb justice."
Leo Terrell, legal counsel for the NAACP, complained "Why are some facts of the investigations being 'leaked' and others not. Is the investigation being carried out in an ethical
manner?" (Jim Newton, "Jackson Being Persecuted, Ministers Say," *Los Angeles Times*,
February 19, 1994.)

[109] Ibid.

up of the best lawyers money could buy, had decided it would be necessary to play the race card. His lead counsel was now flanked by a black attorney, well-connected in the community from which some Superior Court jurors will be drawn, and the spin doctors had floated the suggestion that O.J. [Michael], like many a poor black defendant, had been framed by a racist cop [substitute racist press.][110]

To introduce a race issue where none exists smacks of the same exploitation used by segregationist politicians in the old south to further their personal lust for power. It's divisive and furthers no cause.

– 24 –

CHRISTMAS 1993

On the home scene, life was still hectic. Evan was the first to rise each morning — up by seven and out the door by seven-thirty. Jordie, who was now attending private school, followed half an hour later, still sleepy-eyed when June honked in the driveway to pick him up. Monique had the choice of sleeping in till nine and spending a few minutes with the baby, or driving Cody to kindergarten before going on to the office. She divided her mornings equally between the two children.

Evan's work schedule followed no set pattern. He could be finished by mid-afternoon or work late into the evening, and he was always at the beck and call of his pager. Saturdays were often busy. And more often than not there'd be a Sunday morning patient as well, usually a close friend or family member, or a jet-setting model with just one day to spare on her way to an exotic shoot halfway around the world.

The near daily sessions with lawyers, psychiatrists and social workers that occurred in September and October were no longer daily, though still frequent. Evan, along with June, was required to take parenting classes and have private, weekly counseling as well. Jordie was also required to see a social worker each week, and Larry occasionally had him scheduled with a private psychiatrist. For Evan and Jordie, there was also the occasional visit to DCS, LAPD or the DA's office.

[110] Harry S. Ashmore, *Santa Barbara Independent*, July 28, 1994.

Monique was not required to have therapy, but her work was demanding and kept her at the office late, and it was not unusual to see her walk in the door after eight. Occasionally she'd join Evan in a late night meeting with the attorneys and not get home until ten or eleven.

With these schedules, there was rarely an evening when the entire family was home before nine. Even then, it was difficult to get the case out of one's daily life, particularly for Evan, who was constantly preoccupied with security precautions, not to mention endless streams of paperwork.

Jordie handled the craziness well; he was old enough to keep himself occupied during the day and still be awake at night to see his parents come home. But the little ones were missing their mom and dad, and it showed. With Christmas just around the corner, everyone was looking forward to a much needed break.

As the holiday grew near, the kids began clambering for a Christmas tree, and each day Monique promised they'd get one — soon. She was hoping for an evening when we could all go tree hunting together, much like the traditional family Christmas she enjoyed as a child in France. But the days slipped by quickly and it was not until the night before "the night before" that the holiday season officially began in the Chandler home. We piled into the car and set out on a quest for the perfect tree.

It was the first time in months our collective minds were at ease, laughing and joking as we wandered through the lots on Wilshire Boulevard, assessing each specimen as if it were a family pet that would be with us forever. Six people attempting to agree on anything is almost impossible, like picking a video or a place to eat. Unless, of course, one stands out above the rest. And one did. A Jurassic Park of a blue spruce.

Evan and I raised the green giant in a corner of the living room, turning her round and round to put her best face forward. Then Monique and the kids took over, adorning her with necklaces of popcorn and cranberries and dozens of brightly colored handmade treasures that had been passed down from mother to daughter. Then came the gingerbread men, candy canes, showers of silvery tinsel, and a sparkling gold star for the top. For a few hours, everyone forgot.

Christmas day at the Chandler's was much the same as any other

American family: the pitter-patter of little feet scurrying downstairs at the break of dawn, followed by oohs! and ahhs! amid the sound of shredding paper; bright red stockings arranged neatly over the hearth, each with a fuzzy name embroidered on the front, each awaiting little hands to pluck their sweets; and last but not least, the traditional afternoon gluttony, followed by the required period of lounging around like so many beached whales. All in all, a relaxing and welcomed break from four whirlwind months of a hell in a fishbowl.

Life was returning to normal, notwithstanding the shotguns and side-arms that were still at the ready.

Late that evening, Monique and the little ones boarded a flight for Paris to spend a week with her family — far from the madding crowd — while Jordie, Evan and I remained at home. Jordie would be spending his vacation playing around the house with friends and strengthening his relationship with the young girl he had fallen head over heels for. He was only permitted to leave the grounds with his friends, never alone, and preferably accompanied by an adult. The fear of being kidnapped, or worse, followed wherever he went.

Evan spent much of his time going over the piles of paperwork that had accumulated over the months. I was there to keep him and Jordie company — a little male bonding with the boys — and to help with security.

All was going according to plan. Then, on the morning of December 30, Santa Claus appeared in the guise of a middle-aged Jewish attorney named Larry Feldman. He had just spoken to Howard Weitzman. "It's over, Evan. It's a done fucking deal!"

"No shit! You're kidding!" Evan couldn't believe it.

Weitzman gave no explanation for the sudden decision, but the reason was obvious, Judge Rothman had refused Michael's motion for a gag order. Not only was Feldman free to release some of the lewd evidence he had collected against Michael, but even more devastating, the court's ruling also permitted him to turn over every scrap of evidence to the district attorney.

In addition, the judge would soon compel Michael to comply with Larry's demand for all records regarding employees and child visitors at Neverland.

And, perhaps the most damaging of all, Michael would now have to submit to a deposition under oath, scheduled for the end of January, where he would be forced to either lie and commit perjury or take the Fifth Amendment.[111]

Larry called again that evening, this time with more great news. He expected the DA would soon announce that having found no evidence, the extortion investigation against Evan was closed. "We got them running with their tail between their legs!" Larry exclaimed.

"Hey, Larry," Evan joked. "Did you see Weitzman on TV warning the DAs he'd sue the shit out of them if they let those pictures of Michael's balls get out?"

"Jesus Christ!" Larry laughed. "Can you imagine waking up to those with your breakfast? Who the hell would want to see 'em anyway?"

But Larry did want to see them. He petitioned the court to allow the DA to give him copies of the photographs obtained at the strip-search.

By the second week in January — after Larry had twisted the knife one more time by asking the court for access to Michael's financial records — an informal truce was established in which both sides agreed to stay out of the press and begin formal talks.

Bolstered by the anticipation of victory — more for the privacy it would bring than the money — the Chandler's began to relax. Best of all, the death threats, which followed in frequency according to the degree of media coverage, began to subside. But not completely.

About 3 AM one January morning Evan was awakened by the dog barking. Normally the giant shepherd would start at one end of the house, then move from window to window, barking his head off as he followed someone down the sidewalk. But this time he stood firmly at the front door.

Evan grabbed his pistol and a flashlight and tiptoed down the stairs. Standing directly behind the door he let Sampson out first, then peered around for a look. There was no one in sight, and no one out of sight either,

---

[111] In a 1994 lawsuit in which he was accused of wrongfully firing security guards because they knew too much, Jackson took the fifth in response to deposition questions about his sexual relationships with children. The case was dismissed because the guards had signed a contract precluding them from suing. (Nicholas Riccardi, "Judge Lets Jackson Plead 5th," *Los Angeles Times,* September 16, 1994.)

according to Sampson's nose. Instead, the beast was sniffing a box lying on the front stoop.

"As soon as I saw it," Evan vividly remembers, "I thought, Oh, shit! A bomb! So I grabbed a broom and flipped the lid off while I stood behind the door. I almost puked when I saw what was in it. A dead rat with its head cut off." On top of the carcass was a flower and a note warning "YOU'RE NEXT." It was signed by "The Hunter-Executioner."

* * *

On January 24, 1994, all parties signed a Confidential Settlement Agreement. Michael agreed to pay Jordie an undisclosed amount in return for Jordie withdrawing his lawsuit. In addition, both sides agreed to keep forever silent.

The scandal was now HIStory.

PART THREE

WAITING FOR THE FAT LADY

UNFORTUNATELY FOR THE CHANDLERS, and Michael as well, the nightmare did not end with the settlement. Michael remained the target of a criminal investigation until the following summer, as well as mired in ancillary civil lawsuits. And the Chandlers continued to be plagued by wacko-Jacko fans from around the world, not to mention a few blood-suckers right here at home just dying to get their hands on all that money.

But worst of all for Evan and his family, the anonymity they desperately craved was denied to them, for it quickly became apparent that Michael had no intention of keeping silent, and that the settlement agreement they had signed was a total sham.

– 25 –

Of all the death threats none were more frequent and ugly as those of Michael's British fans. The primary voice in this group was a young woman named Denise Pfeiffer. After eight months of death threats made by phone from Europe, Pfeiffer showed up in person at Evan's office on the morning of April 4, 1994.

At about five feet four inches and one hundred pounds, the intruder posed no physical threat, but the office staff was primed with fear from numerous telephone threats and recognized Pfeiffer's voice immediately. Not only had the staff been subjected to the death threats, but also they had recently been through a bomb threat against the office tower where Evan's office was located. There was no doubt that Evan was the target.

Pfeiffer tried to convince the receptionist that she had a dental emergency and needed to see Dr. Chandler immediately. The staff was afraid that Pfeiffer might have a gun in her purse, so they played along and told her that Evan was not in the office but that she could make an appointment for a later date. With this, Pfeiffer abruptly left.

If nothing else, Pfeiffer was resourceful. She managed to track down Evan's unlisted home address, and on the afternoon of April 7 she knocked on his front door. As it turned out, I was the only one home at the time.

"Who is it?" I asked, peering through a side window.

"Is Mr. Lewis home?" the stranger answered, her thick British accent instantly setting off an alarm in my head.

The waif I saw through the window was so contrary to my image of a would-be assassin that it was difficult to take her seriously. My first impulse was to throw her over my knee and spank her. But first I needed to know what was in the large black purse she was carrying.

"There's no Mr. Lewis here," I said, through the triple-locked door, semi-automatic in hand. We both knew that the other knew, but we played the game anyway.

"I want to talk to Mr. Lewis," the voice persisted.

"Go away! There's no Lewis here!"

Rather than become more aggressive, as I expected she would, Pfeiffer trotted down the driveway out of sight.

I was in my stocking feet, and there was no time to put on shoes. With the pistol tucked in the small of my back I trailed Pfeiffer around the corner to a parking lot where I assumed she'd left her car. Perfect! I thought. All I have to do is copy the license plate and give it to the cops — they'll do the rest. Instead, Pfeiffer walked into a store and disappeared. So I hid behind a dumpster and waited.

A minute later she reappeared, but instead of heading for a car, she took off down the sidewalk. I followed about twenty feet behind, assuming still that she had a car and that it was parked nearby. People were staring at my feet.

Suddenly Pfeiffer spun around and walked straight toward me, then past me. I avoided eye contact and kept walking, then turned and came up behind her, intending to confront her up close so I could belt her if she went for a gun. Unless she was a martial arts expert I had no doubt that I could overpower her, so I kept my gun in my belt.

As I approached from behind, Pfeiffer abruptly wheeled around, placing us nose to nose. We were both surprised as hell. "Are you the one looking for Mr. Lewis? I asked. "Don't I know you?" she asked at the same time. A minute later we were sitting on a park bench talking things over.

Denise was twenty-four, unmarried, had never had a boyfriend, and had never been kissed. Michael Jackson was her only love and she hoped one day to marry him. She told me that her parents had died when she was a child and that she went to live with her older brother and his wife in Leicester, England. By the age of twelve she was madly in love with Michael, and by sixteen she was working and saving her money so she could follow him around the world. She'd been to as many concerts as she could afford, returning to England between tours just to save enough for the next.

Michael knew her well, Pfeiffer claimed. She had been invited to his hotel suite three times over the years. The last time was in Mexico City just before the *Dangerous* tour was cancelled. She called him Pan. He called her Wendy.

I asked Pfeiffer why she was so convinced of Michael's innocence. "Because Michael loves children," she replied, regurgitating the standard Jackson mantra. "He would never harm a child."

I wondered if this deluded creature could grasp the contradiction. "Let me see if understand you correctly," I asked. "Michael would never harm a child, but in his name you threaten to kill an entire family including three children?"

Pfeiffer made it clear that she was not angry with "the boy"; he had been brainwashed by his father. It was Evan she hated, because he had deliberately gone to the media with the idea of ruining Michael after unsuccessfully trying to extort him. She knew that for a fact because she had heard the tapes Pellicano played and she had read it in the papers.

Despite her naiveté, Pfeiffer was intelligent and willing to listen. For the next two hours I went through the entire story: the leaked DCS report; the edited tapes; the false child support claims; the so-called custody battle; the cops, social workers and psychiatrists all believing the boy's story; and on and on, the whole megilla.

We also discussed the nature of child sexual abuse, the M.O. of the typical offender, the abusive history of the Jackson family and the personality of Michael himself. Periodically Pfeiffer would react by saying, "Mmm-hmm, I can see that" or "Oh, I didn't know that." Although she steadfastly adhered to the ideology that Michael loves children and was therefore incapable of hurting them — to believe otherwise would be tantamount to admitting that her entire life was built on a lie — Pfeiffer conceded that the factors involved in driving a person to such behavior were similar to those found in Michael's past.

Throughout our conversation I was trying to decide what to do with this poor soul — whether to release her or call the police. But first I had to be certain she wasn't armed. Pfeiffer had refused several requests to search her bag, which only made me more suspicious and less willing to turn her loose. She swore that if I let her go she'd return to England and never bother us again. She insisted that her purpose was not to harm Evan, only to scare him into recanting his lies so Michael could have his life back.

Eventually we struck a deal. I would "consider" releasing her in exchange for a peek in her purse. I found no weapon, but as I was rummaging through her bag it dawned on me that if I decided not to let her go and she took off anyway, I'd have to restrain her, something I did not want to do in full view on a public street. So I took her passport. She wasn't going anywhere without that.

By 7 PM it was dark and chilly. With no meat on her bones and wearing only a thin blouse, Pfeiffer began to shiver. So I took her back to the house while I decided her fate.

Once the police became involved there would be additional publicity, which the family did not want. On the other hand, making an example of her might discourage others. The deciding factor came when Pfeiffer revealed that she had traveled to the U.S. with a group of Jackson fans and that they were all staying at a local youth hostel. Young males had made some of the death threats, and I was concerned that they were more likely to be violent than Pfeiffer.

When the police raided the hostel they found a diary in Pfeiffer's handwriting, containing evidence of her death threats, her visit to the dental office, and the lewd graffiti she had written in huge red letters on the sidewalk outside Evan's office.

At the very least the Chandlers wanted Pfeiffer barred from the U.S. for several years, until she grew up. She was arrested for terrorism and stalking, but the charges were reduced to vandalism and petty theft as part of a plea bargain. "Wendy" received three years probation and was deported without restriction. She was free to return to the U.S. at will.

On April 20, Larry Feldman retrieved his voice mail only to hear that his office would soon to be blown to smithereens. Federal Marshals were assigned to protect him.

Evan and his family continued to receive death threats for more than two years after the settlement. According to Rhonda Saunders, Deputy District Attorney of L.A.'s Organized Crime and Anti-terrorist Division, these threats should be taken seriously. "One of these nuts can snap at any time," Saunders warned. "You never know where or when." Detective Bill Dworin of LAPD's Sex Crime Unit agreed, and he hit the nail on the head when he said, "You'll be looking over your shoulder for the next few years . . . maybe longer."

It was about this time, April 1994, that the DA began putting pressure on Evan to have Jordie testify at a criminal trial. The authorities had uncovered allegations of sexual misconduct on Michael's part with a second boy, and they had discovered what they believed to be a third boy as well. They also had one adult who testified that she saw Michael acting inappropriately with a child. This testimony would be supported by the child pornography seized at Michael's home, and by Jordie's accurate description of Michael's privates.

Evan was torn. He didn't care all that much about helping the DA, who Evan believed had dragged his political feet rather than do his duty. But he felt a strong loyalty to the LAPD officers who had worked so hard to see that justice was done. Detectives Frederico Sicard, Vincent Neglia, Rose Ferrufino, Bill Dworin and DCS Investigator Ann Rosato had put their hearts and souls into this and would be disappointed, to say the least, if Michael was not brought to trial.

Evan felt particularly obligated to Detective Sicard, a kind and gentle man who had been accused publicly by Jackson's people of improper conduct while questioning other children who might have been victims of Michael's abuse. Evan knew all too well what it was like to be branded by a lie, and he wanted to give Fred the chance to clear his name.

On the other hand, Evan was concerned for the safety of his family. The fear that had been slowly diminishing would soar to even greater heights if Michael were to be indicted. In the mind of the Jacko-Wackos, poor innocent Pan had just paid the evil Captain Hook all that money to go away, and now the SOB was pulling a double-cross and trying to get their hero thrown in jail. Even worse, Pellicano was still on the loose, and no one knew exactly how far he'd go to get his revenge.

As for his obligation to society to prevent further molestations, Evan felt that the entire world was now on notice that no parent should leave their child alone with the singer; it was not necessary for him to risk his family's safety to ensure that Michael go to prison. Evan also believed that for Michael, the loss of his career was a horrendous punishment. He would continue to make music and sell records, but he'd never be one iota of what he had been. And worst of all, his dream of becoming King of the Silver Screen was dead.

"I got close enough to Michael to understand his dreams," Evan commented, "and I knew that his fall from grace would be like a stake through his heart. In that way, at least, justice had been served."

Evan and his family mulled over the decision carefully, and in the end told the DA that they would consider testifying if they were placed in a witness protection program immediately after the trial. For reasons that were never disclosed, their request was turned down.

Nevertheless the DA was insistent that the Chandler's testify, and at times Evan came close to giving in. "The overriding factor was always the safety issue," Evan commented. "But I also had this gnawing feeling that the DA was more concerned with saving face . . . with the politics and notoriety of it all, than with seeing justice done. It would have been their O.J. before O.J. ever happened. Maybe I'm wrong, but that's the feeling I got — from L.A., that is, not Santa Barbara. I mean, Tom Sneddon wanted us to testify, too. But he seemed genuine, like his entire motivation was to put this criminal behind bars. He understood my fears and my need to protect my family, and he didn't try to push me around. I have a lot of respect for Sneddon."

– 26 –

After the bomb threat and the episode with Pfeiffer, the office staff was too freaked out to come to work. The dentist with whom Evan shared an office insisted that Evan move his practice. And the building management insisted that he hire a private security service.[112]

Evan understood their fears better than they did. "It was unfair to put them through any more of this," he agreed. So he turned his appointment book over to his colleague and sent a letter to his patients telling them he was taking a temporary leave and that they'd be in good hands until he got back.

Evan believed he would return to work within six months, but as it turned out he had filled his last cavity. "It was a mixed blessing. Leaving dentistry was something I wanted to do for years. But this was not the exit I had in mind."

There were those who believed that Evan now had gobs of money and could pursue his real desires, the ones for which he had extorted Michael in the first place. "The next time you see a screenplay by Evan Chandler, you'll know it was paid for with Michael Jackson's money," a prominent radio personality commented on the day the settlement was announced.[113]

This joker was just one of many in the media who incorrectly reported that Evan was in control of Jordie's money. More concerned with ratings than with the truth, they were oblivious, or perhaps just unconcerned, with the effect their words had on people's lives.

---

[112] Evan checked into it and not only found the cost prohibitive, but each of the companies he contacted told him he would be a difficult target to protect.

[113] The John & Ken Show, a call-in type talk show on KFI radio in L.A.

After the media announced that Evan controlled his son's fortune, several of Evan's patients all of a sudden threatened malpractice suits against him. Most of these claims were so frivolous they died a quick death. One or two were paid because the amount was so small it was more costly for the insurance company to defend than to fight. And one went to trial, but was dismissed when the plaintiff, knowing she was losing, attempted, in the middle of the case, to admit new evidence that a repressed memory had surfaced of her being sexually molested while under sedation in the dental chair.

Next in line was Ernie Rizzo, the colorful P.I. from Chicago who had a long-standing history as Pellicano's archenemy. Rizzo went on national TV and announced that Evan had hired him. The following day Evan's criminal attorney, Richard Hirsch, went on TV and fired Rizzo, just to make sure there were plenty of witnesses. Hirsch also sent Rizzo a letter to the same effect.

Rizzo claimed that since Evan had hired him, only Evan could fire him, and after the settlement he sent Evan a bill for fifty grand and sued Evan in Chicago. Rizzo never received a dime, but ten years later he was back on TV pitching his old story.

In the scheme of things, the patients and Rizzo were minnows; there were bigger fish to fry. Unfortunately, it was Evan who was everyone's catch of the day.

– 27 –

Although June had told DCS she was willing to let Jordie decide when he wanted to see her, she apparently was not willing to wait too long. According to Evan, she hired an attorney and threatened to sue him for interfering with her parental rights. She accused him of influencing Jordie not to see her.

Jordie had mixed feelings toward his mother after the settlement, Evan said, but he continued to maintain a relationship with her. June would pick him up at Evan's in the morning and take him to school. On weekends they'd have lunch, take in a movie, maybe drive to the beach. The one thing Jordie would not do was spend the night at June's house. It gave him the willies.

In August of 1994, when Dave sued Michael for causing the breakup of his family, Dave added his seven-year-old daughter, Kelly, to the lawsuit by claiming Michael was the cause of her estrangement from Jordie. "They didn't even tell Jordie in advance," Evan said. "He heard the news on TV."According to Evan, Jordie reacted by exclaiming, "That's bullshit! I don't want to go over to that house. It has nothing to do with Michael."

Dave's willingness to drag Jordie back into the fray was the last thing the boy needed. June, though not a party to the lawsuit, did not protest when Dave included their daughter in the action.

"Michael did not break up Dave's family," Evan commented. "He and June were on and off — mostly off — long before Michael came into their lives. As for Jordie, Dave ended that relationship when he cooperated with Pellicano."

I was visiting with my family in April of 1995 when June called and asked for Jordie. I answered, said a brief hello, and handed Jordie the phone. "Shit!" he exclaimed, holding his hand over the mouthpiece. "I told her not to call me."

Contact between mother and son has remained minimal, if any.

Besides suing Michael for destroying his family, Dave sued Evan for assault and battery. (The altercation on Evan's doorstep after the failed meeting at June's.) Larry Feldman's advice to Evan was to counter-sue Dave and June. (June was certain to be witness for Dave.) As a defendant, Evan would incur enormous legal fees, even if he won. But as a plaintiff he would receive money if he won; at least enough to recover legal fees. And Larry was certain Evan would win.

Although Evan's attorney made it clear that Jordie was his most important witness, Evan refused to drag his son back into the spotlight and instructed his attorney to word all court documents so that Jordie would not be included.

Apparently June did not share the same concerns for Jordie. She answered Evan's complaint by claiming that his suit was an attempt to extort money from them by using his son. Jordie would now *have* to be called as a witness.

Robert Shapiro made a statement back in September of 1993 that was so simple its profundity did not register at the time. "Don't for one minute think this will all be over when the suit against Michael ends. There will be all kinds of lawsuits after that; there always are when large amounts of money are involved. But know this, no matter what anybody accuses anybody else of doing, it will always come back to the same question, did Michael Jackson molest Jordie? Whichever side of that question a person is on, will determine their guilt or innocence."

Without June's cooperation Dave's lawsuits against Michael and Evan didn't have a prayer. At court, Evan took June into a private room and begged her to tell the whole story just as it had happened — about Fields, Pellicano and the extortion claim. June refused.

If Dave or June really gave a shit about Jordie," Evan commented, "they wouldn't put him through this. Everything they do tells him money is more important to them than he is, yet they expect him to love them."

June may think it was only Evan she was hurting, but it went much deeper than that. "What she failed to realize," Evan commented, "was that each time she had the opportunity to own up and chose not to, in Jordie's mind she was making the same choice she had made each time she allowed Michael to take him into the bedroom."[114]

– 28 –

Another lawsuit that came about as an offshoot of the Jackson scandal was brought by Barry Rothman against Michael Jackson, Bert Fields, Howard Weitzman and Anthony Pellicano. He sued them for defamation for publicly branding him an extortionist.

As part of his defense Bert Fields claimed that even if he did call Rothman an extortionist, he was immune from liability under an obscure but powerful California law commonly known in legal quarters as "the litigation privilege."

The privilege is based on one of the fundamental principles of our legal system, the right to be represented by an attorney. But an attorney cannot vigorously represent his client if the attorney is constantly worried about

---

114 The lawsuits were voluntarily dismissed by each side before going to trial.

being sued for every negative thing he says about the other side. So the law provides immunity.

In plain English, the statute says that if an attorney and his client are involved in a lawsuit, or even if they have a reasonable expectation of being involved in a lawsuit, they can make any accusations they want about the other lawyer and his client as long as those accusations are related to the dispute.

In his complaint Rothman described his role in the scandal as the attorney who was hired by the Chandler family to provide legal services, specifically, "to obtain compensation" for personal injury, meaning the molestation of Jordie by Jackson. Fields cleverly agreed, and concluded that "this can only mean that (Rothman) was hired to pursue legal action against Jackson."

Fields then argued that since he was involved in a legitimate legal dispute against Rothman, he could call Rothman and Evan extortionists and could not be sued for defamation.

Fields made the following claims in his defense.

> Assuming . . . that defendants did accuse plaintiff of extortion, and did file false police reports, **said conduct took place in connection with personal injury court action which the Chandlers filed or contemplated filing.**

> Assuming defendants made an alleged extortion charge, it clearly relates to the underlying action because it was in direct response to Rothman's allegations of child molestation against Jackson. . . . It is evident therefore **that defendants so acted (if they did) for the purposes of discouraging the Chandlers from pursuing legal action against Jackson.**

> The communication to the media is privileged if it relates to the litigation. . . . Rothman contends that although he made a twenty million dollars **settlement demand** to Jackson on the child molestation charges, the alleged extortion retort did not occur in a "judicial proceeding" under Civil Code 47(2) because there was no actual lawsuit yet filed. Rothman's argument is plainly erroneous . . . the privilege to defame **in the course of a judicial proceeding** 'is not limited to statements made during trial but can extend . . . to steps taken prior thereto' and 'communications preliminary to a proposed judicial procedure.'

Contrary to the public claims made by the Jackson camp in 1993, Fields did not argue that he was involved in a criminal plot by Evan and Barry to extort money from Michael. Not at all. He was quite clear that he was involved in a legitimate legal dispute brought by an attorney who was trying to negotiate a settlement on behalf of the Chandlers. *Precisely what Evan and Barry Rothman claimed all along!*

You don't have to be an attorney to understand that the privilege works both ways. If Evan and Barry did call Michael a child molester, they did so not as part of a criminal extortion attempt, but for the same reason Fields, Weitzman and Pellicano called them extortionists, in the vigorous defense of their legal rights.

Three years after the scandal ended, as a witness in a lawsuit unconnected to Rothman's, attorney Bert Fields made the following claims under oath:

> Pellicano never worked for him.
>
> He never heard any tapes.
>
> He didn't know that Pellicano had played any tapes.
>
> He had heard that Pellicano was acting as some sort of spokesperson but he didn't know that Pellicano had publicly called Evan an extortionist.
>
> He was away on vacation when the story broke and had no idea what was going on.
>
> He doesn't recall where or when he went on vacation. He lost his passport and keeps no records.

And on and on it goes.

✳   ✳   ✳

Evan was not surprised by Fields' defense in the Rothman case. What upset Evan the most was that the media did not understand the significance of what Fields had said, and allowed it to go largely unreported. Here was Michael Jackson's lead attorney stating that Evan's claims against Michael, true or untrue, were made properly and legally. It should have been a headline as big as the ones that called Evan an extortionist. But it got buried.

– 29 –

On January 25, 1994, on the steps of Santa Monica courthouse, Johnnie Cochran announced to the world, "The time has come for Michael Jackson to move on to new business, to get on with his life, to start the healing process, and to move his career forward to even greater heights." Jackson also "recanted his charge that he was the victim of an extortion attempt by the boy's father."[115]

At the same press conference, Larry Feldman announced that the boy's civil suit had been dropped and that his client, like Jackson, "needs closure and wants to get on with his life."

The terms of the settlement were not made public, but there is no doubt that one of the conditions was that both sides promised not to accuse the other of any wrongdoing or exploit the issue in any way. In other words, everyone agreed to keep their mouths shut.

Jordie and Evan kept their word; they made no public statements or appearances. Unfortunately the same cannot be said of Michael and his henchmen.

They began slowly, almost innocuously. On January 16, 1994, while Cochran and Feldman were at the bargaining table, a feature article on Jackson's manager, Sandy Gallin, appeared in the *Los Angeles Times'* Calendar section. Gallin referred to the molestation allegations as "just another extortion attempt," but he also stated, "when all the facts come out and people find out how Michael was taken advantage of and extorted, I believe the public sympathy will be enormous toward him."[116]

One week later, at the settlement press conference, Jackson's lawyers announced that Michael "will soon speak out about the agony, torture and pain he has had to suffer during the past six months." According to Evan, the prepared public statement that he approved did not contain any words to the effect that Michael would be permitted to speak out.

Following Gallin came Anthony Pellicano, who completely ignored the

---

[115] Jim Newton, "Jackson Settles Abuse Suit but Insists He Is Innocent," *Los Angeles Times*, January 26, 1994.

[116] Claudia Eller, "Managing in Turbulent Times," *Los Angeles Times*, January 16, 1994.

terms of the settlement and started in on Evan *the very day* the agreement was announced in the press. On January 26, 1993, Pellicano told the *Los Angeles Times* that "the settlement merely reaffirmed his (the boy's) family was after the singer's money. . . . Obviously there has been an exchange of money to settle this case. It all boils down to money."

In September 1994, Pellicano increased his attack by appearing on the TV program *American Justice,* in which he spoke openly and often about Evan and Jordie. A picture of Evan was shown on the screen while the narrator discussed "Chandler's threats to go public with the allegation (against Jackson)." Evan's name was read aloud while his picture was shown.

Almost every sentence in this broadcast contained violations of the agreement.

"(Chandler's) demands for money";

"Pellicano's alleged extortion scenario now began to seem, at least to the public, more plausible";

"The police search of Jackson's ranch found nothing incriminating";

"Pellicano said the allegations (against Jackson) were nothing more than a blackmail attempt".

Portions of the Rothman-Pellicano tape were also played. And the program was aired again in 1995.

– 30 –

One month after *American Justice* aired, in the October 1994 issue of *GQ Magazine,* Mary A. Fischer published a fourteen-page cover story titled "Was Michael Framed?" Fischer offered her readers "a persuasive argument that Michael molested no one and that he himself may have been the victim of a well conceived plan to extract money from him."

The full analysis of the Fischer article is lengthy and can be found on the Web site. For now, a look at Fischer's use of Dave's tape recording of Evan will provide an insight into her journalistic standards and integrity.

Fischer sets up the scene with this quote of Evan's.

I had a good communication with Michael. We were friends. I liked him and I respected him and everything else for what he is. There was no reason why he had to stop calling me. I sat in the room one day and talked to Michael and told him exactly what I want out of this whole relationship. What *I* want. [Fischer's italics.]

Fischer stopped the quote here, leaving the reader with the same implication that she would be pushing throughout her article, that Evan wanted money. But the quote was cut short, leaving a false impression. Evan's statement continues:

What I want, okay, so he wouldn't have to figure me out. And one of the things I said was that we always have to be able to talk to each other. That's the rule. Because I know that as soon as you stop talking to each other weird things start going on and then people [tape irregularity]. (169)

The conversation at this point on the tape finds Evan lamenting to Dave about how June and Michael have refused to talk to him about his concerns for Jordie. By cutting the quote short and taking it out of context, Fischer leaves the impression that Evan wanted to talk about money.

Fischer then quotes Evan again, twice. (This will be referred to later as quote "A".)

There are other people involved that are waiting for my phone call that are in certain positions. I've paid them to do it. Everything's going according to a certain plan that isn't just mine. (220) Once I make that phone call, this guy [his attorney, Barry K. Rothman, presumably] is going to destroy everybody in sight in any devious, nasty, cruel way that he can do it. And I've given him full authority to do that. (29)

(The numbers in parentheses did not appear in Fischer's article, they were added for this book and their significance will be discussed shortly.)

In the context of Fischer's article as a whole, the implication here is that if Evan doesn't get the money he'll unleash his "certain plan" to falsely accuse Michael in public of child molestation. Fischer continues (this will be referred to later as quote "B"):

Chandler predicted what would, in fact, transpire six weeks later. "If I go through with this I win big time. There's no way I lose. I've checked that inside out. I will get everything I want, and they will be destroyed forever. June will lose (custody of the son) . . . and Michael's career will be over."

"Does that help the boy?" Schwartz asked.

"That's irrelevant to me," Chandler replied. (134) "It's going to be bigger than all of us put together. The whole thing is going to crash down on everybody and destroy everybody in sight. (206-207) It will be a massacre if I don't get what I want." (27)

And with this Fischer continued her "theory" that Evan had a plan to "win big-time" money by threatening to ruin Michael's career, and that Evan didn't give a damn about the "irrelevant" effect his plan would have on Jordie.

The numbers in parentheses refer to the pages of the official court transcript of the tape on which each sentence can be found. Notice that Fischer pulled sentences from all over the place, sometimes more than one hundred pages apart, and strung them together with no indication to her readers that she had done so.

In quote "B" Fischer took the "irrelevant" sentence from transcript page 134, and then added sentences from pages 206 and 27, both of which refer to destroying Michael. By stringing them together Fischer made it sound as if Evan only briefly addressed Dave's question about Jordie's welfare — answering that it was "irrelevant" — and then immediately went back to his main concern about threatening to destroy Michael if he didn't acquiesce to his extortion demand.

What follows is the relevant section of official transcript. The three sentences Fischer linked together appear in bold type.

Pages 133-134

EVAN: I don't know where it'll go, but what I'm saying is that when people — when you — when people cut off communication totally, you only have two choices: To forget about them, or you get frustrated by their action. I can't forget about them. I love them. That's it. I don't like them. I still love Jordie, but I do not like them because I do not like the people that they've become. But I do love them, and because I love them I don't want to see them [tape irregularity]. That's why I was willing to talk. I have nothing to gain by talking. **If I go through with this, I win big time. There's no way that I lose.** I've checked that out inside out.

DAVE: But when you say "winning," what are you talking about, "winning"?

EVAN: **I will get everything I want, and they will be totally — they will be destroyed forever. They will be destroyed. June is gonna lose Jordie.** She will have no right to ever see him again. That's a fact, Dave. That's what . . .

DAVE: Does that help . . .?

EVAN: **Michael's career will be over.**

DAVE: **Does that help Jordie?**

EVAN: Michael's career will be over.

DAVE: And does that help Jordie?

EVAN: **That's irrelevant to me.** The bottom line to me is, yes, June is harming him, and Michael is harming him. I can prove that, and I will prove that, and if they force me to go to court about it, I will [tape irregularity], and I will be granted custody. She will have no rights whatsoever.

Pages 205-207

EVAN: Easy to say that, Dave, but when you tell me you're in a survival mode so you can't pay attention to your children, it doesn't jive with "I would die for that kid."

DAVE: Wait. I'm ashamed of that. I'm not proud of that, but when you . . .

EVAN: I mean, how do you . . . I mean, which of those two statements should I choose to believe, because they're both entirely opposite each other? "I would die for that kid" or "I'm in a survival mode and I . . ."

DAVE: I would do anything for Jordie. I would lose everything. I would die for Jordie. That's the bottom line.

EVAN: Then why don't you just back me up right now and let's get rid of Michael Jackson.

DAVE: Because I don't know the facts.

EVAN: Okay. Well, when you know the facts, when you see the facts come out, then you'll make a decision at that point.

DAVE: Right. That's fair. I mean, that's more than fair, but this . . .

EVAN: It's unfortunately gonna be too late, then, and nothing's gonna matter at that point.

DAVE: Why?

EVAN: Because the fact is so fucking overwhelming that everybody's going to be destroyed in the process. The facts themselves are gonna . . . once this thing starts rolling the facts themselves are gonna overwhelm. **It's gonna be bigger than all of us put together, and the whole thing's just gonna crash down on everybody and destroy everybody in its sight.** That's [tape irregularity] humiliating, believe me.

DAVE: Yeah. And is that good?

EVAN: Yeah. It's great.

DAVE: Why?

EVAN: Great, because June and Jordie and Michael have forced me to take it to the extreme to get their attention. How pitiful — pitifuckingful they are to have done that. I've tried to get their attention. I've cried on the phone, I've talked on the phone. I have begged on the phone, and all I get back is, "Go fuck yourself" on the phone, and so now I'm still trying to get their attention. . . .

Pages 26-28

EVAN: This is life and death for my son. I have to get their attention. If I don't get it, if I haven't gotten it on the phone and I don't get it tomorrow, this guy will certainly get it. That's the next step. And you want to know something? I even have somebody after him if he doesn't [tape irregularity]. But I don't want [tape irregularity]. I'm not kidding. I mean what I told you before. It's true. I mean, **it could be a massacre if I don't get what I want.** But I do believe this person will get what he wants. So he would just really love [tape irregularity] nothing better than to have this go forward. He is nasty, he is mean, he is very smart [tape irregularity], and he's hungry for the publicity [tape irregularity] better for him. And that's where it'll go . . .

DAVE: You don't think everyone loses?

EVAN: [Simultaneous, inaudible] totally humiliate him in every way . . .

DAVE: That . . . everyone doesn't lose in that?

EVAN: That's not the issue. See, the issue is that if I have to go that far I can't stop and think "Who wins and who loses?" All I can think about is I only have one goal, and the goal is to get their attention so that [tape irregularity] concerns are, and as long as they don't want to talk to me, I can't tell them what my concerns are, so I have to go step by step, each time escalating the attention-getting mechanism, and that's all I regard him as, as an attention-getting mechanism.

Here is the breakdown of Fischer's first quote of Evan, quote "A" above. The conversation concerns the meeting Evan demanded between himself, Jordie, June and Michael when he left a message on June's answering machine.

Pages 220-224

DAVE: But I want to be there.

EVAN: Well, then you have to be there at 8:30. It's already set. **There are other people involved that are waiting for my phone call that are intentionally going to be in certain positions [tape irregularity]. I paid them to do it.** They're doing their job. I gotta just go ahead and follow through on the time zone. I mean the time set out. **Everything is going according to a certain plan that isn't just mine.** There's other people involved. . . .

DAVE: How about 8:37?

EVAN: Nope. Eight thirty-one is not even going to work. I mean, they're going to have to be there or not be there. It's up to them what happens now. I mean, it's not going to be [tape irregularity] whether they're there or not. But if they are there, it's going to be far better than if they're not . . . I mean, they're going to have a chance to make things a lot better if they're there.

My instructions were to kill and destroy [tape irregularity], I'm telling you. I mean, and by killing and destroying, I'm going to torture them, Dave. Because that's what June has done to me. She has tortured me, and she's gonna know that you can't [tape irregularity].

I'll tell you one thing that Jordie has no idea about, and that's what love means. He doesn't even have the remotest idea. He can't learn it from June. She doesn't know what it means. She has no conception of what it means. So maybe, you know, I can get [inaudible] teach him that. I don't know. Part of it [tape irregularity] other people and communicating, and those are three things that must be in place in order for a loving relationship to exist, because all of those things show that you care about that other person. Not one thing [tape irregularity].

DAVE: Yeah, but it was there.

EVAN: No, I don't think it ever was, now that I look at her behavior, I'm just saying that June is a brilliant and pathologic personality. What you see on the surface ain't even remotely related to what's really going on underneath. And I believe that that will come out in lie detector [tape irregularity] psychological evaluations which they're all gonna have to do.

DAVE: And you think that's good for Jordie?

EVAN: I think that in the long run — of course it's not the best thing for Jordie. The best thing for Jordie would be for everybody to sit there and peaceably resolve amongst themselves [tape irregularity], but because they're not willing to do that, I'm not allowed to have a say in what the best [tape irregularity]. I'm not even allowed to [tape irregularity] Jordie is. I'm not allowed to have a say in anything about Jordie. So when you ask me that question [tape irregularity], I would welcome them to do that, but they don't care. They don't care about what I think, so they don't ask me that question. Do I think — I mean, just to answer your question, I think that [tape irregularity] for Jordie either way in the short [tape irregularity], in the short term. I think in the long term he's got a [tape irregularity] a chance of being a happy human being if I do what I have to do than if I let things go the way they are.

Now the second sentence from quote "A", that Fischer lifted from page 29 of the official transcript, one hundred pages *before* the first sentence.

EVAN: All I can think about is I only have one goal, and the goal is to get their attention so that [tape irregularity] concerns are, and as long as they don't want to talk to me, I can't tell them what my concerns are, so I have to go step by step, each time escalating the attention-getting mechanism, and that's all I regard him as, an attention-getting mechanism.

Unfortunately, after that, it's totally out of [tape irregularity]. It'll take on so much momentum of its own that it's going to be out of all our control. It's going to be monumentally huge, and I'm not going to have any way to stop it. No one else is either at that point. I mean, **once I make that phone call, this guy's just going to destroy everybody in sight in any devious, nasty, cruel way that he can do it. And I've given him full authority to do that.**

To go beyond tomorrow, that would mean I have done every possible thing in my individual power to tell them to sit down and talk to me; and if they still [tape irregularity], I got to escalate the attention-getting mechanism. He's the next one. I can't go to somebody nice [tape irregularity]. It doesn't work with them. I already found that out. Get some niceness and just go fuck yourself.

Basically, what they have to know, ultimately, is that their lives are over, if they don't sit down. One way or the other, it'll either go to the next step or the [tape irregularity]. I'm not stopping until I get their attention. Do I [tape irregularity] the only goal is right now I have to do what I think is best for Jordie. . . .

The official transcript is 224 pages. Fischer used sentences from page 26 to 220. Clearly she had access to the entire tape or transcript; she could not have committed these mutilations otherwise. One year previous to Fischer's article, Maureen Orth quoted from some of the same places on the tape in her exposé for *Vanity Fair.* Orth's quotes match the official version perfectly.

Having made every effort to convince her readers that Evan must have been after Michael's money, Fischer then set about explaining how he planned to get it. In half-inch bold-black letters at the top of the page, she quoted Evan again.

> This attorney I found, I picked the nastiest son of a bitch I could find. All he wants to do is get this out as fast as he can, as big as he can, and humiliate as many people as he can. He's mean, he's smart, and he's hungry for the publicity.

Taken out of context it's easy to claim that Evan was talking about going to the media. But he never says that. In fact, he never says directly how his attorney plans to "get it out." But he does say so indirectly, and often. Fischer had the entire tape and knew that Evan had made copious statements about being "forced to go to court" (134, 155) to prove that Michael and June's actions "are extremely harmful to him [Jordie]" (137, 140, 150,154, 155, 156, 182, 195, etc.), about being "granted custody" and June having "no rights whatsoever" to see Jordie (134), about putting June, Michael and Jordie "on the stand" where "they will all be asked questions, and they will all have psychological examinations" (153), and on and on.[117]

Many lawyers spend their entire careers hoping for that one big case to catapult them into the limelight and set them up for more big cases. Indeed, although some of the lawyers involved in the 1993 scandal enjoyed a degree of notoriety beforehand, they all became well-known national figures because of that case: Fields, Weitzman, Cochrane, Feldman.

Barry Rothman wanted that too. So when Evan said that Rothman wanted "to get this out as fast as he can" and was "hungry for the publicity," he did not mean that Rothman was going to go to the media; that would have done nothing for Rothman's career. He meant that Rothman wanted to file and win a lawsuit. Which is exactly what Feldman did two months later, and no one called him an extortionist. And, like Feldman, Rothman's first move was to do everything he could to settle the case privately.

---

[117] The numbers in parentheses are the pages of the official transcript where the quoted statements can be found.

All Fischer had to do to figure out what Evan was talking about on the tape — and thus understand Evan and Barry's "certain plan" — was to look at what they did when June and Michael refused to meet with Evan the day after the tape was made. Less than forty-eight hours later they did just what Evan said he was going to do at the meeting, he presented June with the change of custody agreement and demanded that she sign it. This is the agreement June signed at Pellicano's office, ostensibily on the advice of Bert Fields.

By omitting vast amounts of dialogue on the tape that make nonsense out of her extortion theory, and by rearranging the dialogue to alter its meaning, Fischer effectively created a fictitious conversation. She had to, because she started out with the intention of making the facts fit her "theory," as opposed to the other way around.

Unbelievable as it may seem, Fischer's article was nominated for a National Magazine Award, the most prestigious prize in magazine journalism. With the current scandal now in full swing, Fischer is out there again, pitching her 1994 article for republication.

✳ ✳ ✳

Evan considered suing Fischer and *GQ* for defamation. But a trial against *GQ* would be exhausting and expensive, and *GQ* would have at its disposal a battery of lawyers to scream about freedom of the press. Even worse, in the courtroom and in the media the case would become a de facto molestation trial, with all of the key figures dragged back into the limelight. The Chandlers did not want to live through that nightmare again. So they turned the other cheek and let it pass.

But the *GQ* article opened wounds that had barely begun to heal. Jordie wanted nothing more than to shed his identity as "the Jackson kid" and be a normal teenager. That was difficult enough to accomplish without the likes of Mary Fischer dredging the story back into the public eye, especially in such a negative manner. Would the parents of his schoolmates read the article and talk about it at home? Would kids that didn't know who he was now find out? Would he be pinned up against the school fence again and threatened? Or worse?

Evan was cut to the core by Fischer. He tried to keep a stiff upper lip, but the pain was evident in his face and in his voice. It was not until years later that I realized how deeply my brother had been hurt. Looking back, I believe the *GQ* article scored such a direct hit that it sent Evan into an emotional tailspin from which he could not pull out. Aided by events that were yet to come, and, in truth, Evan's own frailties, it would eventually cause him to crash and burn.

– 31 –

With the publication of the *GQ* article it became crystal clear that the agreement between the Chandlers and Jackson to keep mum was a farce. Too much had been said about the alleged extortion, by persons within Jackson's inner circle, to believe that these were isolated events and not part of a plan to resurrect Michael's career.

Conspicuously missing from the plan, however, was direct participation by Jackson himself.

On June 14, 1995, all that changed. Emboldened by the Chandler's turn-the-other-cheek response to the indirect attacks, Michael took center stage and appeared on a *Prime Time Live* interview with Diane Sawyer. As tens of millions across the globe watched and listened, Jackson and his wife, Lisa Marie Presley, talked openly about the events surrounding the molestation scandal.

ABC advertised the show as they would an important news event. They promised the public an independent, "no-holds-barred" interview in which nothing was off limits. They led the world to believe that the truth would be revealed. A child claimed he had been molested. These were serious charges.

After a detailed investigation of the backstage deals between ABC and Jackson, journalist Maureen Orth concluded that *Prime Time's* viewers got "something less than the truth." In her September 1995 exposé of the interview for *Vanity Fair*, Orth wrote that "many with a detailed knowledge of the case were appalled by what ABC News let Jackson get away with." Santa Barbara District Attorney Tom Sneddon felt so strongly about the inaccuracies of the broadcast that he felt compelled to set the record straight.

In response to Sawyer's question about the police photographs of his genitals, Jackson said that "there was nothing that matched me to those charges. Nothing! Nothing! Nothing! The whole thing is a lie!" Sawyer did not challenge the denials.

Sneddon told *Vanity Fair*, "his [Jackson's] statement on TV is untrue and incorrect, and not consistent with the evidence in this case." Jordie's description was an accurate match to the police photographs.

When Sawyer asked about the searches of his Santa Barbara and Los Angeles homes, Jackson replied, "they found nothing, nothing, nothing that could say Michael Jackson did this."

DA Sneddon responded. "The idea that there are not any photos or pictures of anything is pure poppycock. The statement there were no books or photos of nude children on his premises is incorrect. That is not truthful."

Maureen Orth reported, "Police found a lewd, commercially published hardcover book of black-and-white photos of nude boys aged about seven to twelve 'at play'." Orth quoted one investigator as saying that the book "is often found in the homes of pedophiles." And she reported, "there was also a picture of a nude little boy, scantily draped with a sheet, found in Jackson's bedroom."

In response to Sawyer's question about "other settlements in process . . . with children making these kinds of demands," Jackson answered, "That's not true. No. No. No. That's not true."

Sawyer let Jackson's answer stand, never reminding her listeners what the district attorney had stated in his press conference nine months earlier. "Investigatory efforts uncovered additional allegations of sexual misconduct occurring between Mr. Jackson and a second boy (and) also revealed the existence of a third alleged victim." After the Sawyer interview Sneddon told the press, "The status regarding those two is basically the same." And Orth reported, "Law enforcement sources confirm that there is another boy who has a lawyer and is currently negotiating a settlement with Jackson."

But it was Sawyer's statement that Jackson had been "cleared of all the charges" that DA Sneddon called the most "glaring mistake." Sneddon had stated in his press conference that Jackson had not been charged "because of the legal unavailability of the primary alleged victim," and not because of "any issue of credibility of alleged victims." "Michael Jackson has not been cleared" the DA told *Vanity Fair.* "The state of the investigation is in suspension until somebody comes forward."

Sneddon was dumbfounded by Sawyer's interview. "I have no idea what the purpose of her show is," he told the press, making it clear that *he had spent three hours with* Prime Time's *producers prepping them about the facts of the case before the interview aired.*

In her in-depth analysis, Maureen Orth wrote,

> It was learned that ABC had swapped the airing of 10 TV commercials for Jackson's new album ads — worth between $300,000 and $1.5 million — for the rights to 'future Michael Jackson music videos.' . . . Executives at CBS and NBC said that Jackson's handlers had clearly been looking for a "package." . . . A producer at one network told me, 'It's difficult to pretend there was no quid pro quo in the ABC deal'.

Jackson, not Sawyer or ABC News, was in control of the interview, an event the *Washington Post* called "an example of masterfully manipulative marketing."[118]

Apparently Sawyer and the producers of *Prime Time* made a conscious decision not to air any of the information supplied by district attorney Sneddon. And though ABC's news division claimed that Michael's video deal was made with ABC's entertainment division, and that the two divisions had nothing to do with each another, the statements from CBS and NBC indicate otherwise. "Surely someone at the top of ABC had to know about both," Orth commented. Surely they did.

But ABC and Jackson went further than merely proclaiming his innocence and withholding the evidence that linked him to the crimes. The interview also included a video of Evan in his car, with a voiceover of Evan from Dave's illegal recording. And just to make sure the audience understood what Evan was saying, ABC placed his words at the bottom of the screen. "If I go through with this I win big time. There's no way I lose."

This is the same quote that was used by Jackson's people in their original smear campaign, and by *GQ* and by other publications. In effect, Sawyer and

---

[118] Richard Harrington, "Is He History?" *Washington Post,* June 18, 1995.

ABC were aiding in the continued portrayal of Evan as an extortionist. ABC never reported that Jackson had publicly withdrawn his extortion charge, and that Evan had never been charged with the crime.

In reality, *Prime Time Live* was an integral part of Michael's campaign to revitalize his image and promote sales of his new album, *HIStory*. Maureen Orth was being tactful when she accused *Prime Time Live* of offering "something less than the truth." What she really meant was, they lied.

For Michael, the *Prime Time* interview was the crowning jewel in a PR campaign to publicize the release of his first post-molestation album, *HIStory*. *Thriller* may have been his biggest seller, but *HIStory* would be the most important album of his life. Michael's career was barely breathing. If the album failed, it would die. (An indepth analysis of the *Prime Time* interview can be found on the Web site.)

– 32 –

Irrespective of the quality of the music, the album was a blatant violation of the settlement agreement. Numerous press reports described several songs as an attack on Jordie, Evan, Larry Feldman and District Attorney Sneddon.

> Through 15 new songs . . . Jackson rants, stutters, hiccups, and screams about the supposed injustices carried out against him. Barely a song goes by without some reference to his newfound status as the world's greatest victim. 'Money,' (one of the songs on the album) seems plainly directed at the thirteen-year-old boy. . . .[119]

> In one of his new songs Jackson used the phrase "kick me kike me, Jew me sue me."

> Semantically, there's a clear distinction being made between the harshly pejorative "kike" on the one hand, and black or white on the other. Syntactically, "Jew" here is a verb, synonymous with sue, what Jews are presumed to do, like some aggressive lawyers much in the news and some whom Mr. Jackson may lately have had some dealings.[120]

---

[119] Karen Schoemer, "Curiouser and Curiouser," *Newsweek,* June 26, 1995.

[120] Richard Klein, "Way Beyond Megalomania," *New York Times*, Op-Ed, June 19, 1995. (Michael later apologized for the religious slur, saying that he had only recently learned that the words were considered anti-semitic. *Hollywood Reporter,* July 13, 1995.)

> In 11 out of 15 new Michael Jackson songs on HIStory . . . the singer uses his music as payback to a world of accusers.[121]

> Sneddon is believed to be the subject of one of Jackson's newest songs, "D.S.", about a "cold man" (described as the "BSTA", as in SBDA), who is out to get him. . . . the liner notes . . . say the song is about a "Dom Sheldon," but the lyrics as sung by Jackson sound more like "Tom Sneddon." [122]

The Los Angeles Times reported that Jackson began the recording of these songs "18 months ago," which places the timing around November or December of 1993, just *prior* to the signing of the settlement agreement.[123]

Image building campaigns of this magnitude are not spur of the moment decisions. They are carefully thought out and planned far in advance by highly trained professionals, and consist of a multitude of public relations maneuvers involving a variety of media formats. Certainly SONY did not commit thirty million dollars on an uncoordinated, hastily designed program.

> Sony Corp . . . is set to launch a $30 million marketing campaign for Mr. Jackson's new album. . . . Sony is counting on the double album . . . to generate sales of at least $500 million worldwide. The company will be "disappointed" if the album . . . fails to sell at least 20 million copies, says Mell Ilberman, chairman of Sony Music.[124]

> Sony Entertainment, which signed a much-hyped deal potentially worth $1 billion with Jackson in 1991, is taking no chances. Still hoping to salvage its investment with the scandal-scarred singer, Sony is reportedly spending $30 million to promote the album in a publicity megablitz.[125]

Some of the top brass at Sony must have known, or at least suspected, that Michael's relationships with young boys was unholy. Certainly none of them would leave their young sons alone in a room with the singer. They also should have suspected that the lyrics to Michael's new songs were a

---

[121] *New York Daily News,* June 19, 1995.

[122] Rhonda Parks, "Magazine Story Sends Media After Sneddon," *Santa Barbara News Press,* August 11, 1995.

[123] Steve Hochman, "Will the Fans Be Thrilled or Chilled by Jackson 'HIStory,'" *Los Angeles Times,* April 11, 1995.

[124] Jeffrey A. Trachtenberg, "Sony Bets Big on Michael Jackson's Comeback," *Wall Street Journal,* May 19, 1995.

[125] *Entertainment Weekly,* June 16, 1995.

violation of the settlement agreement. Nevertheless they invested thirty million dollars in hopes of making a huge profit.

> Jackson's larger audience, the one Sony is hoping will buy his album and generate sales of $500 million, may not be as easy to please. Sony execs are said to be worried that Jackson decided to address the 1993 scandal so bluntly in *HIStory.* But no one tells MJ what to do.[126]

The Sony deal was potentially as lucrative for Jackson as it was for Sony. In his widely acclaimed 1991 Jackson biography, *The Magic and the Madness,* author J. Randy Taraborrelli reported that Jackson's own recording label, *Nation Records,* would get a 25 percent royalty from Sony. This could amount to as much as several hundred millions dollars. The advances alone were worth $50 million.[127]

That Michael had a lot to lose if he could not resurrect his "scandal-scarred" career does not begin to describe what was at stake. Besides the loss of income from the Sony deal there would be no product endorsements, no concert tours, no further appearances with presidents and kings, and most of all, Michael would lose forever the one thing he wanted most, his dream of becoming a movie star.

All Michael had ever been, and all he hoped to be, was riding on the sale of *HIStory,* and he was prepared to do whatever it took to recapture his fame.

– 33 –

With the *Prime Time Live* interview, Michael had destroyed whatever pretense might have existed regarding the agreement to keep silent. Not only had he appeared before a worldwide audience and lied to their face, he had solicited a major media conglomerate to help him convince the public that he was the innocent victim of an extortion attempt by Evan. Things were back to where they had started in August of 1993. Where would it end?

---

[126] *Entertainment Weekly*, September 16, 1995.

[127] J. Randy Taraborrelli, *Michael Jackson: The Magic and the Madness* (New York: Ballantine Books), 547. (All references to this book are from the paperback edition).

No one knew. But it was not likely to get better until Michael had recaptured his success and no longer felt that he needed to clear his name. Or until he gave up trying. That could take years, and the Chandlers were no longer willing to stand idly by and be attacked. Turning the other cheek was not working.

Evan filed a lawsuit against Michael for breach of contract, and against Diane Sawyer and ABC as well. (The case was filed in Santa Maria, California, the same location as the 2004 criminal trial against Jackson.) Because of provisions in the settlement agreement, the case was split in two, with the allegations against Michael going to a private binding arbitration while the allegations against Sawyer and ABC remained in the public court.

ABC and Sawyer's defense was centered on their First Amendment free press rights to report the story as they had. Evan alleged that they had stepped over that constitutional line by either intentionally lying, or by acting in reckless disregard of the truth. The court dismissed the case almost immediately, based on a California law that required Evan to show that he had a "probability" of succeeding.[128]

Ironically, the original purpose of the law was to protect "the little guy" from having his free speech rights thwarted by large corporations who would tie him up in a frivolous lawsuit, effectively silencing him, while they went about doing whatever it was the little guy had spoken out against. Giant media corporations quickly latched onto the law to protect themselves from claims of defamation.

The California law does have a provision in which the judge can allow a plaintiff to conduct discovery — that part of a lawsuit in which the opposing parties gather evidence from each other. After all, how can you show that you're likely to win if you're not allowed to gather evidence? It's a Catch-22. So Evan asked the court for permission to see ABC's documents and to question Sawyer, Jackson, Presley and anyone else connected to the interview. But the court denied Evan's request and the case died before it got off the ground.

---

[128] California Code of Civil Procedure Section 425.16, also known as the anti-SLAPP statute. SLAPP stands for "strategic lawsuits against public participation".

Considering the public lambasting Sawyer and ABC took from their media peers for "bending" news standards, and the report by Maureen Orth that ABC withheld evidence of Michael's guilt and Evan's innocence, it seems odd that the court did not allow Evan the opportunity to confirm what the press had already reported.

✳ ✳ ✳

The results of the lawsuit dealt a heavy blow to Evan. Before the *Prime Time Live* interview he wanted only solitude and anonymity, but once he decided to fight, his goal was to a have a public airing of the entire scandal once and for all. He wanted Michael and the media to be shut down forever from calling him an extortionist.

Evan poured himself into the battle, working night and day to help his lawyers build their case. He became obsessed and put his entire life on hold, neglecting his health and his family in his quest to clear his name.

Evan rationalized his actions by believing that the lawsuits were a temporary detour, and that once they were over, life would be better than it had ever been — that he would have all the time in the world to spend with his children.

But life did not become better than it had ever been. It became much worse. Evan lost the lawsuits, his health and his family. The last two through no one's fault but his own. But whatever faults Evan may have, whatever demons possess him, one thing he has never been and will never be, is an extortionist.

Today, Evan is alone and penniless, living as a recluse from the world around him. He remains close to only one person, Jordie. His son, now an adult, has in many ways become his father's father, supporting him both financially and emotionally. Jordie is forever grateful that his father rescued him from Michael Jackson.

As for Jordie himself, it hasn't been easy, and it may take many more years for him to find full closure. But Jordan Christopher Chandler is a happy, healthy, heterosexual young man who has lived through an unprecedented ordeal and survived with flying colors. Of all the main participants in this sordid tale, Jordan is the only one who has escaped with his character and dignity intact.

– 34 –

In January 2004, a former secretary of Barry Rothman published a book titled *Redemption* in which she pulled no punches in labeling Evan Chandler and Barry Rothman extortionists.

Geraldine Hughes claimed to have twenty-three years experience as a legal secretary, but she exhibits an astounding lack of knowledge about the most basic of legal principles.[129] Hughes complained that Jackson's motion to stay (postpone) Jordie's civil lawsuit until the criminal statute of limitations passed should have been granted. Among other reasons, Hughes stated that "the civil lawsuit allows hearsay and circumstantial evidence to be admitted, while the criminal case does not."[130] This is not true.

Hughes also stated that "Michael faced double jeopardy" in having to defend against the criminal and civil case, "even though the law is clearly designed to prevent a defendant from having to be tried twice on the same issue at the same time."[131] This, too, is incorrect. The constitutional protection against double jeopardy applies only to a defendant facing repeated *criminal* prosecutions, not a criminal and civil lawsuit.

Hughes misstatements of the law *might* be excused if she had limited them to disseminating benign falsehoods. But she went far beyond benign — all the way to dangerous. Hughes recognized that as an employee of Barry Rothman she was bound by the attorney-client privilege, yet she claimed that she did not breach that privilege by publishing private communications between Evan and Barry.

Hughes based her claim on California Evidence Code Section 956, which states that "there is no privilege" if the client hires the attorney "to commit a crime or fraud." Hughes believed that Evan hired Barry to help him extort Jackson, and therefore no attorney-client privilege ever existed.[132]

This self-proclaimed redeemer of Michael Jackson's innocence also fancies herself the sole judge and jury of Evan Chandler's guilt. The district

---

[129] Geraldine Hughes, *Redemption* (Branch and Vine Publishers, LLC., Radford, VA., 2004), 22.

[130] Ibid, 114.

[131] Ibid, 108.

[132] Ibid, 140-142.

attorney's office stated that no evidence of extortion was found and declined to press charges against Evan or Barry. In January 1994, Michael Jackson publicly withdrew his extortion charge. Yet Hughes would have us believe that even in the face of such statements the law gives a legal secretary the right to unilaterally decide that the authorities were wrong and that she can reveal privileged communications. And further, that she doesn't even have to reveal them to the police or district attorney — she can do it in a book ten years after the fact!

The case law is clear, only a judge can decide if the privilege has been defeated by a crime or fraud.

Hughes' book is replete with biblical references to good and evil; Michael the good and Evan and Barry the evil. Hughes likened herself to the biblical "ram in the bush" and claimed that Michael has had "The creator of the universe on his side from the very beginning of these false allegations," for God has given him "a witness who can attest to his innocence."[133] This pious witness, of course, is Hughes herself. But she seems not to have heard of the Ninth Commandment.

Hughes wrote that Evan needed to get custody of Jordie in order to carry out his extortion plan, so:

> On July 12, 1993, immediately after gaining custody of his 13-year-old son, Dr. Chandler demanded that June Schwartz sign a stipulation prepared by Mr. Rothman. . . . The stipulation stated . . . 4) That all outstanding child support obligations from Dr. Chandler be deemed paid in full and that no further child support be required as long as he maintained full physical custody of their 13-year-old child.[134]

The July 12 stipulation, signed by Evan and June, contains no references to child support.†

Hughes claimed to be the "sole legal secretary to Barry Rothman" in the summer of 1993.[135] But her initials do not appear on letters until late in July. A letter from Rothman to Evan, dated July 16, 1993, and containing the secretary's initials "jd," states:

---

[133] Ibid, 20
[134] Ibid, 78.
[135] Ibid, 22

> Enclosed please find a letter from the Pellicano Investigative Agency trans-
> mitting a fully executed copy of the Stipulation Re Child Care Custody duly
> executed by June Schwartz. This document has now been filed with the
> court.†

Hughes correctly reported June's claim that she signed the July 12 stipulation under duress because Evan threatened not to return Jordie if she
refused. But Hughes, who had access to all of the files, did not report that
Pellicano had agreed in writing to aid June in facilitating the stipulation and
that June had signed the stipulation at Pellicano's office. Hughes knew that
Pellicano worked for an attorney, Bert Fields. As an experienced legal secretary she should have known that June had been advised — by Pellicano,
if not directly by Fields — regarding whether or not to sign the stipulation.

On July 20, after Jordie had admitted to Evan that Michael had touched
his penis, Barry Rothman presented June with a much stricter stipulation
that would have given Evan legal custody of Jordie and would have settled
all possible claims that Evan and June might have against each other,
including child support claims. June did not sign this stipulation.

On July 29, 1993, Hughes typed a cover letter to June's attorney, Michael
Freeman, memorializing an agreement between Rothman and Freeman to
have their clients sign a new stipulation. This stipulation was less restrictive
on the amount of time June would have with Jordie, and it contained no references to child support. June did not sign this stipulation either.†

On August 16, at 5 PM, Rothman was notified for the first time that
Michael Freeman had filed for a court order requiring Evan to pay eight
years of allegedly unpaid child support. June and Dave would later testify
that no child support was ever owed and that the court order was sought for
the purpose of putting pressure on Evan to return Jordie to June.

On August 19, 1993, the day after June conceded to DCS that Jordie had
been molested, Freeman and Rothman met at Rothman's office. Hughes
then typed another letter to Freeman memorializing the agreements
reached at this meeting. The letter stated that Freeman had agreed not to
go forward with his child support order and that June had agreed to sign a
new stipulation in which she waived any child support claims against Evan
as long as she remained married to Dave.† Dave's testimony confirmed that

this was the original gentlemen's agreement between himself, Evan and June in 1985.

If Hughes was as knowledgeable about this case as she claimed to be, she should have known the true facts about the stipulations and the child support issue, and she should have reported them.

On the last page of her book Hughes presented "Excerpts From the Recorded Telephone Conversation Between Dr. Chandler and Mr. Dave Schwartz."[136] The first of these is a quote of Evan's, which reads:

> I had a good communication with Michael. We were friends. I liked him and I respected him and everything else for what he is. There was no reason why he had to stop calling me. I sat in the room one day and talked to Michael and told him exactly what I want out of this whole relationship (169). I've been rehearsed about what to say and what not to say (9).

Throughout her book Hughes not only relied heavily on Mary Fischer's 1994 GQ article for her "facts," she apparently emulated Fischer's writing style as well. As was previously reported, Fischer used the same quote, minus the last sentence, to imply that Evan wanted money. (The full quote, which appears on page 169 of the official transcript, is presented in the previous discussion of Fischer's GQ article on page 233 of this book.)

Like Fischer, Hughes cut the quote short to imply that Evan wanted money. Then, like Fischer did on other quotes, Hughes lifted a sentence from page 9 of the transcript — one hundred and sixty pages away — and stuck it on the end. Hughes didn't even quote the sentence correctly!

Hughes attempted to justify her accusations against Evan and Barry Rothman and her breach of the attorney-client privilege by claiming that the police investigation into the extortion allegations was inadequate.[137] She incorrectly reports that the extortion case "was never resolved, just dismissed."[138] The facts are that there was no case to dismiss because none was ever filed, and the matter *was* resolved by a public statement from the authorities that no evidence of a crime had been found and that Evan would not be charged.

---

[136] Ibid, 184.

[137] Ibid, 92, 103.

[138] Ibid, 149.

Nevertheless, Hughes complained that she was never subpoenaed by the district attorney[139] and she laments that "all of the information I provided went nowhere."[140] However, she states that it was Pellicano she provided information to in 1993, and never claims to have voluntarily taken her story to the police.[141]

It comes as no surprise, then, that on the dedication page of her book Hughes offers a special thanks to Anthony Pellicano for his "extensive investigation efforts in digging up all the facts surrounding this case."

Coming from Hughes, such accolades are as appropriate to Pellicano as the pin-striped suit recently provided to him by the California Department of Corrections.

(For more on Hughes go to www.allthatglittersbook.com.)

✳ ✳ ✳

---

[139] Ibid, 92.

[140] Ibid, 149.

[141] Ibid, 56-57. This experienced legal secretary reveals that prior to meeting Pellicano she thought that private investigators work for the district attorney's office.

PART FOUR

AND THE SINS OF THE FATHER...

– 35 –

THROUGHOUT THE COURSE OF THE POLICE INVESTIGATION Jordie was interviewed by some of the best experts in the field of child abuse, and all unequivocally believed him. But Larry Feldman knew that convincing a jury against a man as beloved as Michael required more than just *some* of the best. It required *the* best.

In October of 1993 Feldman sent Jordie, accompanied by his mother, to New York to be interviewed by *the* man, Dr. Richard Gardner, the nation's leading authority on false claims of child abuse. More often than not, Dr. Gardner appears as an expert witness for the defense. If anyone can poke a hole in a kid's story, it's Gardner.

Gardner put Jordie through a battery of psychological tests, written and oral, including face-to-face interviews. The most revealing of these was the direct question-and-answer session in which Jordie related his experiences with Michael Jackson. The entire transcript of this session is posted on the Web site.[142] What appears later in this part are excerpts from that session.

---

[142] The names of all the boys mentioned by Jordie have been changed to protect their privacy.

Dr. Gardner concluded that Michael had molested Jordie. Had Jordie's 1993 civil case not settled, Larry Feldman was prepared to have Dr. Gardner testify as an expert witness against Michael.

✳ ✳ ✳

I first learned of Jordie's budding relationship with Michael during a phone call from my mother, Jordie's grandmother, in January of 1993. Naturally Grandma and I were happy for him. But a friend who overheard the conversation was wary. "Remember when Michael won all those Grammies, he was sitting with Brooke Shields next to him, she was lookin' so fine, and when they called his name to come on stage he just left her there and picked up Emmanuel Lewis. That's weird, Man. That's very weird."

"Nonsense," I protested, offering many of the trite explanations for Michael's behavior I would soon come to find so naive: "He loves children." "He's a child himself." "Look at all the wonderful things he's done for children." By the end of October I found it mind boggling that any adult with the power to add two and two could still be spouting these truths as self-evident of Michael's innocence. Even when Pellicano put the two "we-slept-in-the-same-bed-but-he-never-touched-us" boys on TV, many people responded favorably with, "See, he never touched them!"

Such blind faith in Michael's innocence was one of the more intriguing aspects of the unfolding public reaction. Sure, we all knew the image, the legend, but who is Michael Jackson the human being? What makes him tick? That's what I needed to know.

Assuming that neither Michael nor his allies would grant me an audience, I did the next best thing — I went to the public library. And it was there that I found my answer, in magazine articles, in books on child abuse, in Michael's and LaToya's autobiographies, and in several unauthorized biographies, including *Michael Jackson: The Magic and the Madness*, by J. Randy Taraborrelli, by far the most comprehensive and well-researched biography on Jackson.

Shy, soft-spoken, childlike. A bit strange perhaps, but nevertheless a decent man, pure of thought and innocent of the ways of the world. That's the Michael we all believed in — who we *wanted* to believe in. Yet according to those who've studied him, the public image is only half of the story.

The real Michael Jackson is described as a split personality, Michael the superstar and Michael the human being. While it may be normal for a popular entertainer to have distinct professional and personal lives, one would be hard-pressed to find anyone in whom the two were more divergent than Michael.

When it came to his career, Michael Jackson was no child. As he explained in his autobiography, "I think some don't think I'm a person who determines what's happening with his career. Nothing could be further from the truth."[143] Indeed, Michael ran his career with an iron fist, often ruthlessly firing those closest to him, as well as insisting on planting wild stories about himself in the media to advance his success, already far greater than anyone's had ever been.

In 1984, Michael wanted to capitalize on Prince's success with *Purple Rain,* so he planned to release a phony story to the tabloid press that he and Prince were bitter enemies. The idea was to whip up a public frenzy just in time for the release of Michael's *Bad* video. The charade would end with Michael and Prince dueling on the video via their music and dance. But the plan needed Prince's cooperation and he wanted nothing to do with Michael's hoax.[144]

At the World Music awards in 1986, Michael concocted the idea of having an adoring teenage girl run onto the stage and grab him while he was standing next to Quincy Jones, who would be accepting the Record of the Year award for *We Are The World.* Michael would then act surprised as the security guards pulled the girl off him. The scheme failed when the hired actor could not work her way through the thick crowd and onto the stage. But had Michael pulled it off, the world's attention would have been focused on him, not Quincy Jones.[145]

Those events never came off, but other, more daring ones did. In 1984, Michael's quick mind cooked up a scheme to parlay a minor wrist injury, sustained during the filming of *Captain EO,* into a sympathy-evoking media

[143] Michael Jackson, *Moonwalk* (New York: Doubleday, 1988), 271.

[144] J. Randy Taraborrelli, *Michael Jackson: The Magic and the Madness,* 422.

[145] J. Randy Taraborrelli, *Michael Jackson: The Magic and the Madness,* 407.

event. The day after the injury Michael claimed to have terrible pain and was rushed to a local hospital where his personal plastic surgeon "examined" him, bandaged his wrist and placed his arm in a sling. As Michael exited the hospital he acted surprised to see the swarm of reporters waiting for him, reporters that had been alerted by his own PR team. The story spread like wildfire.[146]

This hoax is reminiscent of the shoulder injury Michael whined about on *60 Minutes* in 2003, allegedly inflicted by the police during his arrest on molestation charges. Or when Michael showed up at a 2003 lawsuit on crutches with his leg bandaged, claiming that he was late for trial because of a spider bite.

And who can forget the 1984 headlines that Michael sleeps in a hyperbaric chamber so that he can live to be 150 years old, and that he plans to take the machine on the road with him on his next tour. Michael invented this scam when he happened to walk by a hyperbaric (oxygen) chamber in a hospital ward.

Through an elaborate and secret plan, the media event was pulled off, causing all the hoopla Michael had wished for. "I can't believe that people bought it," Michael said. "We can actually control the press."[147]

In 1987 Michael came up with a new scam that could have been more sensational than the hyperbaric chamber story. Michael had his agents spread the word that he had made an offer of five hundred thousand dollars to a London hospital to buy the skeleton of the Elephant Man. According to Jackson's public announcement, his desire to buy the bones was based on "ethical, medical, and historical" grounds. The story caught on fast, making news around the world.

But when the press found out that no offer had actually been made, Michael found himself in the embarrassing position of having to make a real offer, this time for one million dollars. He was convinced that the hospital would accept, because "every man has his price." But hospital officials were insulted by the cheap publicity stunt and refused to sell.[148]

---

[146] J. Randy Taraborrelli, *Michael Jackson: The Magic and the Madness*, 425.

[147] J. Randy Taraborelli, *Michael Jackson: The Magic and the Madness*, 425-429.

[148] J. Randy Taraborrelli, *Michael Jackson: The Magic and the Madness*, 431-432.

In 1989 Michael was livid when Madonna was pronounced Artist of the Decade by media polls. He believed the title belonged to him. So he had MTV make up a new award for him, *The Video Vanguard Artist of the Decade*. It was presented to Michael at the 1989 MTV Awards. "That'll teach the heifer," Michael said of Madonna.[149]

(Apparently Michael liked the word "heifer." "No wenches, bitches, heifers or hos," was something of value to wish for in life, he counseled Jordie.)

In 1987 Michael co-produced a one-hour TV special called *Motown on Showtime — Michael Jackson*. Michael had complete control over the content and placed people on the show who would lavish great praise on him. Additional self-serving documentaries would follow, causing people to wonder about Michael's mental health. Why did the world's greatest superstar need his ego stroked in such an artificial manner?[150]

Even the royal title "King of Pop" may have been self-proclaimed. It originated as part of a deal with MTV for exclusive first-showing of Jackson's *Black or White* video In January 1002, *Rolling Stone Magazine* revealed an official MTV memo that required the term 'King of Pop' to be used on TV during the weeks that the video aired.

Whether these hoaxes Michael perpetrated on his public are to be considered fraudulent or just savvy PR is a matter of opinion, but they certainly did not originate in the mind of an innocent. They were the work of a calculating man. As Steven Spielberg said, Michael is "in full control . . . there is a great conscious forethought behind everything he does."[151]

Spielberg meant it as a compliment, but those who felt Michael's sting, those closest to him, didn't see it that way. Michael fired many of his closest advisors without warning and never in person. Ron Weisner, his manger in the 1980s, John Branca, the attorney who had negotiated some of the most lucrative record deals in history, and Frank Dileo, the man who handled *Thriller* and *Bad*, were all coldly dispatched.

According to Taraborrelli, Michael's reputation in the industry took a big

---

[149] J. Randy Taraborrelli, *Michael Jackson: The Magic and the Madness*, 446-447.

[150] J. Randy Taraborrelli, *Michael Jackson: The Magic and the Madness*, 456.

[151] Dave Marsh, *Trapped: Michael Jackson and the Crossover Dream* (New York: Bantam Books, 1985), 210.

hit when he fired Dileo. People no longer trusted him and began to feel that "Michael would screw you if you worked for him."[152]

The more I read about Michael Jackson what leapt from the pages was not the man that I or any of his adoring fans had ever heard of. It was the man who had perpetrated the cold and calculated seduction of my nephew, one filled with lies, false tears and false emotions, and a complete lack of concern for others, especially the child.

In all of Jordie's court documents, and in everything he told me in our talks together in 1993, nothing was more revealing than when he told Dr. Gardner about the point in his relationship with Michael when Michael began masturbating him. "He stopped everything else that we were originally doing together . . . " In other words, the kissing and hugging stopped once the masturbating started.[153] No tenderness, no foreplay, just sex for sex sake. Manipulation for self-gratification.

While none of the books I read allege that Michael is a child molester, what they do reveal is that regardless of the myth, the real Michael Jackson has the capacity to be tough-minded to the point of being callous, even toward those who considered themselves friends. And he has the capacity toward premeditated deceit for the purpose of achieving a calculated goal.

– 36 –

But what of the "other" Michael Jackson? Jane Fonda described Michael as one of "the walking wounded . . . making contact with people is hard enough for him . . . ." Fonda relayed that those who worked with Michael in *The Wiz* thought of him as someone who "almost faded away" when he wasn't on stage.[154]

Time and time again the point is driven home that Michael had a hard time dealing with life — especially with adults — when he wasn't being

---

[152] J. Randy Taraborrelli, *Michael Jackson: The Magic and the Madness*, 492. Quoting "a leading publicist".

[153] Had the molestation story been a lie planted in the boy's head by his father, as some claimed, Evan would have to have studied child molestation in great detail to have included this in the brainwashing. Why in God's name would a child even mention it if it weren't true?

[154] J. Randy Taraborrelli, *Michael Jackson: The Magic and the Madness*, 263.

the superstar. The following is Michael's description of the character he played in the *The Wiz*, the scarecrow, followed by Michael's description of himself.

> He knows that he has these, uh . . . these problems. . . . And he understands that he sees things differently from the way everyone else does, but he can't put his finger on why. He's not like other people. . . . So he goes through his whole life with this, uh . . . confusion. Everyone thinks he's very special, but really, he's very sad.
>
> When I can't get onto a stage for a long time I have fits and get real crazy. I start crying. . . . Onstage is the only place I'm comfortable. I'm not comfortable around . . . normal people.[155]

The problem is that you can't always be singin' and dancin'. You need to eat, sleep, and do all the other things humans do — to touch and be touched, to be intimate.

When people, including Michael himself, are quoted on their experiences with Michael Jackson the superstar, they speak of a tough, take charge, knows-just-where-he's-going kind of guy. When they talk about Michael the human being, he's shy, quiet and meek.

Given the immense public exposure that comes with superstardom, and the degree to which Michael has introverted into his own private world, these two personalities — and the joys and sorrows that accompany them — are separated by as huge a gap as one could imagine. Unfortunately for Michael, both personalities live under one skin.

According to Michael, his relationship with his father was less than desirable. "One of the things I regret most is never being able to have a real closeness with him . . . he found it hard to relate to me. . . . I still don't know him, and that's sad for a son who hungers to understand his own father."[156]

Joe Jackson, Michael's father, believes that it was his strictness that was responsible for his children's success. "I think children should fear their parents more. . . . It's good for them. . . . I don't think I have ever once let my boys down. If I did, too bad for them."[157]

---

[155] J. Randy Taraborrelli, *Michael Jackson: The Magic and the Madness*, 216.

[156] Michael Jackson, *Moonwalk*, 17.

[157] J. Randy Taraborrelli, *Michael Jackson: The Magic and the Madness*, 215. (There is no evidence that Joe Jackson sexually abused Michael.)

Both Michael and Joe were being kind. Taraborrelli quotes Marcus Phillips, a Jackson family friend, about Michael's plastic surgery: "If he couldn't erase Joe from his life, at least he could erase him from the reflection in the mirror."[158] A girlfriend of Motown Records' mogul, Berry Gordy, has known Michael for years. She claims that Michael told her directly that, "he would do anything not to look like Joe."[159]

Though everyone acknowledges that Joe Jackson is greatly responsible for the fame and fortune achieved by his family, Michael and LaToya have also acknowledged that their father did not spare the rod when it came to disciplining his kids. Joe may not believe he abused them, both physically and emotionally, but many would disagree, including, apparently, his own children.

Taraborrelli sums up the-apple-doesn't-fall-far-from-the-tree relationship between father and son by reporting that to a great extent Michael became "as cold and calculating" as his father who "had been a bully for years" and "was suspicious of everyone because he expected others to be as unethical as he was."

Taraborrelli also points out that when it came to integrity Joe Jackson provided a poor role model for his sons because of his long term practice of "openly conducting affairs with other women" during the course of his marriage.[160]

As for Katherine Jackson, the literature is filled with testimonials describing the great love between mother and son. But was it a healthy love? While young Michael was witnessing his father whore around behind his mother's back, Katherine was indoctrinating the boy with the virtues of being a good Jehovah's Witness.

"Neither fornicators, nor idolators, nor adulterers, nor effeminate men, nor abusers of themselves with mankind" will inherit the Kingdom of God. (Corinthians 6:9) According to Witness' doctrine, the sexually perverse includes just about everyone and everything, "not only all oral and anal sexual activity, homosexuality and extramarital intercourse, but holding hands, kissing, and passionate gazes. All are regarded as perversions or as

158 J. Randy Taraborrelli, *Michael Jackson: The Magic and the Madness*, 253.
159 J. Randy Taraborrelli, *Michael Jackson: The Magic and the Madness*, 414.
160 J. Randy Taraborrelli, *Michael Jackson: The Magic and the Madness*, 491.

potentially evil occasions of sin."[161]

Caught between the rigid sexual morality of a mother he loved dearly and a stern (if not abusive) father who was unfaithful and sexually perverse (according to Witness beliefs), Michael, "the most sensitive" of the children, reacted as one might predict. He became withdrawn and confused, especially about sex.

In his autobiography Michael suggested that he has had several romantic relationships with famous women. But Diana Ross, Brooke Shields and Tatum O'Neal have all denied ever having an intimate relationship with him.[162]

There are numerous anecdotes and comments about Michael's sexual development scattered throughout the biographies, but suffice it to say that in young Michael's Jehovah's Witness eyes, sex was a sin that would make one ineligible to enter the Kingdom of Heaven. But more than that, it was the weapon his "devil" father used to hurt his beloved mother. How that must have ripped at Michael's heart.[163]

– 37 –

On September 5, 1985, Michael issued a strong public statement denying his homosexuality. But Michael made the statement through surrogates, "which gave his declaration of 'manhood' little credibility"[164] Taraborrelli therefore concluded that Michael, then twenty-six years old, was a virgin. In 1994, this widely respected expert on Michael Jackson asserted that Michael was asexual.[165] After all, if a person is neither homosexual or heterosexual, or a combination of the two, he must be asexual. What else is there?

In her excellent book, *The Silent Children: A Book for Parents About the Prevention of Child Sexual Abuse*, Linda Tschirhart-Sanford writes:

---

[161] Dave Marsh, *Trapped: Michael Jackson and the Crossover Dream*, 15.

[162] J. Randy Taraborrelli, *Michael Jackson: The Magic and the Madness*, 190.

[163] According to *Vanity Fair*, Michael described his father as the devil. (Maureen Orth, "Nightmare at Neverland," 136.)

[164] J. Randy Taraborrelli, *Michael Jackson: The Magic and the Madness*, 391.

[165] "Dodging the Bullet," *People Magazine*, February 7, 1994, 67-68. (Taraborrelli said this again on CNN Live in 2001.)

In addition to the terms 'heterosexual' and 'homosexual' to describe adult sexual preference, we need a third category . . . A child molester is neither heterosexual or homosexual; he is a child molester."[166]

According to the American Counseling Association:

Current research suggests that pedophiles have certain characteristics in common. . . . A significant number of offenders have experienced or observed deviant sexual behavior at an early age, usually prior to puberty. In essence, the pedophile becomes fixated on children as a result of an "arrest of psychological maturation resulting from unresolved formative issues. . . ." [167]

The average pedophile looks just like you or me, and unless we are schooled in the signs and symptoms of such individuals, we will never notice them. Michael Jackson, of course, doesn't look or act anything like you or me, and we all did notice him. But not as a child molester. In our minds we made an exception for his behavior and bought into the image that millions of dollars and hordes of professional ad men sold us, that of an innocent man in search of his lost childhood. A real life Peter Pan.

"I am Peter Pan . . . In my heart I am Peter Pan," Michael told the world in his controversial 2003 interview with Martin Bashir. The real-life creator of Peter Pan, British playwright J.M Barrie, drew the inspiration for "that terrible masterpiece" from his relationship with several young boys that he was in love with.[168] Like Jackson, Barrie experienced a youth torn by extreme sexual mores that resulted in an innate shyness. Barrie was impotent when it came to women; his twenty-year marriage was never consummated. He spent much of his time with "my boys." According to several biographies and his own writings as well, Barrie was a man who refused to grow up and preferred the company of children — young male children.[169]

---

166 Linda Tschirhart-Sanford, *The Silent Children: A Book for Parents About the Prevention of Child Sexual Abuse* (New York: Anchor Press/Doubleday, 1980), 127-128.

167 Ronnie Priest & Annalee Smith, *Counseling Adult Sex Offenders: Unique Challenges and Treatment Programs:*, Journal of Counseling and Development, September/October 1992, Vol. 71, p. 27, published by The American Counseling Association.

168 "That terrible masterpiece" — The description of Peter Pan by one of the boys who, as an adult, had come to understand Barrie's affection for him as somewhat of a love affair. (Janet Dunbar, *J.M. Barrie: The Man Behind the Image* [Boston: Houghton Mifflin, 1970], p. 165)

169 Andrew Birkin, *J.M. Barrie and The Lost Boys: The Love Story that Gave Birth to Peter Pan* (New York: Clarkson N. Potter Inc, 1979); Janet Dunbar, *J.M. Barrie: The Man Behind the Image*; Cynthia Asquith, Portrait of Barrie, (New Jersey: Dutton, 1955) Asquith was Barrie's longtime secretary.

Jackson, and perhaps Barrie as well, are among a subclass of pedophiles known as "fixated pedophiles." Fixated pedophiles "desire to remain child-like" and "adapt their behavior and interests to the level of the child."[170] "They are identified mainly as men and their primary interest is in boys, with whom they develop boy-to-boy relationships."[171]

According to A. Nicholas Groth, Ph.D., a well-published forensic psychologist and former director of a prison sex offender program, many pedophiles exhibit common psychological traits: "A sense of isolation or alienation from others, an ineptitude in negotiating interpersonal relationships, deep-seated feelings of inadequacy, and a tendency to experience themselves as helpless victims of an overpowering environment."[172] Michael Jackson, beaten and alienated from his father, infused with a repressive sexual morality by his mother, unable to have intimate relationships with adults, unsatisfied with his success . . . truly one of "the walking wounded."

Unlike the adoring multitudes, child abuse experts were not fooled by Michael's Peter Pan persona. To them, this "female acting, sissified acting" superstar, as Louis Farrakhan described him,[173] with his unusual dress, heavy makeup, and prevalence for hanging out with young boys, stood out like a huge red flag. Joan Johnson, a licensed clinical social worker who has worked with child abuse victims at UCLA's Neuro-Psychiatric Institute, said that if she had heard of an adult cultivating close relationships with children and sleeping in the same bed, she would have immediately launched an inquiry.[174]

But you and I and Taraborrelli are not experts. And so those of us who did not think Michael was asexual (if we thought about it at all), thought he was gay. And with good reason, by anyone's definition he certainly didn't

[170] Ronnie Priest & Annalee Smith, *Counseling Adult Sex Offenders: Unique Challenges and Treatment Programs*, Journal of Counseling and Development, September/October 1992, Vol. 71, published by The American Counseling Association.

[171] "Pedophilia," *The Human Sexuality WEB*, a Web site maintained by the University of Missouri-Kansas City; Dr. Paul A. Gore Ph.D. (2004). www.umkc.edu/sites/hsw/issues/pedophil.html

[172] Linda Tschirhart-Sanford, *The Silent Children: A Book for Parents About the Prevention of Child Sexual Abuse*.

[173] J. Randy Taraborrelli, *Michael Jackson: The Magic and the Madness*. Farrakhan deemed Michael "not wholesome for our young boys nor our young girls," as a role model.

[174] *StarMagazine*, September 14, 1993.

appear to be straight. The tabloid press constantly hounded Michael with these allegations, which he vehemently and truthfully denied.

Tschirhart-Sanford explains:

> Same-sex offenders (an adult with a child of the same sex), do not identify themselves as homosexual, and in fact, may have never had sexual relations with an adult male. . . . If the issue was as simple as desiring sex with another male, same-sex offenders would molest each other. Given a choice between sex with an adult male and sex with a child, the same-sex offender would choose the child as a sex partner."[175]

One of the oft touted rebuttals to the molestation allegations was the notion that a thirteen-year-old boy is too old to be fooled and must have willingly gone along. And it may be that some thirteen-year-old boys are worldly enough to know better, but according to statistics "Boy victims average in age from twelve to fifteen, which is older than the average girl victim."[176]

According to the American Psychiatric Association, pedophiles are often attracted to children of a particular age range, "which may be as specific as within a range of only one or two years. Those attracted to girls usually prefer eight- to ten-year-olds . . . whereas, those attracted to boys usually prefer slightly older children.[177]

– 38 –

Regardless of who the offender is, the seduction and molestation of a child often follows a common pattern, or profile. "Considerable thought and planning go into the offense. After choosing a specific victim, the offender may ingratiate himself with the child's parents to gain their trust and diminish any suspicion."[178]

"One of the more common approaches," Tschirhart-Sandford tells us, "is for the offender to enlist the child in 'the shared secret.' Children are very

---

[175] Linda Tschirhart-Sanford, *The Silent Children: A Book for Parents About the Prevention of Child Sexual Abuse*, 127.

[176] Ibid., 124.

[177] *A.P.A. Diagnostic and Statistical Manual on Mental Disorders*, 1987, p. 284.

[178] Linda Tschirhart-Sanford, *The Silent Children: A Book for Parents About the Prevention of Child Sexual Abuse*, 85-86.

vulnerable to this." The motivation behind the offender's 'shared secret' is transparent. It is, of course, designed to forestall or prevent discovery.[179]

In his interview with Dr. Gardner, Jordie told of the "little box that only him and I could share . . . you put the secret in the box and nobody can know about what's in the box but him and me."

Another "tool" of the molester is "the bribe."

> "The offender has needs, sexual or emotional, that he wants met, and sees the offering of a reward as an expedient way to accomplish this purpose. In doing so, the offender is relying on the child's lack of sophistication in understanding what is to be done to get the reward."[180]

"We'd play video games," Jordie told Dr. Gardner. "There was a carnival . . . a movie theater . . . some golf carts that you drive around in . . . a lake . . . this custom-made water fight place . . . Giraffes, elephants, a lion, horses, a petting zoo, reptiles . . . for just a regular kid it seemed pretty fantastical and overwhelming."

"The bribe varies," Tschirhart-Sandford explains, "depending on the age and desires of the victim. Toys, food, trips, movies. In using the bribe, the offender wants to control another human being. He hopes the victim will focus on the reward, rather than the sexual activity."[181]

Taraborrelli's description of Michael's relationship with a young boy named Jimmy Safechuck is eerily similar to Michael's relationship with Jordie: the toys, the shopping sprees, expensive gifts to the parents, taking the boy on tour, wearing identical clothing. It was a relationship that "most people found strange," Tarborrelli wrote.[182]

According to Tschirhart-Sandford, another "tool" of the molester is "the threat." If the child is unwilling to comply or the offender senses the child is about to break off the relationship or tell someone, a threat may be used. Sometimes it is violent, but more often it is emotional.[183]

---

[179] Ibid., 235.

[180] Ibid., 248.

[181] Ibid.

[182] J. Randy Taraborrelli, *Michael Jackson: The Magic and the Madness*, 469.

[183] Linda Tschirhart-Sanford, *The Silent Children: A Book for Parents About the Prevention of Child Sexual Abuse*, 254.

As Jordie related to Dr. Gardner, Michael not only threatened him with juvenile hall, but also said that the relationship would end if Michael didn't get what he wanted, "If he wanted me to do something [sexual] with him, he would say that Tommy did that with him, so that I would do it. And like, if I didn't do it, then I didn't love him as much as Tommy did."

Tschirhart-Sandford counsels that "The offender relies on the child's wish not to displease him even though to the child the request may have seemed unpleasant or distasteful or even bizarre. . . . In other words, the child's need and wish to please was exploited by the offender."[184]

"He was a friend so I didn't stop him," Jordie told Gardner. "He would cry. He would say 'You don't love me anymore.' It would be, like a whole deal, you know . . . it was hard."

Tschirhart-Sandford continues, "In some instances, the child was assured that what was requested was perfectly normal and proper between them. . . . "

Michael assured Jordie "there's nothing wrong with it. . . . He said that we weren't conditioned . . . like regular people of today's society, they're conditioned and so they would believe it was wrong."

✳ ✳ ✳

The difference between Michael Jackson and any ordinary pedophile is one of degree, not kind. Using his stardom and the fantasy world he created at Neverland, Michael could entice a child in a way that no other pedophile could hope to match. But beneath the façade of fame and fortune lies a child molester no different than the one down the street. "Come to my house, I'll give you candy." It's as old as the hills.

✳ ✳ ✳

---

184 Ibid., 84.

EPILOGUE

THE KEY WORD IN ALL FORMS OF SEXUAL ACTIVITY — and indeed, all forms of human interaction — is consent. With consent one borrows; without it one steals. With consent one makes love; without it one rapes. Children may enter into a relationship with a pedophile without a fuss. But they have not the slightest concept of where the relationship is going, anymore than a fly knows it's headed for the spider's web. They do not consent. They are seduced and molested.

Child protective services (CPS) agencies in the United States collectively receive more than fifty thousand referrals *per week* alleging child abuse or neglect. In 2001 there were nearly three million reports involving five million children.[185]

Of these three million reports 870,000 were never investigated by CPS. No one will ever know how many of these children were abused; only the results of CPS investigations are listed in the national statistics.

Of those reports that were investigated by CPS in 2001, about one-third were "substantiated." The remaining two-thirds were listed as "unsubstantiated," although this does not necessarily mean that they are untrue. In many cases there is insufficient evidence to make a determination one way or the other. Unfortunately, most states list the results of their investigations

---

[185] Unless otherwise noted, all statistics in this epilogue are from the National Child Abuse and Neglect Data System (NCANDS), developed by the Children's Bureau of the U.S. Department of Health & Human Services.

as substantiated or unsubstantiated. If abuse cannot be substantiated, it is therefore considered unsubstantiated.

A small number of states use a third category, "indicated." These are cases in which the strict evidentiary requirements to list them as substantiated are not met, yet the CPS worker suspects they might be true. The statistics from the states that use the "indicated" category show that the number of substantiated case and indicated cases are, at a minimum, equal.

California does not use the "indicated" category, but in California there were 128,000 substantiated victims of abuse or neglect in 2001. If California did use the "indicated" category there would be another 128,000 possible victims. Florida reported that 42,000 children were substantiated victims in 2001, but listed another 81,000 as indicated.

Nationwide, of the three million children who were the subject of child abuse investigations in 2001, over 900,000 were substantiated victims. Half were victims of neglect, 170,000 were physically abused, 87,000 sexually abused and 62,000 psychologically abused. There were also victims of medical neglect and other forms of abuse.

Most experts believe that the majority of child abuse is unreported. "Virtually every study of the crime problem acknowledges the fact that only one to 10 percent of the incidents are ever disclosed."[186] A nationwide poll by the Los Angeles Times found that 27 percent of women and 16 percent of men were sexually abused as children. One-third of the victims said they had never told anyone. In those cases where they did tell someone, only 3 percent were reported to the authorities.[187]

Of sexual abuse in particular, even Dr. Gardner, the expert on false child abuse claims, believes that "sex abuse of children is widespread" and that perhaps as much as 95 percent or more of such allegations "are likely to be justified."[188]

Michael Jackson epitomizes the cyclical nature of child abuse. "And the

---

[186] Investigating Child Sexual Exploitation, F.B.I. Law Enforcement Bulletin, January 1984.

[187] Lois Timnick, "The Times Poll: 22% in Survey Were Child Abuse Victims," Los Angeles Times, August 25, 1985.

[188] Richard A. Gardner, M.D., Sex Abuse Hysteria: The Salem Witch Trials Revisited (New Jersey: Creative Therapeutics), 7.

sins of the father. . . . " He is both a victim to be pitied and an abuser to be loathed. Yet conspicuously absent from the media in both the 1993 and 2003 scandals were articles and discussions about the larger issue of child abuse. When I asked a prominent journalist why the media did not use these golden opportunities to enlighten the public or generate a discourse about this heinous national epidemic, the answer I received was astounding. "It's pretty much a taboo subject. The public does not want to hear about it, it's too dark, so editors won't print it."

It is my hope that this book will help to bring the issue of child abuse into the forefront of American consciousness, and that both the media and child abuse professionals will be more outspoken about this plague.

Michael Jackson has for decades been hailed as an advocate for children around the world. Perhaps, even in his infamy, he can do more to advance the cause of children's welfare than he ever dreamed possible.

* * *